P9-BYO-252

THREADS

Threads

MY LIFE BEHIND THE SEAMS IN THE HIGH-STAKES WORLD OF FASHION

JOSEPH ABBOUD

with ELLEN STERN

HarperCollins*Publishers*

THREADS. Copyright © 2004 by Joseph Abboud. All rights reserved. Printed in the United States of America. No part of this book may be used or reproduced in any manner whatsoever without written permission except in the case of brief quotations embodied in critical articles and reviews. For information, address HarperCollins Publishers Inc., 10 East 53rd Street, New York, NY 10022.

HarperCollins books may be purchased for educational, business, or sales promotional use. For information, please write: Special Markets Department, HarperCollins Publishers Inc., 10 East 53rd Street, New York, NY 10022.

Grateful acknowledgment is made for permission to reprint lyrics from "The Living Years." Words and music by Michael Rutherford and B. A. Robertson © 1988. Reproduced by permission of Michael Rutherford Ltd/R&BA Music Ltd/Hit & Run Music Publishing Ltd, London WC2H 0QY.

Grateful acknowledgment is made for permission to reprint the following photographs: *GQ* cover photo © Sam Jones; courtesy of *GQ*, Condé Nast Publications Inc. *DNR* cover photos courtesy of Fairchild Publications. All other photographs courtesy of the author.

FIRST EDITION

Designed by Elliott Beard

Printed on acid-free paper

Library of Congress Cataloging-in-Publication Data is available upon request.

ISBN 0-06-053534-2

04 05 06 07 08 ❖/RRD 10 9 8 7 6 5 4 3 2 1

For Lynn, Lila, Ari, Jeanette, Mara, and Nancy—
the women in my life

And what is it to work with love?
It is to weave the cloth with threads
drawn from your heart, even as if
your beloved were to wear that cloth.

—KAHLIL GIBRAN, *The Prophet*

CONTENTS

1. *Guy in the Gray Flannel Suit*   1

2. *The Home Team*   11

3. *Visionaries, Decisionaries*   24

4. *Air Play*   32

5. *Personal Appearance*   41

6. *The Hero Was Always Dressed Right*   46

7. *Joe College*   54

8. *Innocent Abroad*   65

9. *Louis, Murray, and Me*   71

10. *Travels with Murray*   81

11. *Polo Player*   90

12. *Pal Joey*   101

13. *The Game of the Name*   113

14. *Getting the Business*   126

15. *Model Behavior*   133

Contents

16. *The Show on the Road*   143

17. *Us Versus Them*   152

18. *Down to Earth*   158

19. *All Those Ties*   166

20. *Designs on Women*   176

21. *The Reality (and Realty) of Retail*   184

22. *Honor Thy Customer*   193

23. *Lowdown on the Markdown*   200

24. *Lucky Charms*   205

25. *Whose Image Is It, Anyway?*   212

26. *Campaign Promises*   221

27. *The Last Row*   230

Acknowledgments   235

Index   236

THREADS

Guy in the Gray Flannel Suit

DOCTOR. LAWYER. Indian chief. Fashion designer.

Most guys don't do surgery on a daily basis, or sue somebody, or open a casino. But everybody deals with what I do: fashion.

"What'll I wear?" Comes up every morning.

The CEO says, "Does this tie work with that suit?" The art director wonders, "Should I wear my cords with a T-shirt or a cable-knit?" Even people who don't give a damn about fashion have to admit it into their lives.

There's covering our nakedness, and then there's image. A man's clothes tell the world how he wants to be perceived. Whether he's wearing a pair of rusty jeans or a beautifully cut Italian suede jacket, he has an image of himself in mind. All clothes make a statement. The *right* clothes make a statement that will open doors.

That's why most businessmen wear a suit. It's easy. They don't have to think too hard about it, and they always—well, almost always—look correct. A suit says, "Take me seriously." It's subliminal, but it's real.

My very first suit was a little white cotton three-piece, bought for my first communion at Holy Name Church in West Roxbury. I wore it with white bucks, a white shirt, and a white bow tie—right out of Truman Capote. I looked so angelic, so *holy*. But a communion suit doesn't count.

My first *real* suit was a beigy, tweedy mod thing from Jordan Marsh, and being able to buy it at a famous store in downtown Boston was a pretty big deal. It made me feel *legitimate*. But I was sixteen, and the suit wasn't expensive, so nobody took my tailoring requests too seriously. When I went to pick it up, disaster! I looked like a *clown*. I'd wanted the sleeves lengthened and the pants shortened, and they'd done exactly the opposite. My first suit experience wasn't a good one.

But it should have been. Buying a suit is a major event, because it makes you look—and feel—important. At twenty-one, every young man should have a great navy or gray suit that he can wear to an interview, a bar mitzvah, a funeral, a wedding. He also needs a navy blazer and a pair of chinos. With those three fundamentals, he's covered for any event. On his feet: anything from penny loafers to wingtips, but shoes should never be outlandish or detract from the outfit.

An observant guy looks around and notices how others dress and walk and decorate their homes. Sooner or later, he makes up his mind how he's going to look—and how he's going to be. Is he going to be flamboyant? Is he going to dress like the guys in the stockroom or dress like the boss? Depends on where he's headed.

A young friend of mine named David Black, who was toiling in the mail room at a publishing company, came in one day wearing a suit, shirt, and tie. "What are *you* all dressed up for?" somebody asked him with a sneer. The answer: for himself. Working in the mail room didn't mean he couldn't dress well and look professional. He wasn't going to let other people's perceptions of him keep him down. And they didn't. He quickly rose through the ranks to become a prominent literary agent in New York. No, it wasn't just the clothes that got him promoted, but he had a certain image of himself, and the clothes helped him project that image. The first time we met, a few years ago, David was wearing a putty-colored dress shirt with a soft collar, a soft-print tie, and a navy blazer—all Armani, so he made some kind of apology. I didn't care whose label he was wearing, because he looked great. He had a lot of other things going for him too, of course, but that strong first impression made a difference. We connected, and now he's my agent.

There's a migratory pattern to developing your wardrobe and taste as you become more successful. It's like traveling. The first time you travel, you feel lucky to get on any flight from anywhere at a price you can manage. You don't care if you sit with the chickens. Then, as you get a bit more successful, you fly coach. When you're a junior executive, you can travel business class. And then, as the CEO, you're going first class. It's an obvious analogy, but it's exactly what happens.

For example, most guys who are starting to move up the ladder relate to a pinstripe suit almost instinctively. They figure, "It's been done before—by my father, my boss, my father's boss—and it's a classic. I'm the boss now, so it's my turn." If you remember the musical *How to Succeed in Business without Really Trying*, you'll remember the final scene of the movie, in which the outgoing chairman of the board is wearing a navy chalk-stripe suit with a soft butter-yellow vest, a white shirt, and a silver tie—and Robert Morse, being introduced as the incoming chairman of the board, appears in exactly the same suit, vest, and tie. He's not just following in the boss's footsteps; he's following in the boss's suit pattern. It's a spoof, but a spoof with a lot of truth behind it.

The other best choice is a beautifully cut solid or chalk-stripe gray suit with a white or white tattersall shirt, a silver woven tie—nothing too bright or too flashy, no tone-on-tone thing happening, no tricks—and a pair of dark brown suede shoes. (Brown with gray shows confidence, and it's one of the dream color combinations for the powerful guy. It's sophisticated, it's soft, and it doesn't scream.) With a fine gray worsted or gray flannel, the fabric doesn't get in the way. You're not hiding anything. You see the cut, the fit, the details, the stitching. And besides, any woman will tell you that the sexiest guy in the room is the guy in the gray flannel suit.

There are more than two hundred steps in making a suit, from measuring to stitching to pressing to pockets to linings. (A cheaper factory might do it in eighty steps.) You've got to go through this little ballet in which the fabric's treated just right, it's sewn just right, the tension of the needles is just right so it doesn't pull, the softness of the shoulder is just right. Then comes the marriage of the inner linings, the shoulder pads, and all the other interior parts to make sure that everything is moving and fluid.

When the front of the jacket is made, the pockets are basted up. This keeps the front of the garment stable while it's being sewn or pressed. When it gets to the rack at Bloomingdale's or Saks, the pockets are still stitched. A good salesman will certainly mention it, or the tailor will open them when the suit is altered. But I've actually had people say to me, "I like your suits, but I don't like the fake pockets."

The final step, the pressing, involves seven or eight steps of its own. The front of the coat gets pressed, the shoulder gets pressed, the lapel gets pressed, the pants get pressed—on computerized machines set to the correct pressure for different fabrics. Overpressing will make the fabric look flat and more commercial, it will make the fabric shine, and it will press the lapel down into the jacket so you see an imprint of the pocket below—like a panty line. So, as with a good sirloin, it's generally wiser to underdo than overdo.

It's these little details that make the difference between a great suit and a not-so-great one. People in the fashion business know what to look for, but the average guy trying on a suit doesn't. And he shouldn't have to. Designing it, sewing it, and pressing it so it looks, feels, and fits right: That's our job.

*   *   *

Our clothes are made all over the world—ties in Italy, sportswear in Hong Kong and China, suits and sport coats in New Bedford, Massachusetts. When we bought the factory in Massachusetts, it had been churning out inexpensive boys' clothing and cheap private label. We installed a great Italian workforce and turned the place around, but before the turn was complete, we had to ride out some serious bumps. Literally.

God does all these wonderful things with Italians. He makes the country gorgeous, he makes the people beautiful, he makes the food fabulous. But just to prove that Italians are human and not divine, he makes it so they can't sew on a button. It was infuriating. It was *insidious.* "Oh, we fix it," they'd say. "No problem. The button's fine." Right. Until the call would come from Nordstrom that the buttons were falling off the suits again.

Then, in the early 1990s, I went to London to launch Joseph Abboud boutiques in Harvey Nichols, Selfridges, and Harrods. Harrods put my clothes in the windows and devoted an entire morning to TV people and photographers. Here came the press, here came the invited guests . . . and here came Joseph Abboud feeling like Prince Charles, descending the staircase to make his grand entrance in a double-breasted navy linen suit. In one smooth, made-for-TV move, I slid my hand over to put it in my pocket—without unbuttoning the jacket. And as the flashbulbs popped, so did the New Bedford button. Flew right off.

There was also the bump in the left shoulder.

On a man's suit, it's the shoulders that matter most. They're the strength of the man, and where you build the suit from. That's where the emphasis has to be, and if you build the shoulders wrong, you're screwed. As Coco Chanel (who took her men in tweeds) once said, "Fashion is architecture; it is a matter of proportions." In the late 1980s, everybody's shoulders got bigger—some bigger than others. At Hugo Boss, they had to turn sideways to get through the door. It was a good thing that went too far, like a melon that goes from being perfect to over-ripe to rotten. The reaction was a total turnaround. Back came narrow shoulders and narrow silhouettes. Where else was there to go?

Narrow or wide, you don't want a bump in the shoulder. And ours was a problem that wouldn't go away. We'd have meeting after meeting. We'd say, "Hey, guys, there's a bump in the shoulder." They'd say, "There's no bump in the shoulder." "Yeah, there *is* a bump in the shoulder." "Okay, okay, we take care of it."

Next season, the samples would come in, we'd put them on the mannequins, and bingo! a bump in the shoulder. The problem: We had been sewing the fabric too tight, and the tension in the stitching of the shoulder created the bump. We may have had the best machinery in the world, but something somewhere in the system was wrong. After a couple of seasons of diligent investigation, the problem was finally resolved.

We were lucky not to lose customers in those early days. We could say to them, "Look, we're working on it," and hold onto them.

Well, most of them.

Neiman Marcus was a major casualty. And a major embarrassment.

I'd bought a beautiful open-weave fabric from Ferla, one of my favorite Italian mills, for some sport jackets. It was soft, beautiful, very expensive stuff, but New Bedford wasn't ready to handle it. The factory was still in transition, and nowhere near as efficient as it is today.

We made the jackets, shipped them to Neiman's, and . . . disaster. It's called seam slippage: The patternmakers hadn't allowed for enough seam, so the stitchers sewed the fabric too close to the edge and it started to shred. If a guy stretched his shoulder blades, the jacket would split. The fabric had no strength, because there were no bindings to hold it in place. It would have been nice to blame somebody, but the slippage was nobody's fault. These were newly developed fabrics, and nobody knew yet how to work with them. Should someone have known? I'd like to say yes, but sometimes you just don't know about a problem until after it happens.

Back came the jackets. *Thunk* went my gut. That was years ago, and Neiman's won't let me live it down. They buy my sportswear, but they still won't buy my tailored clothing. Even with the magnitude of my business, I've never gotten over that.

A well-tailored suit almost dictates good posture. But most guys don't know what to do with their hands. Go to a party, and you'll see every other guy crossing his arms (unless he's Prince Charles, who avoids the problem by clasping his hands behind his back). It betrays insecurity, makes you look like a wimp. And besides, there's nothing worse for the drape of a double-breasted suit, unless it's standing there with your thumbs forward on your hips, which is feminine.

Kirk Douglas addressed the issue on the Op-Ed page of the *New York Times* in 2003. "Many actors have trouble with their hands. Should they put them in their pockets? Should they put them behind their back? Do they have them at their sides? The cigarette answered the question. You take one out of the pack, you tap it, light it and inhale deeply," he wrote. "You can point with a cigarette. You can tap the ashes into an ashtray, and put it out gently in the ashtray or fiercely—whatever the scene requires." But for most guys these days, that prop is gone.

So they play with their pockets.

It's extremely uncool to put your hands in your jacket pockets. Number one, you've got a flap to maneuver through, unless you've got patch pockets, so you look silly. Number two, you put a lot of pressure on your jacket. Number three, if you don't look like you're scratching your armpits, you look like a seagull because your elbows are sticking out. I've always believed that we put pockets on pants just to solve the problem. At least they let you keep your arms close to your body.

But the pockets can get overloaded. In days of yore, when men wore suits to baseball games and tweeds on the train from London to Edinburgh, jackets were truly utilitarian. A ticket pocket held a ticket, a watch pocket held a watch, and a storm latch wasn't just some cool

Ralph Lauren detail. Today's man has a lot more freight, and it has to be dispersed with aplomb.

Consider the wallet. If he wants to carry a very thin wallet in his pant pocket, that's fine. But most guys are collectors, so if they get a business card or a girl's phone number, the wallet starts to expand. The best style is long and flat like a passport case, and it slips neatly into the inside jacket pocket (which is called, in fact, the passport pocket). Otherwise, the guy is walking around with a bulky double-fold either in his side pant pocket, which makes a lump in the front, or in his rear pocket, which looks like a tumor on his tush.

Then there are the glasses, the keys, the change, the cell phone. When clothes were big and baggy, men had plenty of room for all this stuff; now, as clothes start moving closer to the body, they don't. So try to streamline. Economize on your cargo, keep it flat, carry it in your pant pocket, and—please—respect the shape of the suit.

If I don't address the subject of pants at greater length, it's because I don't find them that exciting. They're boring to design, and you're always dealing with the crotch. Pants are funny. We *need* to wear them, because we can't go out in our shorts, but there isn't much to say about them. Women have a capri pant or a cropped pant or a low-rise pant . . . so many possibilities. We have a dress pant, a casual pant, jeans—and not a hell of a lot in between. I mean, how glamorous can you make a pair of pants? Especially with the wallet and the tush and the fit and the pleats and the zipper and the stains. They're very unromantic.

Day after day, you see articles about how suits are back in the workplace. When the stock market is on a respirator, the business world is not an environment for flashy fashion. People are looking for real jobs again and need a competitive edge. This means they're getting interview suits again, and, as a result, wearing shirts and ties again.

Corporate casual arrived on the scene in the late 1990s, around the same time as the Internet. It was a laissez-faire period when anything went. Some people started dressing down, bringing casual into Wall

Street and the legal community. Others thought they'd make a killing (or at least a living) by staying home in their bathrobes and slippers, punching their brilliant new concepts into the computer. But commerce is driven by the oldest concept—you give me something, I give you something—and in real life, people have to do business face to face. That's where dress comes into play.

One morning, two young money managers from Goldman Sachs come to the office and pitch me; they want to manage my portfolio. Obviously they know I'm in the fashion business, but they figure this whole corporate casual is happening, so they show up in shirtsleeves with their collars open and their sleeves rolled up.

Bad choice. I'm wearing a shirt and tie. But I don't say anything. I just watch them try to give me the message that they're cool and hip—while the message I get is that they'd look swell if we were meeting for a cappuccino on Madison Avenue, but here on the twentieth floor they don't fit the part they've come to play. They want to sell me something, to represent me, but they don't project any sense of professionalism or respect. However, I'm not going to base my decision just on how they're dressed, because if they're the right guys, I can look beyond that and it's fine.

Okay. So one of the money managers now picks up a baseball picture from the table. It's a picture of the moment in 1978 when the Yankees' Bucky Dent hit Mike Torres's pitch out of Fenway Park, ending the Red Sox's World Series bid that year like they always do. (Mike Torres gave me the picture, which he and Bucky both signed, and it's really a bittersweet thing for me. Being a Red Sox fan costs me thousands in therapy.)

But the money manager, who doesn't know what it means to me, and who figures he's got a little making-up to do because he's noticed he isn't dressed properly, picks it up and says, "What a great, great moment! I'll never forget it. An unbelievable moment!" You couldn't make it up. He's thinking I'm a Yankee fan, and I'm thinking he's an asshole.

These guys? They could be wearing the best tailored suits ever made, but they're not the right guys for me. They just don't get it. And I just don't hire them.

If you have any doubts that the suit is back in full swing, go to lunch with the power brokers. If you drop in at the Four Seasons in New York, you won't find a drapey suit or trendy Euro-schmatte. You'll see the custom-tailored guys—in their dark suits, crisp shirts, and striped ties—and they look great.

Their clothes aren't the highest priority in their lives, but their clothes define them. They're not fashion plates, but they've got the right spread collar, the Charvet or Turnbull & Asser shirt, the English shoe, the Cartier or Rolex.

They also know their shoes. Shoes reveal a lot about a guy (and this has nothing to do with foot size in relation to other measurements). There's nothing worse than wearing a $3,000 suit with a pair of cheap shoes, so classics are a must. It's extremely cool to wear an English tie shoe in dark luggage brown with a pair of jeans, or a cap-toe with a softly constructed suit, but you can't mix funky footwear with a serious business suit. And the shoes have to be shined. "I love the smell of napalm in the morning," Robert Duvall said in *Apocalypse Now*. Well, I love the smell of Kiwi in the morning. To each his own. Whatever it takes to go out and do battle.

Gap, which was a great beneficiary of corporate casual, isn't pleased that it crashed and burned when the stock market tanked and doesn't want to hear that men are getting dressed up again. Everybody's got an agenda, but nothing stays the same. The mood will swing back, times will become more affluent, and fashion will change. It's what keeps us all on our toes.

TWO

The Home Team

DESIGNING DOESN'T HAPPEN according to schedule. I don't wake up and say, "At eight o'clock tonight, I'm going to put on some soft music and design a suit." I get hit with ideas everywhere, all the time, and scratch things on a pad or envelope or napkin. I don't have to be on the Côte d'Azur or the Via Condotti with my shades, my collar perfectly turned up, and my scarf perfectly knotted. I can be in the hardware store, in the farmers' market, or even lying around at home in my boxer shorts and Red Sox T-shirt reading my daughters to sleep. The pictures in two of their favorite storybooks are such masterpieces of color harmony and delicate design that I get carried away and stop reading, until I hear *"Daddy!"* and get a swift kick in the shin.

The Mitten, by Jan Brett, is illustrated with paintings "sewn" on a background of birch bark (texture on texture) and adorned with embroidered rosettes, paisleys, tulips, or leaf patterns—any one of which would make a beautiful tie design. *The Magic Nesting Doll*, by Jacqueline K. Ogburn and Laurel Long, uses captivating color combinations and patterns-on-pattern. Every picture contains at least twenty-five non-primary colors, and every picture is framed by an ornate border, just the way I'd finish a scarf or pocket square.

That's the gift of daughters. If I'd had little boys, I'd be doing camouflage and cowboy stuff.

Fabric is the beginning, the heart, and the essence of my clothes. It's the touch and the feel—and it tells me what to do. The material is always the dictator. Louis I. Kahn, the great architect, put it like this: "You say to brick, 'What do you want, brick?' Brick says to you, 'I like an arch.' If you say to brick, 'Arches are expensive, and I can use a concrete lintel over an opening. What do you think of that, brick?' brick says, 'I like an arch.' "

My fabric tells me if it should become an unconstructed suit, a weekend sport coat, or a formal jacket. It tells me what kind of shoulder to do (with flannel, I know I'm going to get a softer, more luxurious shoulder; with gabardine, the shoulder's going to be a little harder). It tells me whether to do casual patch pockets or dressy besom pockets. And it's fascinating how the same pattern can look and fit and feel so different when you change the fabric.

A gray flannel suit is going to be rich, fully tailored, and structural, even if the structure is soft. But a linen suit should be unconstructed, like a guy who just woke up on a Caribbean island. It should have patch pockets, no vents, and no lining, so all you see is fabric. Linen is the Rodney Dangerfield of fabrics. It wrinkles, it droops, and it's tragically misunderstood—but I love it. A great image: *The Silence of the Lambs*, last shot. Lecter's on the lam, somewhere in the tropics, disappearing into a crowd, wearing a perfectly wrinkled double-breasted ivory linen suit. Always a man of taste.

Fabric is color, and best when inspired by nature. When I'm driving through the Berkshires in Massachusetts on an October day, I see tweeds in the mountains. With the blue sky as the shirt, and the burnt oranges, reds, and golds below, it's an outfit. But I see outfits all around me—even from my office window. If I look down Fifth Avenue at dusk, the Empire State Building is the guy in the gray flannel suit with a dark blue shirt.

Even small stones will tell me what to do. In the 1980s, I decided I wanted to have sweaters knit in the same beautiful colors I was seeing all over the beach at Nantucket.

I drove way out to Great Point, a treacherous eight- or nine mile strip at the northernmost tip of Nantucket; it's about 100 yards wide, with water on both sides. The best finds were on the Nantucket Sound side, because the sound is choppier than the ocean. I worked the waterfront, gathering the stones in both hands and depositing wet, sandy piles on the floor of the car. When I hauled my load of inspiration into the house, I washed them in the sink and buffed them with butcher's wax to seal in their true color. Then I edited them into five color groups—the black and gray combinations, the blacks and browns, the grays and browns, the khaki-ambers, the russets: eighty pounds of stone reduced to twenty-five, covering the kitchen counter and keeping my wife from fixing lunch.

When I checked in at JFK, lugging my canvas tote bag, the security guards at British Airways chuckled indulgently at my lunatic explanation. Did I have rocks in my head? Absolutely.

First to London, then by shuttle to Scotland and a little mill in East Kilbride, near Glasgow. "These," I said, "are the colors I want for my yarns." And Hunter's, a yarn-spinning company in Brora, about 300 miles north, made it happen.

Two weeks later I returned. The stones were on the table, and this time, placed next to them on parchment-colored sheets of paper, were perfectly matched little twists of yarn. It was alchemy: The stones had been turned to wool. Each yarn had been spun from twenty or thirty fine threads dyed different shades, then twisted to produce a marled effect. It took twelve colors to replicate the nuance of one tiny pebble.

We'd gone from an idea to reality, from the stones on the beach to the shelves at Bergdorf's.

I love to work from the ground up.

Sometimes it's fun to think, "Here's what I'd normally do with this fabric, this is what people *expect* to see, but what if?" That's the role of a designer. So when I use a black-and-gray herringbone *not* for a sport coat but for a dinner jacket with a satin lapel, it can be a beautiful twist. On the other hand, when it's "Here's a pink paisley for a woman's dress—what if I make it into a man's jacket?" it's never going to work. That's not innovative design, it's just bunk to get some fashion editor's attention. So as amusing as it can be to slide the pieces around to create different permutations, the "what if" has to be tempered by common sense or you'll end up with a circus act.

I'm not Versace or Dolce & Gabbana, experimenting for experimentation's sake, going for provocation—and press. I'm not Jean Paul Gaultier, putting skirts on men. A toga party at the frat house or a kilt in the highlands is fine, but at a board meeting? C'mon! I don't want my clothes to be so ridiculous no one can use them in the real world, or so basic I run the risk of losing the essence of who I am. If zip jackets are selling like hotcakes across the country, but we aren't about zip jackets, should we do a zip jacket? I don't think so. If the salesmen suggest we start doing narrow lapels because Kenneth Cole is doing them, no good. If the business guys say, "We can sell lavender button-downs, so let's do lavender button-downs," they're wrong. We'd lose our identity.

It's like two parallel sets of train tracks. One takes the route of glam and gloss, the other takes the route of marketability and wearability. Both might get you a certain amount of public awareness, and both may lead to success. It's just a question of which train you want to get on.

But no matter how strong your creative vision is, no designer is an island. Let's say you're Michael Jordan, the greatest basketball player in the world. You can be playing the worst team in the NBA, but if you're only one guy against five guys, you'll never win the game.

Likewise, the designer is the leader, and it's his vision, but he can't do everything. Some designers have one top assistant to do the work (or most of it) for them. This phenomenon seems more common in women's wear, where the trusty right hand almost assumes the persona of the designer. Calvin Klein used to have a guy named Zack Carr, who probably preferred working under the cover of a big name. Some people said he was more Calvin than Calvin, which must have had an interesting effect on Calvin.

I've never had or wanted a Zack. I think a strong operational partner who respects the designer's vision and brings it to fruition is much more important than the assistant designer or the designer behind the designer. The operational partner makes sure that the factories are functioning efficiently, that the product is delivered on time and priced right, that the sales force is doing its job. In that department, Calvin has had a great business partner in Barry Schwartz. At Polo Ralph Lauren in the formative years, Ralph had Peter Strom, a wonderful alter ego who helped forge the empire. Same with Yves Saint Laurent and Pierre Bergé, Giorgio Armani and Sergio Galeotti. In my early career, the guy was Guido Petruzzi of GFT, an elegant Italian who was a true architect of businesses—and my white knight. In the *real* success stories, that relationship is crucial.

On the design side, I like having a crackerjack team, all of whom I depend on. Most of my young designers and merchandisers are women. It's all about sensibility: Women see the aesthetic, not the hype. They're able to be more experimental and reach farther than men, who are pragmatic and literal. Women designers can't try the clothes on and feel how they fit, but they're more intuitive and know what they want to see a *guy* wearing.

The male designers, on the other hand, often seem less interested in learning the craft than in making a splash. It's good to have faith in yourself, and a certain amount of ego is necessary, but some think they can do it *better* even before they can do it *as well.*

Regardless of gender, regardless of their patience threshold, most young designers still have a lot to learn. Design schools like Parsons and FIT are wonderful in certain ways, but they provide an incomplete education. They're great with sketching and draping, but don't put half enough emphasis on teaching retail, wholesale, and PR so young designers can get a true look at the world in which we sell clothes—because in the fashion business, no matter how thrilling the headlines, if we don't sell clothes we're not going to be here. Knowledge is power, and they could be so much better armed.

Doing an exquisite illustration or fluffing the taffeta just so for a runway show is far removed from the nitty-gritty on the floor of a department store. Fashion exists in the real world, but these kids are being nurtured in a greenhouse. They don't see what happens to the cashmere blazer that's fallen off the hanger, or when the $200 sweater gets marked down to $59.95. They don't see the cockamamie floral jacket that looked so good on paper attracting not one of the twenty people walking through a shop at Saks. They don't see the pressure the retailers put on the manufacturers and designers.

These kids need practical experience, on-the-job learning, eyes open, and not just "Let's get press." They need to understand that a designer's greatest concern, once he gets to the point at which he has his own business, is staying there. Look at Isaac Mizrahi, who burst onto the women's wear scene as a darling of the press. Ten years later the press still loved him, but he had no business; while he'd been engaged in witty repartée and the making of *Unzipped,* a very successful documentary, he'd neglected the operational side of things. The fact that Anna Wintour and *Women's Wear Daily* adored his great personality wasn't going to pay the bills. So he took a break, branching out with a one-man off-Broadway show. Then he bounced back as an important label for Target. Now, through his visibility on television, he has, in some strange way, become the voice of reason in the unreasonable and illogical world of fashion.

If the design schools paid more attention to the nuts and bolts and taught their students what they should know, they'd be doing us all a favor. The kids would gain insight into their future customers. They'd begin to understand the integration of art and style and commerce. Without being blinded by the footlights, they'd have a clear view of the industry they aspire to.

When I hire designers, I care less what school or design house they've come from than where they're *coming from*. For me, the color palette comes first and foremost. I want to see how well developed it is intellectually and the kinds of accent colors they'll bring in to make it unique. Then I look at their books and portfolios. When they tell me their ideas and show me their sketches, I can see how they think.

Every step of the interview process shows me their interactive and communicating skills, which are essential. Can they verbally illustrate a collection, as if it already existed, and explain who would want to wear it and why? They might be the greatest creative people in the world, but if they can't convey their ideas, I can't use them. If someone wants to make reference to Victorian military outfits, tell me why, and then show me how it translates—not into costumes, but into clothes that people could wear.

A designer business is never going to be democratic (somebody has to be the editor in chief and decision maker), but it relies on give-and-take. At a design meeting a few years ago, one of my young twenty-something designers has an idea. "What about a band-collar jacket?" Now, back in the 1960s when we had free love and medallions, we also had the band-collar jacket, known in those days as the Nehru jacket. It came in light-blue polyester and was an easy laugh. Ancient history. This young guy, however, doesn't know that. He doesn't know what a joke it was then, and that's *good*. If I were relying only on my own experience, I'd say, "It's the ugliest thing in the world. Let's not do it." But a whole generation has never seen it, so we do it again. And this time it works. Not only does the band-collar jacket become a great commercial success for us, but we follow it with a band-collar sport shirt and a band-collar dress shirt—which is, of course, an oxymoron, because you can't wear a tie with it, but it sells like hotcakes anyway.

The design house is a cornucopia of ideas, the place from which all blessings flow, the heart of the designer name—and a form of bedlam. There are many moving parts, and much detritus, all of which get filtered into the meat grinder. Outsiders see a world of beauty and glamour and lipstick and flannel and cashmere and silk, but inside is a world of stubby pencils, plastic bins, tweed in your tea, and skeins of raw emu yarn that could tear your skin off. There are fabulous moments, unattractive moments, tensions, and time-frame issues. There are design meetings, strategic meetings, button meetings, color meetings, and silhouette meetings. There's no beautiful fountain pen on the polished art deco desk where someone's quietly sketching, and there's no gorgeous view of some far-off horizon, but there are books filled with raggedly cut swatches and identifying labels in the House of the Designer that resemble the book of secret formulas in the House of Frankenstein. It's not all attractive, but it's very exciting.

This is where we spend the most intense part of our daily lives, so we're dramatically bound by various dynamics and relationships. People connect, flirt and dally, form cliques, turn savage.

Way behind the scenes are the assistant designers, whose tasks depend on the needs and spirit of the head designer. They usually help organize swatches, help put color groups together, and help make up the "flats," which are the technical drawings indicating the dimensions of a garment for the manufacturer. Often they sit in on meetings, for more exposure to the process, and contribute when they feel comfortable. They might even be asked to bring in, say, seven ideas of their own for dress-shirt collars and four for pockets.

The more senior designers clearly have more experience. They know what the head designer is thinking, and they're involved from the very beginning with the initial concepts of the collection. They are truly collaborators.

But they're also rivals—all vying for the attention of the head designer, his touch on the shoulder, his blessing. Everyone wants to come up with the best idea. Everyone wants to be teacher's pet. It's a turf war, but because this is a business of image, the shots are subtle. Nobody attacks anybody's *integrity*. It's more common to hear, "His taste isn't *that* good," or "Armani did that two years ago"—feline snipes *about* someone but never to the someone's face. Then, at the first sign of favoritism, it becomes the group versus the individual—Who does he think *he* is? What does she think *she's* doing?—and the favorite becomes the outcast. It's like *Lord of the Flies*.

Nobody wants to see his designers go to the competition, but it's going to happen. Fashion, like any other dynamic profession, is an ongoing game of musical jobs. Young designers crave change, new experiences, new playgrounds; and established designers crave new blood. When I was at Polo, there was such heavy traffic moving back and forth between Ralph and Calvin we couldn't keep track. They were the two top guys, and working for either of them was like going to Harvard or Yale: lots of status, a great pedigree—and the invaluable opportunity to actually learn something. But their rivalry was intense, and snagging somebody from the other side was always an attack.

One of Polo's design assistants was a knockout named Kelly Rector. She was year-round tan, saucily dressed in provocative T-shirts and cowboy boots. In addition to being the lust object of every red-blooded guy there, she was one of Ralph's muses: the quintessential Ralph Lauren girl. I don't know exactly how and when it happened, but along came Calvin and away went Kelly. Ralph and Calvin have long done battle in the ranks of retail, vying for the crown—almost like Mohammed Ali and George Frazier or Larry Bird and Magic Johnson, in a slightly different context—and Kelly was the catch. So she went to work for Calvin, and then she married him. While I can't say for sure if Ralph considered it a great loss, I know it had to burn.

No one stays forever. But it's tough to accept. For one thing, you don't want to lose poeple because they're talented and you've invested a lot of time and energy in them. For another, you don't want to lose them because they know all the dirty laundry—the weaknesses and frailties of your place—and the designers on the other end can't wait to get the scoop. So when any of my team leaves, I say, "Just do me a favor. Whatever has gone on here, keep it closed and personal." But you can't count on it. Nobody signs a confidentiality agreement. Wherever they come from, wherever they go, what everyone wants to know is: How is it over *there*?

The mood of the workplace always comes from the top down. I don't hire designers for the way they look or the design house they came from. I don't dictate how they dress or part their hair, and I don't need to own their souls. But when I worked for Ralph Lauren, I was surrounded by Ralph: the right green and the right navy and the right wood and the right tweeds and the right M&Ms in the right bowls. Beauty is a danger, though, like a siren luring sailors to their death upon the rocks. The Polo mystique possessed me. The aura there was so seductive, so addictive, that it was like being on drugs. Life in the cocoon actually started to limit my thinking.

At Donna Karan, it's a lion's den—or so I've been told by designers seeking a little peace in their lives. Crazy, they say, and so schizophrenic they don't know what the hell they're doing from day to day. Translation: There's not much discipline going on. We're in a creative business, sure, but we're not painting some masterpiece for the Louvre here; we're just producing clothes, sticking to timetables, honoring commitments. Donna is widely known for changing her mind at the last minute, and it creates havoc. I don't respect that in *any* designer, a prima Donna or anyone else.

When you first kick off a design concept, there's time to play with a lot of ideas. But if you wake up in the middle of the night in the middle of the process and say to yourself, "I was really crazy about all those camel-hair colors, but now I'm just interested in black and white," you'd better blot those creative juices. Because once you decide on your fabrics and colors, once the sample yardage starts to come in, you're at the point of no return. You can still make tweaks, you might have room to veer from double-breasted to single-breasted, but it's too late to change the overall look. Any designer can futz and fiddle forever, but that's not the way the business works. Ignoring your deadlines isn't artistic. It's irrational. And it can destroy a company.

Not only will you have just spent a wad of money on sample yardage that you're not going to use, but you're creating a terrible bottleneck further on in the process because the new fabrics aren't going to get here fast enough for you to build the collection in time for Market Week, when you show your line for the first time.

And if you miss Market Week, you miss the out-of-town buyers. They may come back to New York, but they may not. Even if you're lucky enough to catch them two months later, you're not in the clear because the production team now has to scramble double-time, and the deliveries to the stores will still come in later than everybody else's. This means less time on the selling floor, less chance of a successful sell-through. It's like a tiny snowball becoming the Abominable Snowman. Your moment of "inspiration" has cost your company serious money.

In June or July, we start attending fabric shows and pondering tweeds, plaids, and fluffy yarns for the fall collection of the *following* year. I'll probably buy more swatches and make up more samples than I'm going to use, but in the creative process, there has to be a certain amount of inefficiency.

It's evolutionary. You don't sit down, create one idea, and that's it. You may have to try ten fabrics to end up with three, test a new one you've never used before, drop it when it wasn't what you'd expected. I remember falling in love one year with a range of textured fabrics from an Italian mill—nubby, tweedy herringbones and houndstooths—and buying a ton of sample yardage. This was going to be the statement of the season. But when the fabrics came in, they tailored up thick and heavy, we couldn't get consistent fit out of them, and they didn't look as luxurious as they'd looked in swatch form. You could say that shouldn't happen, but unless you *try* it, you never know. And if a fabric is going to be your statement, you can't just try *one*; you have to try six or seven or eight. You just can't go crazy. If you do, you overshoot your budget and create financial chaos.

The swatches we choose then go into the "mood" or "inspiration" boards we use for reference. These are collages of images—tweeds, autumn leaves, roaring rivers, dappled roads—that will set the color palette. Then come the "presentation boards," which are presented to the company, the licensees, the buyers, and the press (which loves an early insider's view). The boards show our patterns, fabrics, silhouettes (or shapes), and, most important, our "color stories"—series of color combinations that make up a group or collection. A blue "color story" might contain three or four shades of blue that will go into all products, and some accent colors such as light gray or burgundy. The components on the board function as the blueprint of a collection, the bones and the structure.

If we've designed a jacket, the illustrator's "flat" is sent to our factory in New Bedford to be translated into a pattern for a prototype. The prototype can be made in any fabric, but I like something absolutely plain, like gray flannel, because it's easier to see the shape. This is usually made in a 40 regular, which is a true medium—and my size. A great advantage: I can try that jacket on and know how it looks and feels.

Sometimes the prototype works, sometimes it doesn't. Maybe the shoulder comes out too square and needs to be rounder, or the lapel's too wide, or the pocket's in the wrong spot. We'll make corrections on the prototype, and back it goes for fixes. Only rarely will the silhouette miss the mark entirely and require a whole new prototype. Once the prototype is perfect, we can make up our salesmen's samples for the showroom. We produce a prototype for every garment, and the good news is that when we're satisfied with the shape and fit, we can vary the colors or add a detail such as a ticket pocket, but we don't have to produce another one unless we're changing the style significantly.

Then we need a handle—the name for a collection—to pull it all together. So we'll sit around and toss words and phrases back and forth, like "Relic" and "Vintage," "Havana" and "Australia," "Passage to India" and "An American at Oxford." The handle is what you grab onto, especially if you're the press.

Very early on we were known for our warm colonial colors, but we couldn't stay there forever. I knew from a merchandising and sales point of view that we needed to change gears. So as a contrast to all the cognacs and tobaccos, we did a collection in black and white, taking our customer from Havana to the Canadian Northwest. Once we had the handle we could start looking at fabrics in another way, and out of the "Canadian Northwest" came black-and-ivory Donegals, glen plaids with dark burgundy, sweaters inspired by Inuit rugs. But you can go just so far. Every pant and pullover, no matter how romantic, has to make it onto somebody's body. The guy on the subway can't get away with what some warrior might wear on the plains. The ombre plaid robe coat has to work in the office and not just in a movie with Daniel Day Lewis. A theme's a theme, but clothes are for people to wear.

THREE

Visionaries, Decisionaries

THE MAJOR Market Weeks come twice a year: Spring-summer clothes are usually presented in July; fall-winter, in January or February.

The week before a Week is a time of mass hysteria. Designers and merchandisers are running amok, bumping into each other, biting and snapping. "Where should I move this table?" "Let's put the suede pieces over there," "*Help* me here!" Assistants are calling the mail room a dozen times an hour to see if the samples have come in—the tailored clothing from the factory in Massachusetts, the sportswear from Asia, the ties from Italy—and making sure that every stand-up carton contains the eight tuxedos it's supposed to, every box contains the thirty-two sweaters or the sixty ties individually wrapped in cellophane sleeves it's supposed to. We're unpacking garments, laying out the outfits, dressing the mannequins, and fraying our nerves just so when the first buyer walks in on Monday morning, we will emanate elegance and pristine order.

At these times, the editing process becomes crucial. It's not what's *in* the line that's important, it's what's *not* in the line. You can have a beautiful collection that works perfectly until you bring in the one thing that doesn't fit and screws everything else up. Your attitude should never be, "Well, let's throw in this other plaid shirt." Every plaid shirt should mean something. Every *shirt* should mean something. And when it doesn't, it shouldn't be in the line. (If you don't have samples ready, you show the buyers hand-cut swatches with frayed edges affixed to beautiful parchment cards with pins through them and handwritten notes alongside. It's very romantic and looks like a work in progress. Buyers love to be a part of that.)

You're doing everything you can to create the best collection. You're hoping they see what you see, and some of them do. But others allow their vision to be clouded by data. Sometimes, even before looking at the clothes, a buyer will walk in, sit down, and pull out his spreadsheets and laptop so he can see how your last collection performed for him. "You had an eighty-seven percent sell-through, so we're going to buy more," he'll say, or "Your sport coats sold only twenty-three percent, so we're going to cut back." For the designer, this is a calamity.

The age of information has attacked the creative process: Sometimes, too much knowledge is a dangerous thing. Before there were spreadsheets, focus group, or laptops, the great merchants—like Stanley Marcus, Marvin Traub, Murray Pearlstein, Cliff Grodd, Fred Pressman, Wilkes Bashford, Geraldine Stutz, Phil Miller, and Allen Questrom—based their buys not on numbers and sell-throughs but on gut reactions. They were the experts, they had confidence, and they knew that if *they* liked the product, their customers would like it, too. They were being responsible financially, but they trusted their aesthetic. If the world had ten more Stanley Marcuses, the retail climate would be entirely different—product-driven, quality-driven, value-driven, intelligent.

When I started out, the specialty stores led the way. The small-store owner could take chances with new ideas because he answered only to himself. But those days are gone. The expense of opening an independent store is prohibitive today without a corporation paying the bills, and specialty stores have become an endangered species. The tragedy is they're still vital to our industry, because they represent personal service in a community and brave new taste.

Big-store buyers, even if they like the product, are afraid to fail. If they say, "I can only sell blue," you can't say, "This mushroom and taupe is a whole new story" and force an untested color palette down their throats, because if it doesn't sell they'll lose their bonuses and even their jobs. For them it's less a matter of creative thinking than self-preservation.

With forty or fifty stores to think about, they're so busy writing the orders, moving them through the system, and getting their budgets approved that it's very hard for them to go down and tell a guy on the floor about a great new suit or tie. While most stores will *say* they want their buyers to be in touch with trends, new colors, what's happening in the market—and to intimately know the quality of the products and collections they're buying—a lot of that is window dressing. What the stores really want is for their buyers to deliver the numbers. But when the numbers drive the purchases, the selection suffers, because they're thinking safety first: Buy what will sell.

Change is the only constant in the fashion industry. No brand can stay the same. Cars get new shapes, the Hershey bar gets a new wrapper, and we have to push ourselves, too. But if buyers are timid and salesmen know only what they sold yesterday, how *can* we change?

The other day, a guy in the elevator saw my beautiful black moleskin suit and asked me, "Is that in the new line?" I went nuts, because no, it's not in the new line, or the old line, or any line. Half the suits I wear *never* make the line because the sellers and buyers don't consider them *safe*. What they don't realize is that playing it safe *isn't* playing it safe.

At a specialty chain like Saks, one person usually buys for all the stores—and different branches usually carry different pieces of the line;

the larger the store, the larger the selection. Let's say a buyer is interested in a collection called "The Great Northwest." He might buy five styles of sweaters, three of pants, and eight of shirts (the more fashiony, aggressive things in the line) as a mini-collection to put in his A doors. (Stores rank their locations by size as "A, B, or C doors": If New York is the flagship for, say, Saks Fifth Avenue, that's an A door, while Minneapolis or Atlanta may be a B or C door.) The B door might get four styles of sweaters, two pants, and a jacket. The C door might get only a couple of shirts and a couple of pants. There's also a lot of transferring of product between stores. If New York does very well with "Northwest" and St. Louis doesn't, Saks will transfer the St. Louis pieces to the New York store.

No store can buy a designer's entire collection, so the integrity of the line gets diffused. The small specialty stores can buy into the theme because they have the flexibility to create *environments* in the spirit of the designer. But because they're small, they may be able to buy only a few pieces. So the sweater or the jacket has to exist independently, whether or not the buyer understands the concept it came from. Add to that a store's sloppy housekeeping, with things falling off the shelf, and now it's not just that the sweater is lying on the floor and getting kicked around, but that it's lying on the floor *alone*, torn from the rest of the collection of which it's an integral part. It makes a designer want to put on dark glasses and pretend to be someone else.

No matter how much you like the independents, once you're geared to selling to bigger stores, it's hard to sell to small ones again. For example, Louis Boston, the fine men's store that was my launching pad into the world of high fashion, doesn't carry my clothes anymore. It used to, when we started the collection, but Louis likes to have exclusive collections with extremely high prices. The bigger our business grew with Saks and Nordstrom and Bloomingdale's, the less feasible it became for Louis to carry us. When we were a small $3 million or $4 million-dollar business, we could sell to a few stores like Louis and that was it. But when we made the decision to grow—by going broader, selling our suits for $700 and $800 instead of $1,500, gaining greater distribution, and becoming a $50 million business—we could no longer sell to Louis.

Or Bergdorf's. Another heartbreaker, because I'd *had* it, I was *there,* but the store needs exclusive collections, very expensive product, and the Joseph Abboud label had become too accessible.

Losing Louis and Bergdorf's was cutting the umbilical cord, and emerging from the luxe retail world I'd grown up in was painful, even if it was part of an evolutionary process. In a perfect world, you could have it all, but Ralph is the only designer who's successfully crossed all those channels of distribution. He's got his Purple Label for Saks and Neiman's, and he's also in Bloomingdale's and Macy's. I'm still in awe of it. Would I love to be there, too? Absolutely. It's not an easy hill to climb.

When I worked at Louis in the 1960s and 1970s, customers would come in and spend Saturday afternoons just hanging out with a cup of coffee. But specialty stores are becoming extinct—and this makes them even more special. Here, while they last, are some of my favorites.

Barneys is in the process of trying to turn things around. Before dropping its downtown roots (and its apostrophe), before spreading itself too thin, the store was hot, filled with European designers and exciting stuff, because Fred Pressman, the visionary who ran it, was dynamic, steely, and smart. He didn't look for cool or hip; he looked at what the clothes could do for his customer. And he knew his customer. He himself was extremely unpretentious (khaki jackets and black knit ties, tuna fish for lunch) and soft spoken—but when he talked, everybody listened. He was the quintessential retailer: in the store all the time, familiar with every product. He wasn't a striver with a lust for the limelight; he was a conduit. His sons, Gene and Bob, went ultracool and moved from Seventeenth Street to Madison Avenue, but they didn't need to—they already *were* cool—and the move put enormous financial stress on the company. Today, Barneys still has a certain cachet, but Fred's legacy has paled.

Bergdorf Goodman represents aristocratic New York, and when I stroll up Fifth Avenue to the main store—near the Plaza Hotel and Central Park—and the magnificent Men's Store across the street, I feel like I'm approaching Mecca. This is the only Bergdorf's on the planet, with all the confidence and independence that allows. With management on the premises and everyone focused on the same organization, Bergdorf's can control its environment. The Men's Store proves that there's room in the market for khaki linen suits, cashmere cable sweaters, unconservative tweeds, gutsy fabrics, pronounced patterns—and that the world of menswear doesn't have to be so homogenized. I like some things better than others, but this is good taste without constraint.

Louis Boston was one of the first stores to bring the big European names to America and pick up an international reputation among designers and manufacturers. Murray Pearlstein was a powerhouse, and everybody wanted to sell to Louis. But in 1988, Murray miscalculated and decided to branch out. Murray knew Boston, but he didn't know New York, and when he opened at Fifty-Seventh and Lexington, he might as well have been in Queens. No New Yorker who can afford Louis's clothes shops on Lexington Avenue below Bloomingdale's. He also got caught, because of the recession, in a switch to less expensive clothing. If a guy was sending three or four kids to school and paying country club dues in the late 1980s, he wasn't going to look at $4,000 suits. So when Murray landed on Lex, his location and high prices were serious issues. Then there was the native competition, and the hackles he raised at Barneys, Bergdorf's, and Paul Stuart. In some naïve, arrogant way, he thought he was going to come in and own the business in New York, and that wasn't the case. Retreating to Boston, he put things right again and kept Louis special. These days, the store is still important, but it's lost its edge since he retired. Murray was such a shining star it's hard for anyone to follow in his footsteps. He's the pinnacle of what Louis was and ever will be.

Mitchells and Richards, connected in Connecticut, prove that if you do it right you'll be embraced by a community and gain stature. Very often, when family's involved, businesses dissipate. But by starting with

Mitchells in Westport, then acquiring Richards in Greenwich, this three-generation business (the late Ed Mitchell; now his two sons, Jack and Billy; and their sons) has done nothing but skyrocket. They carry men's and women's—Chanel, Gucci, Hermès, all the best international brands—and dress just about every CEO on the New York-Connecticut border. When the Mitchells unveiled their newly renovated store last year, they had James Brown performing and fashionistas from Zegna and *Harper's Bazaar* blending like a perfect martini.

Paul Stuart has adhered consistently to its design philosophy of updated traditional clothes with great style and beautiful quality. It's still one man's domain, the man being Clifford Grodd, president and CEO. He's one tough cookie (he was a tail-gunner in World War II), but he has wonderful taste and is tremendously respected. Paul Stuart was at its zenith in the 1970s and early 1980s (the days of "Think Yiddish, dress British"), when the height of fashion was the Madison Avenue executive, the natty guy, with a collar pin, full tie, and gray flannel suit cut fairly close to the body: Ivy League with a schmear. These days, the store still represents natural shoulders and side vents, pinpoint-cotton-oxford dress shirts and Italian foulard-silk ties, suede wing-tip balmorals and Donegal tweeds, walking sticks and umbrellas—all the true stuff of classic menswear. Everybody else has forgotten the corduroy suit with leather buttons, the seersucker suit, the linen suit. But Cliff Grodd hasn't. He makes them all part of his tapestry.

Wilkes Bashford is the consummate class act in San Francisco. Wilkes himself has always been influenced by European collections, and his devotion is reflected in the store, which does a grand job in presentation—displays, windows, architecture, imagery. But here's the rub: As more and more designer companies are opening their own stores, less and less of their stuff is going into stores like this. So, like Barneys, Bergdorf's, and Louis, Wilkes Bashford is backing away from designer labels and depending more on his own private-label collections.

And here are two icons.

Brooks Brothers. After falling into the hands of Marks & Spencer (who didn't know what they had), after trying to be Gap and Banana Republic with windows full of knit shirts and chinos; after abandoning its culture and core constituency, this 186-year-old company has finally found its way back to its rightful place as chief purveyor of American traditional. The store is doing younger things now, but it still excels in tweed jackets, ancient madder ties, and the trademark button-down shirt (still made in America). Now owned by Italians, who have an almost fawning respect for its image, Brooks is the player to watch—as long as it stays true to that image.

Abercrombie & Fitch. Once the preeminent purveyor of safari gear and picnic baskets for the Harvard-Yale game, A&F is now outfitting the carriage trade's grandchildren. Fifty years ago, you'd go in and see a real rhino head on the wall. Now every store has a fake moose head. The old rhino was talking to Teddy Roosevelt, Admiral Peary, and pals. The new moose is talking to sixteen-year-old girls who speak another language. But never mind. The young people running up and down the stairs may not know every reference here, but somehow they *get* it. A&F has taken the old fuddy-duddy elements, such as Aran sweaters, herringbones, tartans, and corduroy, and reinvented them. They haven't "reinterpreted the classics." They've reconstructed a dinosaur from the mosquito in the amber, but the dinosaur's a little different this time. The old A&F sold cargo pants to carry bullets, bowie knife, and canteen. The new one sells them to kids with cell phones and credit cards. My daughter Lila fell for a tweed cardigan with elbow patches. It's a far cry from the tweed jacket with elbow patches I knew back in the 1960s when I was trying to be William F. Buckley (stylistically, not ideologically), but she loved it and it's authentic for *her* generation.

Life without the specialty stores would be very difficult for new designers and new brands entering the scene, because the specialty stores have always been the leaders, always provided the platform. If they go under, we're all sunk.

FOUR

Air Play

"HE'S A SECOND Ralph Lauren," people were saying.

"He is not a second anyone," the influential fashion writer Clara Hancox answered back in *DNR*. "He is today, without question, 'the first Joe Abboud.'" But by the early 1990s, even such a stellar endorsement wasn't enough. I'd won some great awards and gotten some great press, but I was in a sophomore slump: not big enough to go up against the established brands like Armani or Ralph Lauren, and not the newest kid on the block either. Without enormous advertising dollars, I still had to find a way to keep up the buzz. I needed a niche of my own.

One day over my cornflakes, it opened up.

I'm listening to *Imus in the Morning*, and he mentions that Saks has just sent over a tuxedo and vest by this guy Joseph Abboud. "Must be one of those European froufrou designers," he adds.

So I pick up the phone. I'm an American designer, I tell him, and a Red Sox fan who's been listening to the show since 1981, when we Polo salesmen would come in at eight o'clock, have our coffee, and turn on the radio. We have a nice talk, and then he asks, "Do you mind if I mention this conversation on the air tomorrow?" Is he *kidding*?

"I'd be flattered," I say.

"Do you mind if I rip you apart? Because that's what I do."

"It's your show," I said. "Do whatever you want."

He's been ripping me apart ever since.

It was a calculated risk. But he had the right audience—10 million to 12 million people who could afford to buy my clothes—so I took it. I knew I was never going to share a pedestal with Tom Brokaw and Tim Russert and the other venerated guests. But I knew there was a role for me, and I didn't mind taking the heat. You've got to know going in that you're going to get destroyed, but if *you* get destroyed and the *product* does well, it's worth it. To this day, the single most important thing I've ever done to promote awareness of my brand is *Imus*.

I know if I dress a certain way I can start a little skit or routine. So I put on a cool outfit and a thick skin. There are days I think, "God, I hate this"—Imus can be brutal—but I keep on playing because even as he's beating me up, he's also giving me this incredible exposure.

He razzes me about Armani and Ralph and loves strumming the gay-designer stereotype. "Joe doesn't really have a family," he'll whoop. "He rents his wife and two kids. He shows pictures." Or, "Joseph Abboud goes in the back door." If I wear an ivory suit, he'll say, "Here comes the ice cream man." If I wear a pocket square, it's "What a goofball, what a poof. But boy, he makes great clothes." It drives my mother-in-law, Jane, crazy, because she considers me a gentleman who shouldn't endure such stuff, but it's built an awareness for me that I could never have achieved through advertising.

One day I was on as guest sports announcer, doing four spots in two hours. So I wore four different outfits, trying to provoke him into doing a shtick. I kept waiting for him to jump on me, but nothing. He calls the shots and never goes where you think he's going to go.

But I got to deliver this:

Top Ten Reasons That Joseph Abboud Should Not Do Sports on *Imus in the Morning*:

10. None of his fellow designers have seen a professional sporting event except ice dancing.
9. There isn't enough time between sportscasts to change his outfit.
8. It's hard to pick point spreads based on sexual preference.
7. His idea of a starting lineup includes runway models and music.
6. Sitting behind the sports desk wrinkles the pleats in his pants.
5. He's not allowed in any locker room for postgame interviews until all players have left the showers.
4. He was disappointed when the Cleveland Browns weren't renamed the Cleveland Khakis.
3. He wonders why the NFL doesn't know that shoulder pads are out.
2. His definition of a flagrant foul is wearing argyle socks with a glen plaid suit.
1. They don't make headsets in earth tones.

Suddenly, I'm all over the place. Not always treated reverentially, but out there. Take this, from *Seinfeld* in 1996:

> Jerry walks into a men's store. An effete Barneys-esque salesman holds up a luxurious two-button cashmere crested blazer. "Joseph Abboud," he intones.
>
> "Oh," says Jerry, nodding. The salesman beams.
>
> "It'll look great with my sneakers."

*   *   *

I'm still knocked out when I see my clothes on a star. In fact, I'm knocked out when I see a star.

It's a gorgeous afternoon at the Beverly Hills Hotel. I'm in town to do some personal appearances and I want a tan, so I'm lying out by the pool. Everybody's basking, everybody's looking at everybody else, and who comes along but George Hamilton.

Now, this guy is one of my Technicolor heroes—impeccably dressed, famously tan, perfectly one-dimensional. I'm actually using some George Hamilton tanning lotion. And here he is, about to go sit in his little private area and catch some rays. I want to introduce myself. Maybe he'll know who I am, and maybe he won't. I don't really care. I just want to meet him.

He does know who I am, and he's charming.

"I just bought this stuff in the hotel," I tell him, showing him the lotion.

"I spent years perfecting it," he tells me.

We talk about fashion and image. He tells me how the studios used to groom their stars when they looked the part, dressed the part, and lived the part right down to the right flannel pants for iced tea on the producer's lawn. I'm riveted by it. This is everything I've ever dreamed about, and I'm hearing it from the horse's mouth. I tell him how I've just done a collection of paisley ties, and he tells me how much he loves paisley ties.

"You know what?" I say. "I'd love to send you some." Graciously, he accepts. When I get back to New York, I send him a dozen paisley ties. And never hear a word.

But they're not all like that.

Gene Pitney, who sang "The Man Who Shot Liberty Valance," "A Town without Pity," and a million other great songs when I was a kid, was another idol I'd never met until I got a nice piece of news in 2002. This guy, whose music still spins around on my CD player, was inducted into the Rock 'n' Roll Hall of Fame at the Waldorf Astoria and came out wearing a Joseph Abboud tuxedo. Which he'd bought himself.

But for star-spangled exposure, there's nothing like the Academy Awards—even when the duds are a dud. I think there are more badly dressed handsome men there than anywhere else on earth. There's still nothing like a beautifully cut tuxedo, a crisp white shirt, and a classic bow tie. With that formula, you can never go wrong.

At the ceremony in 2004, a lot of guys went wrong. Caught up in a tidal wave of ordinary ties with tuxedos, they ended up looking like funeral directors. But a few bow-tied purists clung to the rocks, like Jude Law, John Travolta, Chris Cooper, and Clint Eastwood (who wore his bow tie with a blue shirt, and if any stylist had suggested otherwise, Eastwood would have blown him away).

You can learn a lot about what *not* to do by watching the Academy Awards. We all remember Kevin Spacey showing up a few years ago in a very, very long jacket. Who told him to do that? Some LA fashionista trying too hard to make a name for himself, no doubt. On the other hand, Robin Williams's long jacket (or was it a short coat?) in 2004 seemed appropriate just *because* he was Robin Williams, and it fit his personality as well as it fit him.

Giorgio Armani has always had a lock on actresses, who go for his serene designs, and actors love his clothes. So, in fact, do celebrities on other stages. At the height of Armani in the 1980s, Pat Riley was his poster boy. With those wonderful slouchy jackets and big shoulders, Pat brought fashion to the NBA floor, and all the coaches in professional sports wanted to slick their hair back and look just like him. Then one day Pat came into my Greenwich store and bought a leather jacket.

Don't tell Armani.

My clothes encounters with the sports and broadcasting world started in 1986 when I met Bryant Gumbel, who was then hosting the *Today* show. A buyer we both knew at Brooks Brothers thought Bryant would be interested in seeing my collection. Fine with me. "Just have him call,"

I said, and, to my amazement, he did. When he came up to the show-room—my first celebrity customer!—it was clear he knew as much about the clothing business as most of the buyers. As he moved through the room, touching fabrics, stroking ties, I could see real passion in his eyes.

We became fast friends. We'd both worked in retail, we both loved clothes and sports. When he asked me to design seventeen different outfits for his gig at the Seoul Olympics in 1988, my company was brand-new, and landing such a marquee name got us press in the *Wall Street Journal*, the *New York Times*, *USA Today*, the *Washington Post*, and others. That opened up the networks to me, dressing the Olympics hosts like Bob Costas on NBC, Jim Nance and the NFL guys on CBS, and a few other high profiles on the TV screen.

When these guys need clothes, they need them yesterday. They've got deadlines, and time is at a premium. So when they come up to the office, they don't sit around and have a lot of coffee. There's no "In two months I'm going to buy some new suits." There's *now*. So we try to make it easy for them: Tell us what you like, we'll get it done, we'll get back to you with the information, we'll let you know when it's ready.

It's like walking into a doctor's office and getting a diagnosis. But the conversations are crucial, because this isn't about Joseph Abboud putting his stamp on their foreheads; it's about these guys and their image. We'll go through suit fabrics and the all-important questions. Two-, three-, or four-button? Side vents or no vents? Flap pocket or patch pocket? Plain front or pleated? Double-breasted or single-breasted? Since they're usually visible only from the waist up, most TV guys prefer single-breasted so they can show off their shirts and ties. Double-breasted doesn't work when they're sitting down, because it gets all bunched up and crossed over. Half the time they're wearing jeans underneath, anyway.

This kind of on-air visibility is invaluable to us, and the cost is relatively insignificant. Yeah, there's a lot of time and effort you can't put a dollar figure on—getting the clothes made, coordinating everything, and doing all the fittings—but it allows us to reach our audience without a tremendous advertising budget. I don't count on the viewers waiting for my name to roll in the credits—"Hey, I like that tie Brokaw's wearing tonight! Let's see who made it!"—so they can run out and buy 200,000 blue-and-ivory ties. But I do count on the association, which is almost subliminal. We get a three-second hold with my logo, and it's powerful stuff. In other words, we get the credit and they get the clothes. And if we get some press from it, that's icing on the cake.

Okay, here comes Bob Costas for the Olympics, and what's the image he wants to project? Fashionable, but not *too* fashionable (meaning clownish or boyish). What's the where and when? It matters, because being out of whack with the seasons presents weight issues, fabric-availability issues, color issues. We'll do fireside clothes like tweeds and suedes for the Winter Games in France and Norway, but when the Olympics play in Australia—when it's spring in Sydney but autumn in New York—Bob needs a wardrobe that will look right to audiences all over the world. (And look right in its environment as well. You can't throw one palette against the other. Is the set brown, with burled wood and soft leather, so he can wear earthy colors? Or is it iron and steel, which calls for blues and grays? And how does it all jibe with the outdoor events? If viewers are going to be seeing a lot of blue sky and ocean, that's a consideration too.)

Public figures have to evolve if they want to stay public, and when it's up to me I try to keep them on the edge without pushing them over. I'll tell them it's time for striped ties or patterned shirts and offer gentle options, nothing radical. But sometimes the most subtle conversion can be cataclysmic. Just try moving Bryant Gumbel from solid ties to more patterned ones, or Bill O'Reilly from two-button to three-button. The audience might not even notice such changes, but to these guys it's like asking them to remove an arm. Some networks provide stylists, but it's usually the network guys who don't need them. They know what they want and what works for them.

Bryant, especially, has very specific fashion dicta. One day he'll ask,

"Does that shoulder make me look like I'm trying too hard?" Another day he'll announce that he won't wear suede shoes because he's too short. I tell him he's not too short. "Well, there's no *shine*," he says, "and duller makes me look shorter." Like that.

O'Reilly's a different challenge. He's no-nonsense, a tough interviewer, and the no-spin zone extends to the wardrobe, too. I love picking clothes with him, but he doesn't have a lot of patience. He comes into our showroom on the twenty-seventh floor, with his phone on his hip, and I already know the game: This is going to be short and sweet. He's got the radio show, he's got the TV show, he's got two minutes for pleasantries—then let's get to it.

Every swatch he picks is blue. I suggest a gray, but forget it. And I know not to even go *near* the B word—brown. So we'll go from a blue shadow chalkstripe to a dark blue glen plaid to a blue nailhead, and anybody standing ten feet away when he laid out the swatches wouldn't be able to tell the difference. But blue makes him comfortable, so that's what it is. He doesn't stand around pondering and musing. Those meetings go *bing! bang! boom!* and he makes his decisions in a shot.

When he can't come up, we'll send about three hundred swatches over to his office (some of them not blue). He's too busy to sit down and be persuaded, so I attach handwritten suggestions—"I think this will make a great suit. Just think about it." Or "I don't know if this plaid works for TV, but you don't have anything like it." You have to move people around gently sometimes.

Tom Brokaw is handsome, dignified, and in great shape, and his approval rating and credibility are astronomical, so he's the ideal model for a designer. We met a few years ago when he was in the process of changing his style. He wore nice clothes, whosever they were, but they were a little small for him. I don't think he wears my stuff exclusively, but he wears a lot of it. One night recently, Tom and his wife, Meredith, came over for dinner. He was wearing a turtleneck and one of our burnished-rust tweed jackets and I thought, "Man, if there was ever the perfect ad, it just walked into my house."

Then there was the pearl-gray flannel pinstripe I designed for him. With his gray hair, he looked fantastic in it—but so fantastic that the suit got too much attention and diminished his authority. He wore it on the air only once. Now he wears it to parties.

When I started doing *Imus*, fashion was kept in its own little media niche. But now it's everywhere—movies, the Internet, and TV. Especially TV. We all watch ourselves on *Full Frontal Fashion*, where they know their audience and aren't going to get too cerebral. With Lila and Ari, I watch *The Makeover Story* and *Extreme Makeover*, and now there's *Extreme Makeover: Home Edition*, where crews run in like little elves and do the gardening. But I'm not crazy about *Queer Eye for the Straight Guy* because I hate the stereotyping. It trivializes everybody and is an assault on our individuality. You can't make every straight guy a Neanderthal and every gay guy an *artiste*, because—look at me, the straight-guy designer—there's often a crossover.

We should all be able to develop our own tastes without worrying about how we're perceived. I can pick out drapes and still make it to the ball game in time for the national anthem.

Personal Appearance

SEPTEMBER 7, 2002. Fenway Park. The Blue Jays versus the Red Sox.

The biggest fashion dilemma in my entire life? What to wear to throw out the first pitch.

If I get *too* dressed up, I look like a poof—and a *designer*. If I don't dress up enough, some jerk from Toronto says, "That shlep is a *designer*?" I end up wearing a white T-shirt and a navy blazer over a pair of jeans, and a navy-and-white Red Sox cap. Cool, but not overly cool.

For the past two weeks, I've been playing to a crowd of two—my daughters, Lila and Ari. I've been practicing in my driveway at home, pitching sixty feet six inches at a propped-up trash can and nailing that sucker. My friend, Fred Wilpon, tells me to just relax. Easy for him to say; he owns the New York Mets. Me, I'm nervous as hell. By the time I get to the ballpark, with 34,000 people there, it's too late to warm up, and I'm worried about just getting the ball over the plate.

"It's the embarrassment factor. The crowd can kill you," I've been warned by Sean McDonough, the veteran Red Sox announcer. (Stephen King, a passionate Red Sox fan, once bounced the first pitch about two-thirds of the way home and was loudly booed.) "So when you go out there, don't throw from the mound, but come up closer to the plate and throw from the grass." Lila and Ari are sure that whatever I do, I'll be fine.

I decide to throw from the mound. When am I going to get another chance to stand on the mound at Fenway?

The loudspeaker announces: "Fashion designer Joseph Abboud, great Red Sox fan." The big screen flashes: "In honor of his dad, Joe Abboud, who was a lifelong Red Sox fan." "The Star-Spangled Banner" is playing, and I'm walking to the mound.

Usually when you throw out the first pitch, there's a backup guy to catch it. But I've asked for my friend Nomar Garciaparra, who's a deity in Boston—*It's Nomah!*—so I know I'm in good hands. I also know I'm going to get a cheer when he comes out. Which I do.

"Let's just go play catch," Nomar says, to relax me. And suddenly it's my big moment. I don't take the big windup I've been practicing, but I get off a decent throw—a little high and outside, but it's over the *plate.* The crowd roars. It's an extraordinary rush, like nothing I've ever felt before. I'm standing on the mound at Fenway and calling up the spirit of my dad, thanks to just one thing: clothes.

I drive up to Boston from my home in Westchester, New York, about twelve times a season to see the Red Sox. In fact, I'll travel practically *anywhere* to see them. Even to Yankee Stadium.

One summer afternoon I was sitting on the third-base line right at the field, with Yankee fans all around. The Red Sox were losing, and I was feeling lousy. This was nothing new. Every single time I go to Yankee Stadium, the Red Sox lose. My Boston friends beg me not to go. They tell me I'm bad luck.

I'm sitting there watching my recurring nightmare, and out of nowhere a bird flies overhead and dumps right on me—*and* my beautiful tan suit. He could have picked any number of Yankee fans. How come he got me? Because he zeroed in and said, "There's the Red Sox fan. Let me *at* him." Forget what you've heard about bird shit being good luck. We lost the seventh game in a row.

But I can make a good impression anywhere.

One day I took my two daughters to Sbarro's at the mall in Stamford, where young Ari dropped a slice of pizza on my lap.

"Aren't you Joseph Abboud?" A radiant grin from the next table. "I really love your stuff." Carefully swiveling my pepperoni'd pants out of sight, I smiled and greeted my public.

Most people assume that the designer's tie is knotted perfectly. His home is flawless. The dog and cat are sitting in the perfect spot. He doesn't have health issues, cranky relatives, or flat tires. This is what *Vanity Fair* and *Hello!*, Palm Beach and Beverly Hills image-makers and dream-spinners would have people believe, but it's not true.

The designer—at least this designer—is just a guy.

And, like most men, enormously susceptible to the opinions of women—no matter what their age. One morning, I was going downstairs in a beautiful gray flannel suit, a woven silver tie, and a white shirt. And there was Lila, then ten.

"Daddy, do you think that tie goes with that suit?"

I looked in the mirror. Maybe she had something. I went upstairs and changed my tie.

"Better," she said, when I came back down. "Much better."

I may be Mr. Big Shot preaching to all the guys, but this mattered a *lot*.

In reality, though, men dress mostly for other men. We want to be appealing to women, we want them to help us look good, but we don't particularly dress for them. The payoff is that when we dress well for *men*, we automatically appeal to women. When I'm trying to figure out what to wear, I think about the day. Am I going to be the designer or the businessman? Am I giving an interview? Teaching a class? Meeting the mayor? I can't just throw something on and dress for *me*. I have to think about the human dynamics of the event and who's going to be there.

I didn't always. Years ago, when I was trying too hard, I showed up at a lunch given by *Forbes* magazine at La Grenouille in an ivory linen suit with an ivory silk T-shirt. I went in as The Designer, but with my ethnic looks and flamboyant getup in this sea of dark suits, I ended up feeling like a gigolo. The irony was that I'd spent my life avoiding such situations. Dressing well had always been my forte; standing out had been my way of fitting in. But this time, I didn't read it right. If I could have done it again, I would have worn a dark navy double-breasted suit, a white shirt, and a silver tie—and I still would have stood out, but within the boundaries. So the message is: Understand how to dress for where you're going. Don't get caught with your pants down.

Which leads to underwear. To me, guys are either "Floyds" or "Tarzans." This came out of my years at Polo, where we decided that "Tarzans" wear briefs and "Floyds" (for Floyd Patterson) wear boxers. The only boxers I wear are the ones with hearts and polar bears that my girls give me to sleep in. Otherwise, I'm a Tarzan, in white or gray. (Bathing suits are also "Tarzans" and "Floyds." Invariably, it's the guys in the Tarzans who shouldn't be wearing them. They've got a potbelly, or their little crack is showing, and you want to tell them No! Meanwhile, the young kids, who *could* wear them, are wearing bathing suits below their knees.)

As for undershirts—don't even start. You always see them through a guy's shirt. My father used to wear the Wallace Beery kind, the tank top, and to me they're of another time. Why buy a beautifully patterned or nicely colored or finely textured dress shirt that's going to be upstaged by a piece of underwear?

If you're going to wear nice clothes, you've got to have a body to hang them on. Lift weights, bat balls, lug rocks—whatever makes your day. I play a lot of sports, but I won't play golf because the clothes are so ugly. Think about this. When a man buys a suit with a lapel that's a quarter of an inch wider than the last one, it's a mammoth decision in his life. But put him on the golf course, and this master of the universe parades around in the most god-awful pink-and-green argyle sweaters and lilac pants. I've never been able to understand it.

In high school, I ran track and played football. To be on the football team, I had to take Hoffman's Gain-Weight pills. They came in a huge can, and I had to take about twenty or thirty of them a day. You chewed them, and they were chalky, and they tasted like *chicken liver*. Horrible. But I went from 167 to 187 pounds.

Now I work like a demon three times a week at a spinning class to keep the weight off. Not the karaoke class, where you get off your bike and stand up onstage at a microphone. Somehow I can't see myself sweating and singing "Hunka Hunka Burning Love." I wear tight bike shorts, but I'm always a little self-conscious about them (especially after a girl on the next bike told me she thought I was a ballet dancer). And I've noticed lately that the hard-core gym fashionistas are wearing cargo pants and regular shirts. Instead of the 1980s-1990s thing, it's now streetwear at the gym as opposed to gymwear on the street.

Then there's the culture of gymspeak.

Women can say anything and get away with it, but there are certain things guys just don't talk about. Women will openly talk about breast implants—"Marcia's look great, don't they? I'd like to get some, too." But a guy doesn't say to a pal, "Hey, I'd like a penile implant." One woman will say to another, "I love your legs!" and it's fine. But if a woman compliments a guy—"You're in great shape!"—he'll grunt back with, "*Yeah*, I'm doin' forty-fives now, better for my back." Always the caveman.

If I were to point to a woman's arms and say, "Great definition," she'd probably be flattered. But if I were to say to some guy, "How'd you get those bulging biceps?" he'd crown me with a forty-five-pound weight. I have a hard enough time being a designer at the gym.

SIX

The Hero Was Always Dressed Right

I'M THREE YEARS OLD. I've just tumbled into the Charles River from the bank where my family is having a picnic, and I'm splashing, flailing, sinking fast . . . when my father dives in to save me.

It's my earliest memory of him, and the bravest, because Joe Abboud was in constant pain. In the early 1950s, when he was doing a job up in Maine, his car was rear-ended, and his back was injured. He'd always had back problems, but this collision undid him forever. He was a master mechanic for the American Can Company, but there was no compulsory insurance, and the guy who hit him was a coworker with a family, so my dad wouldn't sue him. He got some disability, but he was finished with a salary. Unable to work, he stayed home while my mother held two jobs to support the family.

Through the years, he'd undergo surgery after surgery for spinal fusions and then have to lie flat on his back for months at a time. I clearly

remember waiting on a swing outside Boston's Faulkner Hospital because I was too young to go in and visit him. Back surgery and pain medication were in their infancy then, and he found some relief in medicine,
but more in drink. I was far too young and self-absorbed to understand
my mother's frustration and exhaustion, and all I remember is feeling
sorry for my dad.

I have a photograph of him in khaki pants and a khaki military shirt,
holding a compass. Very Abercrombie & Fitch, except that he didn't
know a thing about Abercrombie & Fitch. Instinctively he had the right
clothes for the part, like any hero. Before the accident he'd been a great
outdoorsman, a member of the National Guard, a survivor. He wasn't
a big man—probably five-foot-seven and slight—but he was strong.

Whenever he shot a deer and brought it home strapped to the hood
of the car, he'd dress it and we'd eat venison for six months. No one
had any moral qualms about hunting in those days. It wasn't politically
incorrect, it was manly. But such good times were rare.

Weak and just able to walk, between those long bouts with his back,
he still wanted to be the guy he'd been and do the things he'd done—
and he wanted to share them with me. He taught me to shoot a rifle and
a bow and arrow (for the kick, not the kill). He couldn't run or throw
a ball, but he took me fishing and to Red Sox games. Nobody used the
word "bonding" in those days, but we were together, just the two of us.
We never talked about my future or his past. It was just me being with
my dad.

When I was born, in 1950, my family lived at 21 Milford Street in
Boston's South End. The South End wasn't exactly a destination. In
the mid-nineteenth century it had been a very fashionable area, but
by the mid-twentieth it was a landing place for immigrants and first-
generation families. Who knew about racial problems? Not us. East
Boston was Italian, South Boston was Irish, the West End was Jewish,
and the South End was an ethnic hodgepodge of everybody—with a
heavy dose of the Middle East. On Shawmut Avenue around the

corner, mothers shopped at Lebanese markets, kids bought nickel pickles out of a barrel and chewy sheets of apricot paste, and grandfathers gathered in murky little storefront social clubs to smoke, sip sludgy coffee, and play pinochle.

Ours was a five-story brick row house, and my father took pride in polishing the brass kick plates and shellacking the double front door. We occupied the first three floors, my uncle Esau and his family the fourth floor, and boarders the fifth. The house was just a house to me then, but when I drive past it now I'm proud to see how handsome it looks in what is now a gentrified neighborhood. Somebody else owns it, but it will always be *mine*.

We had no yard, so we used the streets. In summer, I sped along on my little red steamroller, and on warm nights we sat out on the front stoop, backs against the wrought-iron railing. Winter blizzards provided huge snow dunes—neutralizing the city, freezing traffic, and transforming our turf into a world of hills and castles.

We were working-class and inner-city, but not poor, and we had pretty much everything we wanted. I never envied anyone else's dad, or car, or stuff. My mother was the love of my life. My three older sisters coddled me like a little prince. I'm convinced that being surrounded by love and a lot of women gave me a sensitive view of the world.

Jeanette wrote music. Mara was a fine artist. Nancy did delicate charcoal drawings. My father painted kaleidoscopic designs on the cement patio, with an engineer's eye for intricacy. My mother was culinarily creative. Nobody was an *artiste*, but we were all able to express our emotions and verbalize the beauty in our lives.

When you're a child, you may look across Boylston and sense it's different over there, but it doesn't really figure in your life. Not unless my father took my mother to the dentist on the far side of town did I get to see the other Boston and start to wonder. We'd drive up Beacon Hill, and I'd gaze at the Public Garden and Common on the right, the mansions—with their pillars, ironwork, handblown lavender glass, and window boxes—on the left. What was this incredible place? It always felt like there was a mystery about to happen, a story to tell.

I was intrigued, but it wasn't my world. Mine was at the movies.

When I was four and five, my parents paid an older kid in the neighborhood twenty-five cents every afternoon to take me to the National Theatre around the corner on Tremont Street. My mother was home with her sewing machine, my father was in bed with his back, and I was in Morocco and Timbuktu with Buster Crabbe and Batman, swashbucklers and swells. There in the dark, I wasn't just some little Lebanese kid with a baby-sitter. I was the Hero, in tweeds and tuxedos, ascots and furs.

That's where I knew that clothes represented a better life. People in the movies were successful and glamorous, just like they were on Beacon Street, and clothes were the ticket.

In 1956, we moved to a modest one-family house in an Irish-Catholic neighborhood of Roslindale, and I transferred my affections to the Rialto in Roslindale Square, where I caught all the B movies and everything else that kids saw on Saturdays. On television, there was Davy Crockett, top of the heap, and a cowboy named Rex Trailer, who had a kids' show and showed cartoons. Trailer had a sidekick named Pablo, a duck named Hubert, and a fringed cowboy shirt. Man, I loved that shirt. These were heroes a Lebanese kid from the South End couldn't begin to identify with, but running around in their suedes and fringes (forget the coonskin hat), they were clearly making an impression.

It didn't matter what I watched, so long as it had action—and style. Whether it was Brando with the black leather jacket in *The Wild Ones*, or Charlie Chan and number one son sleuthing around in fitted three-piece gabardine suits, or Robert Donat in *The 39 Steps*, running from the bad guys while his tweed suit got crumpled and his lapel flipped up, the hero was always dressed right. There's no question that those early associations—as well as later images like Redford and Newman's great corduroy and leather jackets in *Butch Cassidy and the Sundance Kid,* the Cambridge freshmen at a candlelit dinner in their *Chariots of Fire* tuxedos, Mel Gibson's murky tartans in *Braveheart*—affected the clothes I design.

And we'll always have *Casablanca,* ever the more intriguing for being in black and white: Humphrey Bogart's double-breasted shawl tuxedo and Paul Henreid's colonial khaki suit, with its beautiful roll-on lapel and the polka-dot tie I've always imagined as ivory on chocolate brown or midnight blue. That tie, with its oval dots, would influence every polka-dot tie I'd ever do in any collection.

I also loved soldiers, onscreen and off. Toy soldiers took over the house. No shelf or windowsill was sacred—not even the little manger scene my mother set up every Christmas. When nobody was looking, I'd pull out the Holy Family and wise men and put in *my* guys.

When *Johnny Tremain* opened in 1958, a toy company came out with a set of Revolutionary War troops. The next year *Ben-Hur* inspired an industry of Roman soldiers, slaves, chariots, and your own little Colosseum. I'd close the door to my room and reenact my battle scenes. And I was a purist. No way would I pit my *Ben-Hur* soldiers against my *Johnny Tremain* guys. Even then, I had different motifs and themes. Even then, I didn't mix my metaphors.

Lila Sallah Abboud, my mother, had always been a seamstress—at least since the 1930s, when she worked at Peerless, a clothing company in Boston. When I was a kid, she was still at it, stitching piecework at home. I remember the wrapped bundles of sleeves and collars and the stop-start whirr of the sewing machine continuing long after the rest of us had gone to bed. She didn't think of sewing as an art form, or have any particular affection for fashion. Stitching paid the bills, and there was nothing romantic about it.

Mom never complained, but nothing in her life had been easy. Her parents had come from Lebanon to Gloucester, a blue-collar fishing town on Cape Ann near Boston, and when my mother was two, her mother died—after being given the evil eye, the neighbors said, because she was so beautiful. The piano was draped for a year of mourning, and when my grandfather went on the road selling barber supplies, my mother had to live with other families, caring for their children. The only doll she ever had was cardboard—Aunt Jemima cut from the front of the box.

But there was another image she cherished more: a photograph of her mother in a full riding skirt and high-button lace collar with a riding crop. It was all she had. From the time I was a little boy, that picture was important to me too. At our house, it stood on Mom's bureau next to her hairbrush and mirror, and it never failed to fascinate me.

I was a mama's boy, and a roughneck too. At seven or eight, I was scrapping with so many other kids in the neighborhood that my mother threatened me with reform school on a daily basis. But that didn't scare me half as much as her anger at night. Whatever my crime, whatever the hour, I would not go to bed until she'd forgiven me. She'd be in her little sewing room off the kitchen, stitching some skimpy sleeve, and I'd be on pins and needles—sitting on the kitchen steps until I could hear a change in her voice.

"Ma, I'm sorry."

"It's okay, Joseph," she'd say, still a little cross. "Go to bed."

"Ma-a-a. I'm sorry."

"Go to sleep. It's fine." But it wasn't fine, and until I knew I was forgiven, I wouldn't leave. This could go on for hours.

"*Ma-a-a. Ma-a-a.*"

Until finally, "All right, Joseph. It's all right. I love you. Come kiss me good night." When her tone went tender, I felt a wild rush of relief. Every single time.

I worshiped her, but I was rattled by the way she sometimes treated Dad. When he was on medication, one drink could really affect him. He wouldn't get surly, but almost silly. His softness made her hard.

All any kid wants is harmony at home, and when my parents got along well, we were all in love. But if he said, "You're full of malarkey," we all knew to head for the bunkers. For some reason that phrase was a trigger, like in *The Manchurian Candidate*. He knew it, but he'd provoke her anyway because *he* was so disappointed in the way his life had turned out.

She wouldn't blow up or be cruel. She'd shut herself down and say nothing at all. And her silence chilled the house.

The aunts and uncles spoke with accents, and when Mom kissed me good night she included a few Middle Eastern endearments that would have killed me in front of my Irish-Catholic friends. But worse was having those friends over for dinner when we ate Lebanese food. There were no forks and knives on the table because we ate with Syrian bread.

This wasn't the cardboard pita bread that comes in packages at Stop & Shop. This was a large unleavened round, maybe fifteen inches in diameter, that my father bought hot out of the oven from a fragrant bakery on Washington Street. We'd tear the bread and scoop up the hummus or chopped meat or beans or whatever, and when we had Middle Eastern food two or three times a week that was the way we ate. On Sunday mornings after church, my uncles would come over and sit around the kitchen table eating olives, spicy cheese, tomatoes, and Syrian bread—with shots of Irish whiskey.

I don't want to paint a picture of the family wearing turbans, but my parents were first-generation, so they kept the traditions of their parents to pass on to us. When you're an adult you can appreciate the beauty of the culture. But kids just want to be like everybody else. I knew we were different, and it bothered me when people didn't know what we were or where we were from.

"What are *you*?" was the oft-asked question at Holy Name School. "What's '*Abboud*'?"

"Lebanese," I'd say, over and over again.

One day, it was a tall, blue-eyed, blond kid who asked. "Hey, Joe, what are *you*?"

I was sick of it, so instead of going through the whole explanation again, I blurted out, "French." French sounded exotic. French sounded good.

A puzzled pause, a quick take on the ludicrous contrast between us—he being this Gallic god who could have stepped right off an Olympics poster and me, a curly-haired kid who looked like an organ-grinder. "That's funny," he said. "I'm French, too."

Caught! "Well . . . we're from *Southern* France," I cracked back. But it wasn't funny. In that mortifying moment, when I hated him and hated myself, the first seed of stubborn pride took root and became my credo: Know who you are, and be proud of who you are. You might as well, because when you try to be somebody else you don't fool anybody.

SEVEN

Joe College

WHEN I WAS coming of age in the mid-1960s, there were two schools (at school) of dressing: the collegiate kids and the rats. The rats wore little Beatle boots and pointed shoes and tight pants. We weren't *The Lords of Flatbush*, but in seventh and eighth grade we thought we were pretty tough, so we slicked our hair back and wore black. The collegiates were wholesome, very Kingston Trio, very Harvard Square— madras jackets, cuffed khakis, navy chinos, blue button-downs, yellow barracuda jackets, and Weejun penny loafers with barrels on the sides.

I started out a rat and morphed into a collegiate. I liked all those interesting madras colors and chino pants I was seeing in the epicenter of Ivy League, Harvard Square, and was beginning to understand that this was how the blue bloods dressed. I never sat down and analyzed the situation or decided that this clothing would make me look more intelligent. I just knew it was a nice way to dress.

Out in the real world, there were other looks happening, too. One was an aberration known as the "continental look": sharkskin suits, trim plain-front pants, skinny ties with little pearl pins in them, skinny lapels, and skinny legs with no cuffs. Very Rat Pack—Dean Martin, Sinatra, Sammy Davis Jr.—and a lot more sophisticated than ours. More accessible to the regular guy was a company called h.i.s., which sold wool-and-polyester suits at moderate-priced stores. For $49.95, you got one jacket, two pairs of pants, and a reversible vest. You could take a solid three-piece suit, you could wear the tattersall side of the vest with the solid jacket and solid pant, you could wear the tattersall pant with the tattersall vest and the solid jacket. . . . you had, say, twelve combinations. It was the most god-awful thing that ever happened to men and boys.

But it didn't happen to me, because I'd been hooked. On went my madras jacket, and suddenly I was president of the ninth grade at Washington Irving Junior High. That jacket—blue and purple, the colors bleeding beautifully—was the first of my life-changing tools. I'd bought it at Surman's, a nice little local men's store in Roslindale Square where I worked as a stock boy, and I wore it with khakis and loafers. Mr. Haberdashing. Once I became president, the girls started paying attention. (Even the rat girls liked collegiate.)

It was the first real connection between clothes and success.

At fifteen, I became a part-time salesman at Thom McAn, not the place where I bought *my* oxbloods and cordovans—that would have been a little shoe store near Surman's—but a nice place to work. I really liked selling, but I remember spending most of my time dyeing ladies' shoes. I'd go in the back room for a can of foul-smelling dye, take the ivory shoe and turn it lime green. One particular week, when there was a prom or wedding afoot, I remember running back and forth, dizzy from the fumes, dyeing and dyeing and nearly dying. But that was also the week of my first check in three figures: $104.

The next year, I moved on to Anderson-Little, and this was high-powered stuff. Now I was selling suits, for $69.50. Nice suits, nice fabrics—but just suits, nothing enchanting about the buttons or the fit. I didn't care. I was getting paid to be involved with what I loved more than anything on earth: clothes. And getting paid to discover just how much I loved selling.

On Saturdays I'd take the T downtown to explore things on a higher plane. I went alone because I didn't want any distraction. I'd check out Jordan Marsh, but I preferred Filene's. I'd spend hours in the tie department—knit ties, club ties with little motifs—where the really good ones cost $2.50. Most were private label; this was before the designer craze. But dessert for me was Filene's world-class sweater department. Every fall they'd get gorgeous heather-colored cable Shetlands in twelve or fifteen colors, and I'd just stand there staring at them on the shelves—so perfect, so pristine, so *expensive*—agonizing over which one to buy. I'd say, "Could I see that one and that one and that one and that one?" and the salesman would lay them on the counter. I didn't want to overstay my welcome, so I'd take just as much time as I thought was proper. The greatest joy was finally being able to casually say, "I'll take *that* one." But I couldn't afford to do it often.

Came the junior prom, I tossed caution to the wind. I had a date with Auta, the most beautiful girl in high school, the girl every guy wanted—a flower child with long, dark hair who looked as if she'd just come from a hootenanny—and this was my moment. First move: the suit. It was a navy three-piece natural-shoulder from Rogers Peet, and it cost an inconceivable $100. I had no right to be spending that kind of money, and if my mother had known she would have shot me, but I was buying more than a suit. Rogers Peet was one of those blue-blood bastions where the customers' first and last names were interchangeable—like Stewart Graham or Patterson Elliot—and even if Joseph and Abboud didn't quite operate the same way, I figured I could work at it, keep my hair short, dress like the establishment, fly under the radar, and be accepted. It was sort of like *The Great Gatsby*. Not as beautiful and sad, not as romantic, but I was buying my way into another class. I thought that by simply showing the salesman that I could afford that suit, I'd make him realize that I was legitimate, and I'd command a certain respect. So I took out my envelope of twenty $5 bills (I didn't have a wallet) and endowed my future.

Next, the tie.

I headed for Louis Boston. For months, I'd been studying the windows—with the beautiful herringbone suits and tweed jackets, the silver ties and striped ties—but had never dared go in. One day, my nose against the glass, I'd even saved the window dresser from embarrassment. I was watching him do a display with a single-breasted navy suit and a double-breasted navy suit, and suddenly I saw him on the lip of the volcano. The navies were exactly the same, but the fabrics were not, and he had mixed the pants! There he was, being very artistic and fluffing the pocket squares, with the *wrong pants* stuffed with tissue paper and ready to go. I didn't know what to do! Was I going to tell the maestro he was screwing up? Me? Somebody had to. I rapped on the window and pointed to the pants, crossing my index fingers. He didn't get it, shooing me away like a fly in his face. I pointed again, gestured again, and finally it clicked. He made the switch.

My favorite window was the Berkeley Shop window on Louis's far left, which is where I'd been eyeing a woven-silk gold club tie with a navy helmet crest. *The* tie. It was bright, bold—very fashion-forward— and it was the most beautiful tie I'd ever seen. It cost an extravagant $5.

The moment was at hand. I had the suit, I had the girl, I had a beautiful French blue shirt, I had seven or eight backup combinations of shirts and ties, but I had to have this one.

Stepping into Louis for the first time was like stepping into the tomb of Tutankhamen. It was the discovery of the ages, a promise and a threat, because I knew there'd be a pack of well-dressed salesmen on the other side of the door—how would they perceive me? There were area rugs on the wood floor, leather chairs, beautiful clothes everywhere, and the pleasant smell of *newness*. There was also a long counter covered with gorgeous ties. But mine, I would learn, was on the third floor, in the Berkeley Shop. And so, boarding the Louis elevator, in the exalted company of Louis staff and Louis customers, I rose to the occasion.

In my memory, it shone like a beacon—this gold tie that had acquired epic significance—and there might have been trumpets playing. Da-*da*.

When the clerk put it in a beautiful black-and-gold box, with tissue, I could barely breathe. I stood stiff at the counter, sneaking a look at the suits to my right, but just a look. I didn't dare go *over* to them because I was afraid somebody would say, "Can I help you?" and then what would I do?

But I was a Louis customer.

Louis Boston, a legend in Boston and in sartorial history, began as a pawnshop in the late 1800s, when Louis Pearlstein bagged his first suit as collateral for a loan. Louis was a lovely guy and a terrible businessman, and a tough-luck story would get him every time. But Saul and Nathan, two of his five sons, had a vision. They opened a little haberdashery store in the Motor Mart Garage building on Eliot Street and built it into a two-trouser-suit joint, like Barneys, and they were on their way. In 1932, thanks to Saul's flair with the customers and Nathan's business sense, they moved to Stuart Street in the theater district. In the 1940s, they upgraded to Boylston Street near Berkeley. Today's elite emporium is ensconced in an appropriately classic temple on Berkeley Street that once housed the New England Museum of Natural History and Bonwit Teller.

If there's one single spot more important than the rest in my life, a crossroads both figurative and literal, it's the corner of Boylston and Berkeley. The land of Louis.

When I discovered it, the store was run by Louis's grandson, Murray Pearlstein, then in his forties, who'd been one of the keys to its ascendancy. He was handsome, blond, and tough—like Steve McQueen—with incredible taste. I can still picture him in a vested suit, a blue overcoat, and a Pierre Cardin hat right out of Robin Hood.

After the gold tie (and the beginning of a six-year romance with Auta, for which I thank the tie), I'd become a regular fixture there, hanging around like a groupie. So one day a soft-spoken salesman named Arthur Jordan, who saw some potential in me, suggested I apply for a part-time job. Really? Work at Louis *and* get a 50 percent discount? I filled out the application.

It was a late autumn afternoon in 1968 when I got the call. I'd graduated from Roslindale High School, had started classes at the University of Massachusetts in Boston, and was living at home. The phone was in our little TV room upstairs, and the lights weren't on yet, so I couldn't even find it when it rang.

Stumbling, muttering, I snatched it up. "Hello?"

"Hello, Joe? This is Louis Pearlstein." Murray's cousin, the business guy. My heart caught. "We'd like to offer you a part-time sales position, if you're interested, at $2.35 an hour."

"I'm interested. Very interested. *Thank* you."

"Fine. If you accept the position, we'll always want you to be well dressed, behave like a gentleman, and keep your shoes shined."

Sitting on the floor in the dark, I accepted. And everything that's happened since has happened because of Louis.

My first Saturday on the job, and they're watching. Life at Louis is a feudal system, populated by high-powered, well-dressed salesmen, and I'm not even a page or a squire. Some of them know me because I've been such a persistent customer, but now I'm in a different position. I'm in the furnishings department, selling.

In comes a woman. Everyone else is busy, so she's mine. She looks like a nice lady, probably wants a shirt or tie. Wrong. She wants a *lot* of shirts and ties. She's just bought a bunch of suits upstairs for her husband, and now she's on my turf. (In those days, the departments were very segregated: The suit guy upstairs sold you the suits, the haberdashery guy downstairs sold you the shirts and ties.) So the suits are brought down and placed on "pull-outs," or easels, and I start putting together shirt-and-tie combinations—looping the tie into a makeshift knot with a little dimple, running my hand over it, puffing the tie up a little bit, stroking, selling, laying it on. She has five suits, I'm banging out these combinations—stripes with checks, paisleys with stripes and plaids, pattern on pattern—and I end up selling her two dozen shirts and thirty ties.

As I'm carrying this fabulous bundle over to the cash-wrap with my arms spread wide, I'm looking around to see if anybody's noticed. I'm beaming, exhilarated, and yeah, I want someone to see this! They've seen. I'm not on commission; these guys are. And they're grumbling, "How did this pisher kid get a $2,000 sale?"

But it wasn't all pinstripes and paisleys. This was the late 1960s, and the world was flying at a crazy pace. The Pill and the sexual revolution had arrived, and they'd had an impact on fashion at all levels—in the less expensive stores and in the more expensive stores. All the rules were being broken, and there was no reference to any tradition. Men were *letting go,* dropping their trousers and slipping into printed body shirts, bell-bottom pants, and chains. Middle-aged guys with potbellies were wearing jump suits and *finding* themselves. They were going to discos, buying jewelry, and carrying bags. The age of innocence had transmogrified into the peacock revolution, and our clothes said it loud and clear. Even at Louis, we were selling double knits and polyesters, popcorn weaves and printed velvets.

While all this was going on, I was concentrating on more sophisticated pursuits. I was learning to discern the differing depth of color in dyed fabrics and wovens, and I was also discovering a new world of murky halftones. I couldn't have articulated any of this then. I just knew what my eyes told me. I had been a student for so long, going from store to store, but now I was coming up with combinations I'd never seen before. Instead of blue and red, I'd combine navy and brown. It attracted customers. "That's good," they'd say. "I never thought of that."

I was even starting to compose my own collections. I'd pull a light beige jacket out of this line or a dark beige pant out of that line and build on it to create a monochromatic look. I wasn't a designer, but I was becoming an editor. And six months later, when I got a raise of thirty cents an hour to $2.65 and was promoted to the Berkeley Shop on the third floor, I felt like king of the hill.

"I see this guy up on our floor one day, in what we called the Berkeley Shop, which was our Paul Stuart kind of section," Murray remembers, "and he's all dressed up, looked like he might have been a boxer or something, kind of rugged. I looked at him, said this kid must be a phony or something—my own personal observation. I was kind of a jock myself, so I gravitated toward his type. And after a while it became evident that he was a ballsy kid who sold very well. Customers loved him, and he had a boss who was a very tough guy, who sat all over him and didn't give him an inch."

As always, my salary went right back into the place that paid me, so I supplemented my earnings by playing poker, which I'd learned at my mother's knee when her cards club met on Friday nights. Clothes were everything. *Everything.* I was just flashy enough to be noticed, but not flashy enough to get myself in trouble.

Except once.

It's eight o'clock on a Saturday morning and I'm on my way to work, all dolled up in my first Ralph Lauren tie—a beautiful purple clock-design I've recently bought for the unimaginable price of $12.50—and a tan herringbone Pierre Cardin jacket with a little purple stripe in it. And I'm feeling great. I get off the T at the Essex Street station, cross Tremont, and start to walk up Boylston when three tough-looking kids come out of an alley and fall in behind me.

"You know what?" says one. "I don't like that tie." I ignore him.

"You hear me? I don't like that tie." I keep walking. But it's early on a Saturday, and there's no one else around.

He grabs the tie, and I smack him—right in the face. Suddenly, the other two join the battle, and I'm fighting all three. I'm getting pummeled, scratched, punched. Am I going to get my nose broken, my arm, my jaw? I don't care. All I'm thinking is, "Please, please, God, don't let me bleed on the tie!"

Louis was close to UMass, so I'd go to classes dressed for work—an aberration in my vest, big tie, and wide-lapel plaid jacket while the other kids were in ripped jeans, scruffy beards, and drug-induced comas. Let's paint the picture: protests coming down Boylston Street, love signs and peace signs, earth shoes and one-nighters—and here comes Mr. Fashion Plate. Half the classes were getting canceled because of the Vietnam War, and I was walking in with my Polo jacket and briefcase because I didn't have time to go home and change.

When I wasn't peddling clothes at Louis, I was pedaling Swan Boats in the Public Garden—the hardest Stairmaster you ever stepped on in your life. The Swan Boats have been plying the pond since 1877, from April to September. The twenty passengers sit on benches and the captain sits behind them, pedaling like crazy and steering with two pulleys. On windy days, your thighs are *burning*. On really windy days, a guy stands on the back pontoon to give you an extra push with an oar in the water. It was brutal work for $1.65 an hour, but I loved being outside and knocking around with a great bunch of guys.

If we liked the passengers and didn't want to scare them, we'd call the rats that sometimes ran through the Garden "bunnies." If we *didn't* like them, we'd take them under the pigeons. There was a little island in the lagoon and a branch that stuck way out, covered with pigeons. We had a way of maneuvering the boats right under the branch and swinging out the driver's side so *we* wouldn't get hit by the bird shit but they would.

One of the crew was George Survillo, president of our senior class in high school, captain of the football team, and the guy who regularly got me out of typing class by demanding over the loudspeaker that Joseph Abboud come to the principal's office immediately. (We got caught, of course. If we'd done it once or twice we might have gotten away with it. But five or six times were too many for Miss MacLeod.)

George was a big powerful guy of Russian heritage (his father was an Orthodox bishop), and another natty dresser. We shared a passion for the movies, Errol Flynn & Co., and riding horseback, so we'd take the elevated to the stables out in Forest Hills and Blue Hills and for $2 an hour take charge of the light brigade.

There were certain sections of the trails where we were allowed to gallop, and we did. We were lunatics. We had no training, wore no helmets, but at seventeen what did we know? One day at Forest Hills we were galloping, the horses going *fast,* and a huge fallen tree lay straight ahead, like the iceberg before the *Titanic.* Our horses leaped right over it, and George remembers seeing me fly out of the saddle and slam to the ground. I don't remember it at all. All I remember is the rush of derring-do.

So where's my pardner, George, now? Back in the saddle again, and playing the hero in his own movie. He's a sergeant with the Boston police department, the commander of the mounted unit, and one day he gives me a call. He wants me to design a new dress uniform for the mounties.

"Remember the capes they wore in *Doctor Zhivago?*" he asks, hopefully.

"George," I remind him, "this is the Boston Police." But he wants to talk about braids on the arms and big brass buttons and helmets with plumes. "George," I say, "if we're not careful here, you'll look like *The Pirates of Penzance.*" He only wishes.

"So how many cops and horses are involved?"

"We used to have over a hundred."

Yeah? I'm picturing a legion.

"Now it's eleven."

Oh. A *light* brigade.

As a kid, I was always in awe of the mounted police and their handsome steeds—deliberately enormous, deliberately intimidating—as they patrolled the Common and the city streets, snorting and pawing the ground. One afternoon when I'm back in Boston, George invites me to go riding. On them. These horses are bigger than any I've ever seen, and it's raining out there. I'm absolutely terrified. But there's no backing out for the couturier to the cops. I climb up, swallow hard, and off we go. George and Joe, two guardians of the public good (only one of whom is breathing).

But at least I look swell. I've refused George's offer of a bright yellow slicker because I prefer the way my black quilted-suede jacket matches my horse.

For the designer, image is everything.

EIGHT

Innocent Abroad

I HAD NO GREAT ambitions, but when Auta, now my girlfriend, decided to go to Paris for her junior year abroad, I suddenly got motivated. No way was I going to let her go without me, so I worked my tail off and won a scholarship to study seventeenth-, eighteenth-, and nineteenth-century French literature at the Sorbonne.

Before I knew it, I was on my first plane, Boston to New York, and my first boat, the *S.S. France* to Le Havre. Then I was in Paris. *Paris!*

Auta boarded with a family on the rue du Louvre on the Right Bank, and I went Left, taking a room across the street from the Jardin des Plantes in the home of Mme. La Jeunesse (a youthful dowager of eighty who had hidden a number of Jews during the occupation). I didn't smoke or drink, but I was in the French Quarter, poised to become another Hemingway or Fitzgerald.

We walked everywhere, splurged (for five francs) on little *biftecks avec pommes frites* at the *self-service*, hung out at the obligatory cafés—Aux Deux Magots, Café de Flore, place de la Contrescarpe—and took it all in. One day a guy handed me a pamphlet, some piece of propaganda.

Auta pulled on my arm. "Know who that *was?*" I shrugged.

"Jean-Paul Sartre!"

With its foggy nights, bells and murmurs, and scents of bread and perfume and garlic and Gauloises, Paris was a sensual paradise.

And then it wasn't. Auta and I started drifting apart, and just when I was ready to leap off the nearest *quai*, things got worse. Back in Boston, my mother was diagnosed with cancer. All at once I was losing the two most important women in my life.

I started to run—run everywhere, from the *boulangerie* to the cleaners to the Louvre to the University. I ran between five and twelve miles a day, *every* day; they called me "Monsieur Coureur" in the neighborhood. I developed blisters, and I ran with blisters. It rained, and I ran in the rain. Fixation? Yes. Sublimation? Probably. But it helped.

And then, one day, the sun came out. At the corner of St. Germain and St. Michel, another one of those life-affirming crossroads, I suddenly saw the Paris that had been in front of me all along. Style! It was all over the place. As I emerged from my self-pity, the beauty of the art, architecture, people, and clothes really hit me. And I knew it was the beginning of something.

What a difference between where I'd been and where I was—between the provincial predictability of Boston and the nonchalant chic of Paris—the cafés, the shops, the parks. Men wore light-colored linen and cotton suits on the *street*; in America, these were the kinds of things you saw only in *Gentlemen's Quarterly*. Not only were the French better dressed, but they moved with an effortless grace, as if they were on a runway all the time. They were aware of their bodies, and their clothes were a part of their lives, not just extra layers.

Even more astounding was the sight of women in evening gowns and men in tuxedos on the Métro, en route to the opera. After a life-time of looking at brown and gray suits on the T, it was a beautiful thing. (The French call a tuxedo a "smoking." *Voulez-vous un "smok-ing"?* I love that.)

For income, I replaced the poker and pedals with wealthy made-moiselles who wanted to learn English. Tutoring paid twenty bucks or so a session, and I was usually invited to stay for dinner, too, in these elegant Right Bank homes. Quite a change from the prison food at the *restaurant l'universitaire.* My three students—aged sixteen to eighteen —were very cute and very sweet, but not dating material. I wasn't about to jeopardize my position.

Nor could I consummate my crush on Mlle. LeBrun, one of my teachers at the Sorbonne. I was mad about her; she was nice to me. I was only twenty; she was twenty-three—and adorable, in a young Diane Keaton way, with big sweaters, big overcoat, little combat boots, cute hats. The closest we ever came to any kind of communion was over coffee at a café, but our entire conversation was in French and I could never say what I felt because I was too unsure of my grammar.

Appropriate dating material, when I finally discovered it, was a complex package. The typical twenty-one-year-old French coquette was more direct and more sophisticated than her American counter-part because French guys were so aggressive. (When they went for the boobs, they'd say, "I want to feel your heart beat." Clever, *non?*)

So how was I supposed to behave? Aggressively? Deferentially? This was a whole new game, a cultural phenomenon, and I didn't know the rules of engagement. So I'd go over to Chanel and buy exquisite foulard scarves for maybe $95 (they'd be $300 or $400 now) and give them to girls I liked, because I thought the way to a girl's heart was through fashion.

Often, it was.

With the rest of my tutoring money, I went shopping for myself. Today, the Champs-Elysées is much like Fifth Avenue or Rodeo Drive, but there was a world of difference then. Parisian shopkeepers were brilliant at display. There were no theme windows; simplicity was the goal. But the windows were *sexy*—and I don't mean open shirts. The fabrics and color themes were irresistible, and they had real balance.

One day I saw a unique sport coat in the window at Pierre Balmain, and the window made me buy it. In a period of big, loud patterns (what we at Louis called "airport plaids"), this brown-and-beige nailhead with a rust-and-brown windowpane was absolutely gorgeous. It was very fitted, non-vented, and *very* European—worn on the mannequin with a ribbed rust-colored mock turtleneck sweater. It was the first time I'd seen tailored clothing combined with sportswear. I wanted to be that mannequin. I could see me, looking out at me. So, with the money intended for books, I bought it.

I also bought a leather coat in russet and bronze (my colors before they were my colors) and a James Dean-style brown leather jacket that's still as supple as it was over thirty years ago. It's too small for me now, and it's so worn that the shoulders are a lighter shade of cognac than the rest, but it has great emotional significance for me, so I'm saving it for Lila.

I discovered new tweeds, bought shoes at Salamander, and shot $500 on a fawn-colored long suede coat. But most French things were skintight and uncomfortable as hell. Tight arms and tight chest were the rage. French men are narrower than Americans—no shoulders, no tush—and in those days, they had no muscles either. Nobody exercised; Monsieur Coureur was an aberration.

So I lived in sweaters, corduroys, and sport coats. Or in my Bohemian wardrobe. There were lots of Algerian shops then, and I loved those white cotton V-necks with big sleeves and embroidery that looked like holy shirts. I'd wear a big belt over them, like a tunic, and with my tight bell-bottom jeans, clogs, and beard I had a little bit of an Omar Sharif thing going.

On my birthday in May, the head of the French department took me to dinner at a café across from Notre Dame. As the bells chimed twelve and I turned twenty-one, he handed me a copy of Hemingway's *A Moveable Feast*, best-known for the indelible line, "If you are lucky enough to have lived in Paris as a young man, then wherever you go for the rest of your life, it stays with you, for Paris is a moveable feast."

I was that young man. And I was lucky. Paris *has* stayed with me, and the dazzle and poignancy of that year affected my life forever. But Hemingway, for all his insight, wasn't exactly on the button. The evocative mix of rapture and longing, smells and sounds, belongs *there*, and only there.

Fifteen years later I was back in Paris, designing. Studying at the Sorbonne had been a Left Bank experience; this was haute Right Bank, and I didn't feel comfortable in that world—ever. I was still the guy from the Left Bank. So I'd decline the invitations to fancy dinners and take a sentimental journey of my own. Maybe it was maudlin, maybe just nostalgic, but I needed it. After going back to the Ritz to change my Mr. Designer clothes, I'd leave Place Vendome and go back to becoming Ernest Hemingway.

I'd cross Pont Neuf from the Right Bank to the Left, because I'm a creature of habit and that's what I'd always done. On the other side I took different routes, but there were always certain things I had to pass. Sometimes I'd work my way down to Ile de la Cité so I could see Café Notre Dame, where I'd turned twenty-one, and have carré d'agneau at Lapérouse, an exquisite eighteenth-century restaurant on Quai des Grands Augustins that I'd stared into from the outside but could never afford in my student days. Émile Zola, George Sand, Victor Hugo, and Guy de Maupassant had apparently been regulars there among the boiserie and paintings, as had Parisian courtesans who'd scratched their diamonds on the mirrored partitions to check their worth; the marks are still there. Lapérouse was worth the wait.

I'd also go back to Brasserie Lipp on Boulevard St. Germain, where

NINE

Louis, Murray, and Me

MY PLAN AFTER graduating from UMass in 1972 had always been to teach, mostly to please my mother. But my year in Paris changed all that. I'd gone over as a kid and come back with some world-awareness, a new language so I could help the guys at Louis handle their correspondence with the French companies (which gave me a touch of status), and a nice Parisian wardrobe. I couldn't wear all of it—I wasn't in the coffeehouses of Paris now; this was Boston—but I did strut around in that long suede coat for a time. It was too expensive not to use.

Out in the world I was grabbing hold of my life, but within the fold I was helpless to save my parents and terrified by my impending orphanhood. After twenty years of anguish from his back injury, my father was now dying of prostate cancer. I'll never stop seeing him try to navigate the stairs in those last few months, pencil-thin in his pajamas and so shaky that a hug and a kiss were all he could manage. He died in May 1972, on the morning of my world history final, just before I graduated from college.

Twenty years later, I did a fashion show at the Museum of Natural History in New York. For the big finale, we played "The Living Years," by Mike & The Mechanics. I came out carrying my one-year-old daughter, Lila, to these lyrics:

> *I wasn't there that morning*
> *When my father passed away.*
> *I didn't get to tell him*
> *All the things I had to say.*
>
> *I think I caught his spirit*
> *Later that same year*
> *I'm sure I heard his echo*
> *In my baby's newborn tears.*
> *I just wish I could have told him in the living years.*

We never really talked man-to-man. No birds and bees; Dad was an old-fashioned guy, and I guess he figured I'd figure it out. We never talked about marriage or family, my career or my future. The only thing we could talk about was the Red Sox. Even now, I can't watch a game without wondering what he'd think of the lineup.

He's always with me.

The other night I dreamed he was alive. Healthy, strong, and standing tall. He needed a suit, a navy three-piece, and I fitted him for it. When he put it on, I pulled down his lapels and straightened his tie.

"Dad," I said, "you really look good." He smiled. The suit fit him perfectly.

It was a great, great dream. Because he *knew* me.

He knew that I was Joseph Abboud.

*   *   *

I'd been offered a job teaching at Brookline High School, which would have gotten me the elbow patches and maybe an apartment at the Brattle Arms in Cambridge—a brick building that doesn't look like much to me now but in those days represented the ultimate in cozy mystique, a place right out of Raymond Chandler. Or maybe I'd go to graduate school. But I was tired of school and wanted to get to work.

And along came a full-time job at Louis. Good-bye, academia! Hello, apparel!

One afternoon I'm straightening the ties, putting new ones on the rack behind the counter, and the elevator door opens. Out steps Ralph Lauren, in an antique leather jacket and fatigues.

This is five years after he's started Polo, and most people know who he is. I certainly do. He's an icon, a celebrity. One of my heroes.

And he's walking right toward me.

Somebody introduces us, and Ralph doesn't say "Hello" or "How do you do?" The first thing he says to me is, "You look just like Dean Martin."

No one had ever told me that, and I probably didn't look like Dean Martin. But Ralph thought I did, so I smiled and shook his hand. I was starstruck. He hung out for a little, talked about what he was doing, and off he went.

(Fast-forward to the year 2000. I've just done an event at Mitchells in Westport, Connecticut, and I've run over to New Canaan to pick up a watch. I'm walking down the street in a gray flannel chalk-stripe suit and a cashmere turtleneck, and who comes along but Ralph and Ricky Lauren.

"Hey, Joey," says Ralph. "Did I ever tell you you look like Dean Martin?" And after all these years, we laugh.)

By twenty-three I'd become a buyer-merchandiser with a big budget and Murray's blessing. I was bringing in product, putting it on the shelves, selling it on the floor, choosing it for the windows. Louis's windows weren't miniature theme parks like so many windows today. The focus wasn't on props or propaganda. It was on clothes—beautiful clothes. Doing an all-ivory window one week with gabardine trousers, a hopsack linen sport coat, soft shantung print tie, and a marble bust of some Renaissance woman (which I accidentally dropped, breaking her nose), I learned how the simplicity of color can make the statement.

At work, things were swell. At home, a disaster. In November 1973, my mother died from breast cancer, and my sister Nancy and I were stuck together roaming around the house like two lost souls. Her boyfriend was heavily into drugs, and I was trapped in a pigsty.

I like things neat and in place. Order gives me a sense of security, and when things are out of control, I lose it. The house I'd known and loved for seventeen years was *filthy*, and—still acting entitled, still the little prince who didn't make beds or wash dishes—I blamed everything on Nancy.

So I went anywhere but home. Squash games, movies, McDonald's. I was making maybe $15,000 a year, had nice clothes and a zippy little black Mazda RX, and should have felt like a man about town—except that I was parentless, girl-less, and wallowing in despair. On Friday nights, a lot of us from the store would go to Mother Anna's in the North End for veal parmigiana, and on Sundays I'd hang out with the Pearlsteins. I'd go over for breakfast and stay all day. Murray and I would jog around Jamaica Pond and then go back and watch football games, and his wife, Dorothy, would feed me. I was voracious and needy in every way, and they and their two daughters became my new family.

I loved Murray like a father, but he was still my boss and could fire me at any time. He had a short fuse, and the only way I kept the job was by making him laugh. If he said, "I *told* you those shirts were too dark," I'd argue with him for an hour, and then, when I knew I was about to get kicked out the door, I'd say, "Yeah, that's what *I* said. The shirts are definitely too dark." I'd break his momentum and it was over.

As a customer, you can try new things, and the risk is yours. But as a buyer, you're taking chances with somebody else's money. Like the wool clock argyles I was buying from Corgi, the venerated knitwear company in Wales that now serves the royal needs of princes Charles, William, and Harry. They were wonderful socks, with a long history, but they didn't fit into the world of modern appliances—because they were wool. I thought my customers understood this, but apparently not. They came out of the dryer looking like tiny doll socks, and I had to stop buying them.

I was always pressuring Murray to let me buy things I loved, but if I didn't *sell* them I wasn't doing my job. I remember a heavy, natural-shoulder brown-and-gray check suit from Lanham, a manufacturer in Lawrence, Massachusetts. It was very fashion-forward, and Murray, to shut me up, said, "Okay, you can buy six of them." The first Saturday we got it in, I sold five. And thank God, because my ass was on the line. And you know how Murray knew? He was the guy who went through the inventory cards. He could see what suits were selling and who on the floor was selling them.

"When I first heard what Joey wanted to do, I closed my eyes," Murray says now. "After I began to look at it for a while, I began to be addicted to the same kind of feeling about colors. He influenced me on that, and in another way too—about balance and taste and how to put things together. His taste was in my vocabulary. He was Mr. Brown—not really brown in the sense of brown, but anything that was off of gray or blue—and when this kid saw it in a line, he wanted to buy it. So I'd let him buy four suits, instead of fifty, and sure enough, when I turned around, my cards would show me that it would go. At first I thought, 'Well, that was a onetime thing. He must have had three friends he sold them to,' but eventually, between the two of us, we probably introduced the idea of 'It doesn't have to be a navy or a black suit' to the market."

Louis had a huge appetite for product, and every manufacturer and de-signer wanted to sell to us. One major source was Hickey Freeman, and once a season we'd go up to the factory in Rochester. I hated Rochester. It was cold and dreary and always winter, four seasons a year. We'd fly through a blizzard to stay at the Holiday Inn, and for two or three days lock ourselves in the factory to select the fabrics and "style out" the suits, which actually meant designing them. Hickey Freeman was used to producing conservative stuff, but fashion was starting to flower. Murray and I did shaped, not sack, suits and brought them to life with such unusual fabrics as off-color flannels in taupe and mushroom and stone, antique "grandfather-striped" worsteds, and sepia tweeds. I was the guy who wanted to put a vest under everything. And guess what? Murray went for it.

I was always saying "What if?" and he was a creative guy open to new ideas. I suggested lengthening the vest (a bonus for any guy with a bit of a belly whose belt buckle always showed), widening the trouser bottom, and making the jacket more fitted. He went for those things too.

This was my first crack at designing, and we were at the source— where the changes would actually be made. But the payoff (literally) was seeing my ideas ring the cash register. When they sold in Boston, I felt the pride of coauthorship.

Back at the store, Murray insisted on sizing the orders himself. If we bought forty different swatches and wanted fifty suits made from each swatch, that would be 2,000 suits. On order sheets, he would then indicate the lot number of each swatch, how many suits we were buying of each fabric, and every size we'd need in each suit. It was painstaking work. Since one order sheet wasn't big enough, he'd tape three sheets together to make one long chart that he could read up and down and sideways.

"On the navy, I'm going to buy a 38 regular, two 39s, three 40s, two 41s, two 42s, and four 44s," he'd say, as I watched. "In shorts, I want one 38 short, one 39 short, one 40 short. Longs, I'll need a 40 long, a 43 long, a 44 long, and a 46 long." He'd make every mark with a pencil in his tight little scrawl, notating, cogitating, erasing, going back and forth until he'd balanced the sizes he wanted to buy and had the right number of regulars, shorts, and longs. It would go on for hours and hours. Once, in a frenzy I'll never forget, he managed to staple the whole enterprise to his antique leather-topped desk.

But I'll tell you something: Because of those sheets and swatches, he knew what he had. He touched it, he felt it, he knew the fabric, he knew if it was single- or double-breasted. Even though Louis was a sophisticated, world-renowned store, it had this touchy-feely entrepreneurial spirit—and that's where I learned the business.

We were buying 4,000 gabardine suits a year from a company called Windsor of Germany. They were made of Italian fabric and manufactured in Germany, where they were fused.

The traditional suit is hand-tailored, made by people who actually sit down and sew. But these suits were . . . the nice industry words are "automated" or "engineered," but in reality, fusing is a form of gluing. It doesn't sound very appealing, but there's an art to it. In many cases the fabric will look smoother *because* the linings are fused—by steam, heat, and adhesive.

Our sales rep at Windsor was a guy named Hans Schultz. We called him "Schultzie," like a *Hogan's Heroes* thing, and we loved him. One night Murray and I were having dinner with him out in Chestnut Hill, and one of us asked, "When did the Germans get so great at fusing? How come you don't do tailored suits anymore?"

Silence from Schultz.

Then, "Don't you know? Most of the tailors in *Cher-many* were *Choo-ish*."

Here was the German salesman with the Jewish retailer, offering a forceful history lesson. The Germans had killed off their workforce, then developed all this great technology to fill the need they'd created. They'd come up with something good, but to us it was now like a weed in a beautiful garden.

Another out-of-town visitor was an Irish salesman named Padraig Ósiocháin of the Galway Bay Sweater Company. He was fair and pale with silver hair and a mighty brogue—a cross between a leprechaun and a mythical Irish king—and he was a vision when he walked into Louis carrying his sample case. Winter, spring, and summer, he always wore the same thing: a three-piece suit—and tie—all of inch-thick black-face-sheep wool. The suit must have been bullet-proof, and it made an indelible impression.

The hand-knit Aran sweaters he sold were of the same fabric. This guy *was* his product. Traditional Arans are ivory, but his were black with white flecks. They were gorgeous, heavy sweaters, and every time my order came in, the shipping room guy would yell, "This box stinks!" because it smelled like sheep and peat. This was the genuine article.

European style fit right into Louis's International Shop—and into my wardrobe as well. One day in July 1974, when we were in New York on a buying trip, a photographer snapped my picture. I was ambling along Fifth Avenue, wearing a Daniel Hechter ivory shirt-and-pants suit and a pair of espadrilles. He didn't tell me his name and didn't ask for mine, just took off. But next day there I was, this anonymous dude on the front of *Daily News Record* with a caption screaming WHITE HOT. My first *DNR* cover. The big time!

Young and foppish, I soon became one of Murray's catalog models. Today the pictures make me cringe, because what was cool in the 1970s is almost cartoonish today.

One shot shows me pretending to be the owner of a horse farm— but I look like I just got off the boat. I'm wearing a stiff tweed suit with epaulets and leather-buttoned military pockets, very tight pants with very big cuffs, a wide tie, and a big collar, and I'm holding a pair of gloves in my hand. The quintessential country gentleman, we thought, but more like something out of *The Sopranos*.

There's another one of me as a bare-chested he-man wearing pleated Ralph Lauren corduroy pants, a Bert Paley shearling jacket, and nothing else. (It did wonders for my dating life.) And one where I'm in a little two-piece safari number, with a matching top and pant. Thirty years later, it looks like a gas-station attendant's outfit. My hair is so huge and the collar's so big that if a strong wind came up, I'd fly away.

But here's the thing: We didn't just *like* this stuff, we *loved* it! Louis was the epitome of good taste, and we were the arbiters. "Art produces ugly things which frequently become more beautiful with time," Jean Cocteau once said. "Fashion, on the other hand, produces beautiful things which always become ugly with time."

I guess in ten years we'll be laughing at today's beautiful things. But that doesn't stop them from looking good now.

The next course in my curriculum was becoming a stylist, and Murray started sending me on location. A couple of those experiences still jangle my wires.

I'm obsessive about my surroundings—happy mood, sad mood, I've gotta get out of here, I couldn't sleep in this room for a million dollars, that kind of thing. So when I have to go with Tyler Smith, the art director, and the team to Rhode Island on a dreary afternoon in late fall just as it's getting dark, I'm already depressed.

We get to this place in the middle of nowhere, and it has sort of a Charles Manson feel. And here comes Myron Taplin, the photographer, bald on top, with a ponytail and a long beard. Today's subjects are shirts, ties, and sweaters that will be draped over tables and andirons—and Myron's our man. As Tyler has told me, Myron is a still-life photographer because he can relate only to inanimate objects. He has an aversion to flesh and blood. Wonderful. Nonetheless, Myron has a big black fireplace where he's got some rotisserie thing for roasting turkeys, and outside there's a one-legged chicken hopping around. I am beyond creeped out. While Myron and Tyler are discussing shirts and ties, I'm thinking: devil worship.

Later, when everybody starts to leave, I have to stay so I can pack everything up that I'll have to drive back to Boston. I'm convinced I'm going to die there and never be found. But guess what. The guy is a tremendous photographer, and we end up getting *unbelievable* pictures.

*   *   *

The photographer was Clint Clemens, a great-great-grandson of Samuel Clemens. The models were Jerry Hall and Appolonia. The stylist was me, a naif in my twenties. This was summer, and we were shooting fall tweeds. Jerry Hall's long blond hair and long blond legs, and the bronzy, tawny clothes . . . words fail me.

We were up at 5:30 in the morning because we wanted to get the sunrise, and Appolonia was about to get dressed. She took her shirt off and I fell in love. There she was in her little bikini underwear and bare breasts, and I was trying to hand her the clothes and not blush. It was my first experience with a naked girl, professionally. Since then, of course, I've learned to take it in stride. Models dress, they undress. Now I'm like a gynecologist. It doesn't mean a thing.

When the shoot was done and the three of us posed for our own pictures, Jerry leaned over and stuck her tongue in my ear! She was just being playful and cute, but I was sure that a tongue in the ear was more than shaking hands. Then she went off to meet Mick.

I also did the styling when we used Susan Sarandon, Andrea Marcovicci, Susan Blakely, and Robert Wagner in our TV ads. Wagner was a real pro. He did thirteen ten-second commercials for us in one day, in a studio down in North Carolina. He was gorgeous, he was trim, and he *looked* like a movie star.

These days I sometimes see Susan Sarandon at the Family Discount Center in Westchester, getting stuff for her kids. I want to go up to her and say, "We did a commercial together for Louis Boston thirty years ago." But I'm usually in my bike shorts, and I worry that she'll think I've become a ballet dancer. So I don't.

TEN

Travels with Murray

EUROPEAN BUYING TRIPS with Murray were always an adventure. In getting to see the sophisticated side of the fashion world—trekking from Pitti Uomo in Florence and the mills in Biella to Sehm in Paris and the spinners in Scotland—I was also seeing another side of Murray.

Like one quiet Sunday morning in Florence, in the middle of Pitti Uomo, the annual and all-important menswear trade show. The custom here is that international buyers come in during the week to see the new goods exhibited by a galaxy of designers and manufacturers, but only the Italians are allowed in on Sunday. But here we are— Murray, Arthur Jordan (the senior buyer), and me (the junior)—on a Sunday, crashing the exposition center. And already Murray's in a foul mood.

We wander into a room to see a line called "Punch," and a little

Italian sales agent approaches. "Yes? I may *help* you? Where you are *from*, please?" Murray doesn't like to say where he's from. He just wants to look at product. Avoiding eye contact, he says, "I'd like to look around." The little guy stamps his little foot. "You must-a *tell* me. Is my *show*room." Murray says, "It's Sunday morning. I just want to look around."

In the background, Italian customers and salesmen are standing there in their fabulously cut flannel suits and their perfectly shaped suede shoes and their handsomely tied ties, smoking cigarettes and sipping espressos. I glance at Arthur, Arthur glances at me, and we know this isn't going well. The guy says, "This is-a *my* showroom. Tell me who you are, or go away."

Arthur and I want to scram. Murray says, "Look. I'm from America. I paid to come over here. I have a store. I'm a buyer. And I'll look at anything I want. And by the way"—pointing his finger in the guy's face—"fuck *you*."

The world stops! The well-turned-out Italians freeze in mid-cigarette. There's a hush in the room that feels like forever.

Now this little guy, who's about four foot ten, jabs his finger at Murray and says, "Fuck-a *me*? Fuck-a-*me*? No fuck-a-*me*. Fuck-a *you*!"

And Murray says back to him, "Fuck *me*? Fuck *you*!"

This is the sophisticated fashion business. We're in Firenze. And all the Italians in their beautiful suits, their jaws are dropping. Arthur and I step in, because in another second, Murray, being Steve McQueen, is going to hit the guy. They're red in the face, close to blows, and suddenly the guy realizes who Murray is. "Ah, Signor Pearlstein," he says with a little bow. "Now I show you the collection."

The thing that saves their lives? Beautiful shirts.

Murray backs off, picks up a gorgeous linen iridescent soft-collar that only the Italians can do, and we all resume breathing.

Punch line: We end up being one of their best customers in the world. And the little guy, Max Fusati, becomes one of Murray's dearest friends. So much for first impressions.

*　　*　　*

One day, Murray, brave and trusting, dispatched me to London alone to meet with John Thorpe, a very proper selling agent who managed different knitting operations. Among his clients were Margaret Seal and Peggy Head, a pair of virtuoso knitters who created the patterns and oversaw a squad of little old ladies to produce them. This was literally a cottage industry; the ladies did their knitting at home. They were all very traditional, used to doing chunky Aran cable knits in bright colors with little Scottie dogs, and we were definitely stretching their aesthetic.

John, Margaret, Peggy, and I gathered in a cruddy, dimly lit office upstairs on Regent Street and sat at a big old brown table. All around the office were sweater samples. This was no tidy Gap presentation. This was heaps of sweaters in every nook and cranny. A 300-year-old hat company was in the next room, run by a pale old guy with bad dandruff and a bad suit like something out of Dickens.

I had a budget to buy the sweaters I thought were right, but I didn't see anything I liked. So I asked my usual question, "What if?" and then, with their encouragement, did a rough sketch of the sweater I'd dreamed of buying. I based it on one of their samples: a traditional English pullover with lollipop pastel stripes. First, I asked the knitters to add a small pocket on the left breast. Then I changed the stripes. Out went the blue, pink, and yellow; in came beautiful, madder, colors—an inky cobalt blue, an oxblood heathered burgundy, a peat brown, and a dark lovat green—all in the same muted tones.

It was the first sweater I'd ever designed. Thorpe was delighted with the order (200 sweaters is one powerful order, and the reason he was probably so willing to make the changes), and I hoped that Murray would be. He was.

As my appetite to do new things grew, Thorpe kept finding ways for me to fulfill my fantasies. As an agent with many clients, he was able to tap into knitters with different specialties. One of the next sweaters I developed was a V-neck Shetland with Corgi (of the socks), whom he also represented. This was a beautiful allover argyle hand-knit (with the knots hand-tied) in olive, russet, and deep umber. Murray liked that one so much he wore it himself, and do I have to tell you what *that* did for my confidence?

So I was doing this early designing, and loving it, and loving it even more when the sweaters would come into the store four months later and I could put them on the shelves. With the sweaters and the Hickey Freeman suits and vests, I was beginning to put a collection together.

As much as I loved Murray, there were days when we made each other crazy. When I had an opinion about product, I'd tell him, and if I didn't get my way, I wouldn't shut up. He was strong, but I was head-stronger.

"He was like a little kid," Murray will tell you now, "the bird that's the baby in the nest, yapping and yapping. So we'd take him along, and the two of us would have a terrible time keeping him down. Every time he'd go into a showroom, he wanted to take over immediately. If we didn't agree with what he wanted to buy, he'd go into a pout that lasted for about a week."

At the Sehm show one day in Paris, we saw two groups of ivory tennis sweaters. One group was trimmed in navy and dark gold, which I liked; the other in red and light blue, which they liked. I said, "You're wrong. It's bad." I wouldn't let up. "It's *really* bad." Finally, Murray got so mad he told me to take a walk and cool off.

We were in a big exhibition hall, and I didn't know where to go, so I just started wandering. I was close to tears. I deserved the dressing-down, because I'd been pushy, but I was embarrassed and depressed and I hated him.

Just then I saw an enormous escalator in the middle of the floor. I got on, and there on the next floor was a sign: *Salon de Maille*. A lingerie show. Downstairs were booths full of men's sweaters, shirts, and Murray. Here was a world of gorgeous, statuesque *parisiennes* in tiny panties and bras.

Me at four, in the original
Joseph Abboud sweater.

The quiet before
the storm:
bracing for a
fashion show.

The torn photo of my
maternal grandmother,
Theresa Latoof Fakhry:
relic of a family mystery.

Theresa and her brother Rasheed, leaning on their father,
Latoof, in the 1890s. Their seated mother (my great-grandmother)
was named Maroon—still one of my favorite colors.

Honeymoon at Coney Island. My parents, Joseph and Lila, in 1932, looking as though they've just walked out of a fashion magazine—with the Cyclone behind them and the world ahead.

My dad and me. One of the few happy times.

With my girls—Lynn, Ari, and Lila—in 2001.

Layers and textures: looks from the 1992 collection.

Murray Pearlstein (*left*) and Luciano Barbera at the Villa d'Este on Lake Como.

The I-Man and the A-Man. With Don Imus at his Radiothon.

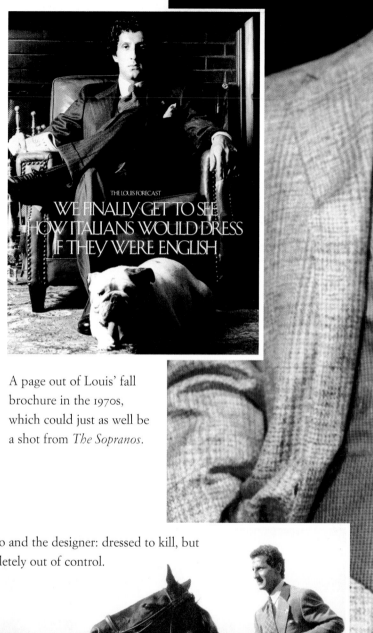

THE LOUIS FORECAST

WE FINALLY GET TO SEE
HOW ITALIANS WOULD DRESS
IF THEY WERE ENGLISH

A page out of Louis' fall
brochure in the 1970s,
which could just as well be
a shot from *The Sopranos*.

Diablo and the designer: dressed to kill, but
completely out of control.

Wynton Marsalis on trumpet, with his quartet: a vision of elegance.

Setting the stage.

The best shirt-and-tie ad I've ever done, shot by Fabrizio Ferri on Eric, my favorite Joseph Abboud model of all time.

My first *DNR* cover, 1986. What a feeling!

White hot: my first front-page appearance, in 1974. Who knew?

Nomar Garciaparra on the left, wearing Joseph Abboud. His inscription meant the world to me.

A banner moment at New York's
American Museum of Natural History.

Joanna Pakula, after
a sleepless night.

Every young man's dream: a
day at the beach with models
Appolonia (*left*)
and Jerry Hall.

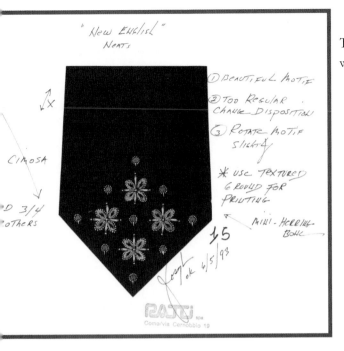

Tie sketches:
work in progress.

The Fabrizio Ferri rock tie.
Fabrizio spent hours
positioning the pebbles
for this ad.

A trio of signature paisleys from Italy.

A romantic sketch for the women's collection. It was always about the fabric.

I wish every man could dress
this way. I love the intricate
use of all the patterns.

Relaunching the women's collection at Saks.

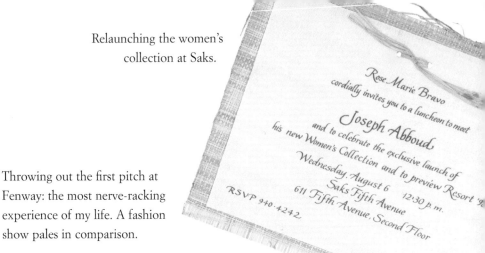

Rose Marie Bravo cordially invites you to a luncheon to meet

Joseph Abboud

and to celebrate the exclusive launch of his new Women's Collection and to preview Resort '9

Wednesday, August 6   12:30 p.m.

Saks Fifth Avenue
611 Fifth Avenue, Second Floor

RSVP 940·4242

Throwing out the first pitch at Fenway: the most nerve-racking experience of my life. A fashion show pales in comparison.

This '70s Louis ad did wonders for my social life.

A parting gift from the women's design team at Polo Ralph Lauren.

An Olympian souvenir.

NO ONE WILL EVER MEASURE UP TO YOU JOEY!!!

BRIGITTE
FEB. 84

The most exciting fashion show I've ever done (1992), especially because I was carrying Lila down the runway.

Cheered me right up.

As for the sweaters, Murray ended up buying both styles (more of the red and blue), and they all sold.

Arthur and I usually shared a room, and that was okay. He was ten years older, but we got along great. Checking into the Majestic in Florence one season, Murray got his single and Arthur and I got the double—except that the double had one big bed and an antechamber about the size of my desk, with a cot. Right next to the elevators.

"Okay," I say to Arthur the first night, "you take the bed tonight, and we'll switch off tomorrow." Fine.

I'm absolutely exhausted and fall into my . . . cot, but no way can I sleep. The elevators are going up and down all night, and Arthur's sleeping like a baby. The next morning he goes into the bathroom, and I hear this terrible *thud*. I run in, and there's Arthur on the floor, holding his head and bleeding like a gored matador. He slipped in the shower, and here he is, naked, holding his underwear to his head, moaning.

I grab a towel to stop the blood, run to the phone and say that my friend fell and hit his head. "*Scusi, signor?*" says the guy on the other end. "The man he break his *leg?*"

This goes on forever. Arthur's bleeding to death, we're supposed to meet Murray at the show, and he's a crazy boss. (He's mellowed now, but in those days he was a very fiery guy.)

Finally, a knock on the door. "*Il dottore.*" He has to be ninety, and he looks like one of my Lebanese uncles. He's doddering, he's got a three-day beard, and he says, "Is somebody broke their leg?"

"No," I say. "Nobody broke a leg. My friend fell and hit his *head.*"

He walks into the room and sees Arthur in a daze, holding the bloody towel to the wound. "Who put-a this on his head?" he asks, picking it up.

"Me," I tell him.

"You must to let it crust," he says, flinging it into the corner. He means *scab.*

Arthur's woozy now. The doctor wraps him in bandages so that he looks like Boris Karloff in *The Mummy,* and tells him to stay in bed. Then, "*Il conto.*" The bill.

"The hotel will take care of it," I say, smartly.

"The hotel, no."

"I have to pay?"

"*Si, signor.*" I hold out all my money, which is 30,000 lire.

"How much?" I ask.

"Thirty thousand lire," he says, sweeping it out of my hand.

Arthur took a week to recover, and I never did get the bed.

Another stop on the Italian map was a company called Ben Sussan in Milan, where it was kind of make-your-own sundae. You'd pick your fabrics and say, "Well, this jacket is going to have an elbow patch and a throat latch, and maybe a leather top collar, and maybe bellows pockets." As you added nuts and syrup and cherries, the price went up.

We'd often bump into Bernie Schwartz, an off-the-wall guy who'd been a schoolteacher in Seattle and now ran a store in Beverly Hills called Eric Ross. Bernie's thing was West Coast slick, and he had a great following. It was in the days of schmaltzy clothing anyway, but this was hyperexpensive schmaltzy clothing. If Ralph Lauren put an elbow patch on a hacking jacket, he did it authentically. Bernie, on the other hand, was doing it from an L.A. standpoint. He had movie stars for customers and he'd convince them that he could design them a suit exactly the way they wanted it; then he'd go to Luciano Ben Sussan, the great Italian tailor, and get it made.

If you could add six details to a jacket, Bernie could add sixty: leather elbow patches, leather under the pocket, side vent with a button in the back, throat latch, contrasting lining, dinosaur stitching, a quilted pocket, a pocket on top of another pocket. He'd go to Ben Sussan and lock himself in a showroom for days, making sketches, every one different. Ben Sussan would be going nuts, saying, "Wait a minute. I'm going to make a special design for one customer?" and Bernie would be saying, "But I'm telling my guy he's the only guy in the world who's gonna have this jacket!"

One day we walked in together. "We welcome *you*, Mr. Pearlstein," said Ben Sussan, who had finally had enough, "but I renounce *this* man," pointing to Bernie. "I *renounce* him."

Bernie Schwartz sold Eric Ross in 1976, and it closed three years later.

Meanwhile, back in Boston, there was this blond.

She was adorable, with cropped hair and beautiful blue eyes. Breezy and quick but somehow not intimidating. And *where* she was was right behind one of Louis's counters. We met in the fall of 1973, and I was incredibly touched when she showed up two months later at the mercy meal following my mother's funeral. (You want to see two worlds colliding? Picture the glamorous gang from Louis meeting my great-aunts in their rolled-up stockings, wrinkled black dresses, and clunky shoes at a Washington Street restaurant called The Red Fez.)

Lynn Weinstein came from a well-to-do Jewish family, and I was the Lebanese merchant. A scary clash of cultures? No. I also fell in love with her family and their friends, my sisters fell in love with Lynn and her family, everybody fell in love right back, and it was enough to smother us all.

We both worked late, sometimes two or three nights a week, in the Boston or Chestnut Hill store. As a big-shot buyer-merchandiser and no longer on commission, I made it my gallant habit to sell a customer thirty shirts and twenty ties, then walk over to Lynn and say, "Would you write this up?" and she'd get the commission. On free nights, we'd sometimes grab a hamburger at Charley's, but our ideal date was the movies and then sitting for hours at the old Café Florian on Newbury Street. For me it was an extension of Paris . . . with, *finally*, the right girl.

Our wedding took place at her home in Newton—Lynn in a tailored ivory silk dress, me in a navy pin-stripe suit with an ivory linen vest and a navy tie with ivory polka dots (the Duke of Windsor standing under a *chuppa*). A Jewish bride, a Lebanese groom, and a marriage made at retail.

It was a small ceremony, and the reception—out at Spring Valley Country Club in Sharon, my father-in-law's club—would be the bigger deal. For this event, where all the Lebanese and Jewish relatives were finally going to meet, Lynn had chosen a form-fitting floor-length cro-cheted gown studded with pearls. She was drop-dead gorgeous and ready to make her entrance.

At this point I'd like to address my unfailing sense of priority.

My wedding was June 6, 1976, also the date of the sixth game of the championship series between the Phoenix Suns and the Boston Celtics (*my* Boston Celtics). What was I supposed to do? Miss the game?

"It's late," cried my bride. "We have to go!"

"Not yet. I've got to *see* this."

"Joe, c'mon! They're waiting for us!"

"Just one more quarter, one more quarter."

I watched the whole game, we were an hour and twenty minutes late, Lynn was going berserk, my new mother-in-law was livid—but the Celtics won.

Married or not, I still went traveling. Hollow-eyed from no sleep or throwing up from food poisoning, I had to crawl out of bed and help keep the show on the road. "These three-week trips are killing me," I wrote Lynn, because they were. In addition to the physical drain, three weeks in close quarters is a long time to spend with two guys—every hour, every meal—and we'd all get testy. "I'm not doing this anymore," I'd write. And keep on doing it.

But not forever. As I approached thirty, it was time to consider the next move. I didn't want to wake up at sixty or sixty-five and be handed a gold watch and a thank-you card. I didn't want someone to take over Louis and get rid of me. I didn't want to wonder years later, "Could I have done more?" The big chill was: I had no control over my future.

I didn't want to leave Louis, but I'd been there for twelve intense years. I was devoted to Murray and his family and loved what I was doing, but I didn't want to spend the rest of my life doing it. When I told Arthur I was thinking about leaving, he didn't seem surprised. "This is as far as I ever dreamed I'd go," he said, "but for you it's only the beginning." I was overwhelmed by a faith in me that I certainly didn't have.

So what to do? There wasn't another store on earth for me. After Louis, anyplace else would have been a step down.

It was.

ELEVEN

Polo Player

I PLUNGED TO A PLACE called Southwick—a short, unpleasant chapter in my life.

Southwick was not a store, not a designer brand, but a manufacturer of tailored clothing in Lawrence, Massachusetts, that did private label for Louis, Paul Stuart, Barneys, and other top specialty stores. When I left Louis, I'd decided to cross from the retail side to the wholesale side because that's where I thought everything was happening. And when Richard and Edna Grieco hired me to style and design for them, it sounded right. Southwick was a bastion of tradition, and I was being invited to help change its face.

Except that I wasn't allowed to. For nine months I served time in Griecoland, trying to do what I'd been hired to do and being thwarted at every turn. Introduce new fabrics and silhouettes? Ship spring product early? The salesmen would look at me through their two-button sack suits, as if to say, "Who's *this*? What does *he* know?"

What I knew was retail. I'd just come from one of the best stores in the country, where we needed products early in order to have a good season. (Fashion-forward customers don't wait until March or April to buy their spring clothes; they buy in January and February.) I was a thirty-year-old guy with bright ideas, and these were sixty-year-old geezers stuck in the status quo. It became a turf war. While the Griecos *intellectually* understood that they were being kept in a time warp, they didn't have the conviction to back me. The machine had run the same way for so long it would have taken great discipline to change it. This was my first hostile environment, and an unbelievable nightmare.

The factory walls and bundled clothing were a grim contrast to the spiffy surroundings at Louis. What's worse, I missed my personal connections with the customers. Southwick was so insulated from the outside world that the salesmen didn't know who they were selling to; they could just as well have been dealing in golf clubs or bird cages. It wasn't that I didn't understand the manufacturing process; I did. But this was production without inspiration, without optimism. Sure, there were great clothes being made, but the environment was demoralizing.

In retrospect, I picture those months as being continually cloudy and rainy, outside and in. That's how I remember them. My only escape was playing squash and backgammon at the University Club every night. Clearly, I'd made a terrible mistake. Instead of jumping on the fast track to a glowing future, I was ready to jump out the window.

Ralph called.

I had loved his stuff from the very beginning. In 1967, the year Ralph Lauren started Polo—and, with it, the American designer era—I was seventeen, and a Yankee Doodle Dandy (a dubious Yankee, a definite dandy). One day, haunting the Berkeley Shop at Louis Boston, I came upon a red-white-and-blue plaid sport coat with gold buttons. It was the most beautiful sport coat I'd ever seen. It was gutsy, with very wide lapels and a flared bottom. Very fitted. The epitome of arrogance and 1960s good taste.

I had to have it.

Most sport coats in the Berkeley Shop cost $79.50, but not this one. This one, designed by Ralph Lauren, whoever *he* was, cost $150.

I went over to the salesman. "Uh, do you have a layaway plan?"

"Yeah, we have a layaway plan."

Okay! I already had the tie, and now I could actually get something substantial at this place! I knew I couldn't have it right away, but if I could just keep paying for it, eventually it would be mine. I tried it on and felt like a million dollars. I gave the guy ten bucks—all I had on me—and every week after that, I'd come in and give him another $5 or $10. It took about three months, which was *forever*, to buy that jacket.

On my next visit to Louis, I fell in love with a belted-back Norfolk jacket of brown-and-white Donegal, with gussets and patch pockets. Another Ralph Lauren, and another knockout. How could I know I was buying into another guy's dream? All I knew was that this piece of clothing was going to substantiate who *I* was.

I buttonholed the same salesman. "Do you have that jacket in my size?" I was a 39 regular at the time.

"No. All we've got is a 40."

"Can you take it in?"

"Of course not," he said, with obvious disdain. "We'd never take it in because of the construction. The belt and the gussets."

I was heartsick. I wanted it more than anything in the world, and this guy wouldn't sell it to me.

"I really want to buy the jacket," I insisted.

He said—and now he had his colleagues gathered around, looking at me, shaking their heads in agreement—"You can't buy the jacket."

I begged. I pleaded. I went back four days in a row, trying to persuade these guys to let me buy the jacket. I said, "I'll tell you what. If you sell it to me, I promise I'll wear a sweater underneath it to take up some of the bulk." Here I am, trying to negotiate with them to sell me the thing, and they're saying, "You *promise* you're going to wear a sweater underneath this?" And I say, "I swear."

It worked. I got the jacket, and I loved it. But you know what? I also loved their integrity. Let people want it and let it be right for them, because if you sell it to them wrong, they'll never come back.

Not only was Ralph Lauren already one of my fashion gods; he now became my guardian angel. Just as my father had pulled me out of the Charles as I was about to go under, Ralph saved me from Southwick.

When he called in the midst of my misery, he offered me the job of New England and Northeast sales representative. This meant I'd be selling Polo menswear to stores from Maine down to Virginia and Washington, D.C., a huge territory. I'd thought I was done with selling, but if that's what it took to join Ralph, I'd do it. The face-to-face customer issues, the windows, merchandising, buying, budgets—I felt sure I had them under my belt. But if Louis had been college, then Ralph Lauren was graduate school.

Lynn and I didn't much like New York. We didn't know where to live, where not to live. So without much of a search, we rented an apartment in a high-rise on West Sixtieth Street. It was a nice apartment in a nice building with nice views—and I hated it. I kept picturing the exact same configuration of apartments above and below me. I was sure people could hear me brushing my teeth.

But I could walk to work, and that made sense. Because I was always working. It's all I wanted to do.

"Hey, Joey, how're things going?" Ralph would ask when he dropped by my desk. "What do you feel like wearing this season?"

Ralph Lauren was asking what *I* felt like wearing!

"Black-and-white tweeds," I'd say, or, "Really dressy stuff," or, "I feel like wearing suits again." If it wasn't exactly where he wanted to go, that was okay. He liked my honesty and seemed interested in my opinion. It was intoxicating.

I was the black sheep in the flock, and not just because I was swarthy instead of blond and blue-eyed. The other guys all dressed in chinos and rep stripe ties, button-down shirts and patch-and-flap sport coats, and I leaned toward the daring side of the line, with the spread-collar and side vent. My taste was a little left-field, but Ralph liked to tap into that.

When he didn't agree, he never pooh-poohed my ideas. But in his genteel, soft-spoken manner he could knock the legs right out from under me.

"This isn't Polo," was all he'd have to say, and I'd feel it like a punch.

The collection was too large to pack up and take on the road, so most of the major accounts came to Polo headquarters on West 55th Street. We wanted them to smell and feel and see and touch. Not only that, it was home field advantage. Always better to have the other guys play in *your* park.

Most of my customers were close enough to drive in or take the train. They came to the showrooms, where I'd present a *concept*, from tuxedos to tailored clothing to sportswear to neckwear. Soup to nuts.

If Ralph was feeling Scottish, or Western, or Caribbean that season, that's what we delivered to the buyers. I've always been a salesman, always sold my way to where I am. If I can believe in it, I can sell it—and I believed in it. I'd try to think about every three-button or double-breasted as if I were buying it for my own store. Sometimes I'd try to move the buyers beyond traditional and sell the more advanced things, like moleskin trousers and stuff that was slightly more Euro. They were in the collection, and I'd just slant it.

We weren't all on the same page. The Southern buyers were traditional natural-shoulder guys, products of a culture you could *never* change, so I had to tread lightly. But I wanted the clothes to sell well for them so they'd come back the next season.

I'd give it the old negative song and dance.

They'd say, "I'll take twelve navy blazers."

We'd size them and then I'd say, "Well, you've got twelve, so maybe we should stop. But you'll probably need a couple of 42 longs or 44 longs." Before you knew it, the twelve had become eighteen. And I'd keep going.

"If you have the single-breasted," I'd say, "you're probably going to have a customer for the double-breasted. But you know what? You can wait 'til next time. We may still have some fabric left. We can check. We might, we might not."

"Well," they'd say, "I probably *could* use some double-breasteds . . ." and think it was their idea. (This was the same strategy I'd used with girls: "I'd love to go out with you on Saturday night but I know you probably can't so we'll do it another time because I know you're busy and I just wanted to ask you but I know you've got exams so I understand why you can't so see ya later good-bye." And they'd say, "But I *can*.")

One of my customers, from Richards in Greenwich, was a gentleman named Eddie Schachter. We'd be at the office late—writing orders until one o'clock in the morning, wolfing down corned-beef sandwiches from the Carnegie Deli—and Schachter would show up. He was endearing in a way, but he was also demanding, condescending, even oppressive, and I always felt challenged to keep things light. I got pretty good at turning a contentious meeting into something more fun.

Every time he came into the office, the first part of the collection I showed him was the socks. Not because I thought socks were the most important part of the collection, but because they gave me the highest commission and because he drove me crazy. I'd bury him in so many argyles he wouldn't have money left for blazers. But he didn't have to buy socks from anybody else for a very long time.

Another good customer was Louis Boston, my alma mater. One morning, I was enthusiastically presenting the line to Murray Pearlstein, now sitting on the other side of the table. "You'll love this," I said, proudly laying out the swatches, and, "This is a great jacket," and so forth. I wasn't trying to *sell* him. I had the same passion and energy that I'd always had. But Murray leaned forward and touched my arm.

"Stop, Joe," he said. "Wait a minute." I looked at him, puzzled. "Joe," he said, "I'll tell *you* what's right for Louis."

I hated hitting the road. I'd been at Louis, and I was a retail snob. I admit it. I didn't *want* to go to cities that weren't glamorous. I didn't *want* to go to Hartford and Providence and Baltimore. That whole mid-Atlantic region—it's like being in one of Bruce Springsteen's nightmares.

And I didn't want to schlep the bags, because I didn't think that was what Cary Grant would do. It was what Willy Loman would do.

But here was my biggest worry: the pocket squares. I had to make sure I represented Polo properly, and it was real pressure, so I'd spend an hour and a half, two hours, trying to figure out which pocket squares to pack. Then there was the matter of arrangement. If it was silk, I'd do a Sammy Davis and stuff it in nonchalantly, like a little cloud. If it was printed cotton, like a bandana, I'd sort of throw it in there like an afterthought.

The worst night I can remember was in Hagerstown, somewhere in the bowels of Maryland. It was late, not many people around, and three of us sales guys were sitting at the bar. I was incredibly depressed; I just loathed the places we were going, and the hotels. They weren't Villa d'Este, you know? But there I was, all dressed up in my beautiful Polo sport coat and pocket square and silk tie and low-vamp shoes and argyle socks . . . and without Lynn.

There was a woman behind the bar, and she had one of those monkeys around her neck. You know, the stuffed monkeys that you wind around your neck so they move when you move. Well, she did it for me. This was the end of the world. The joint you'd come to just before committing suicide.

I promised myself I'd get myself out of sales.

But not yet. There was still a tremendous upside to selling. For one thing, there was the Polo knit shirt. That logo shirt with the polo player on it was one of the greatest market phenomena I've ever witnessed, and an *enormous* part of the success story of Ralph Lauren. When it first appeared, it had a limited color range and was just another item in the line. But once it caught on, it hit like a tidal wave.

Lacoste had been there first, with the crocodiles, and its cachet came about almost by accident. It was just one of those things, like a Rolex watch, that become status items without intending to. This knit shirt, Ralph's version, now became the status shirt. During my tenure, it went from seven colors to forty-four.

Comfortable, casual, very Hamptons—it was The Shirt. And an easy sell. With stores like Jordan Marsh and Filene's, Bamberger's and Hanes, when we allowed them to buy it, we couldn't write the orders— million-dollar orders!—fast enough. Our arms ached (this was before computers, remember). It was incredible what that shirt did. To this day, I can't think of another single item that's had such an impact on the menswear industry: millions sold, a multimillion-dollar business. There are lots of knit shirts out there now, including ours—and we've built a significant business with them—but nothing comes close to the triumph of the Polo polo.

It was the right shirt at the right time. The Lacoste was getting tired, being distributed and discounted in too many stores and losing its cachet. Polo was the new kid on the block, offering instant status for only $32.50—a lot less than the cost of a ranch—in a staggering range of colors. The message was clear: Wear this shirt and you have style.

The Ralph mystique was unfolding, and it all looked glamorous, but there was always a big push to *do business*. We were salesmen, and we had to perform. The knit shirt was a blockbuster, but not every- thing else was.

No matter. The job was to sell. If we had a big inventory of blue button-down shirts and the stores didn't want them, Peter Strom would say, "I don't care if they have too many blue button-downs. You sell blue button-downs." He put the fear of God into us. We didn't have a choice; our asses were on the line. So we tried anything we could, used all the finesse in our repertoire, to navigate the customer into the right position without showing weakness.

We never wanted to say, "Look at all these blue button-downs. You've got to help us out." So we'd say, "Ralph *really believes* in the blue button-down this season, and if he visits, he'll want to see that blue button-down."

"You really think Ralph will come by the store?"

"Well, you never know. He loves to drop in."

Peter directed the operational side, and he was truly one of the reasons for Ralph's early success. Here's what I admired most about him: If Ralph held up a yellow book and said, "Don't you love this black book?" Peter would say, "That's the most beautiful black book I've ever seen." Whether he agreed with Ralph or disagreed, he was Ralph's greatest supporter. If they had any discord, it was never in front of us. They sent out a unified message: Ralph had the vision, and Peter was going to get it done.

One day, Peter says to the sales guys, "Wear your crummy clothes, because we're all going out to the factory to pick orders. We need to get this stuff shipped out." That meant he was short of manpower and we were going to New Jersey to be factory workers for a few days. Peter would do whatever he had to do, and if it was picking orders, you'd better be there. "Picking an order" meant pulling different polo shirts out of different brown cardboard boxes and putting them together to fill an order. You became a picker and a packer.

If Mitchells of Westport was buying a bunch of thirty-six red shirts, for example, you'd go pick three from a box of red smalls, twelve from a box of red mediums, twelve from a box of red larges, and nine from a box of red extra-larges. You'd put them into a shipping box and circle them on the packing slip. (That was the one I most hated picking, because I just hated the red.) Then you'd go over and pick the yellows (which I hated, too, because most guys look lousy in yellow). Then the navies, and so on.

Here was the worst part: You couldn't always fill the orders completely. Say the customer wanted twenty-four pink (four small, eight medium, eight large, and four extra-large). You'd go to the pink smalls and pick four. Fine. Then to the pink mediums and pick eight. Fine. Then to the pink larges. But there weren't eight larges; there were no larges. This was a crisis, because the customers wanted you to ship complete. So you'd have to take the pinks you'd already picked and put them back in their boxes. It was horrible.

It's not that it was demeaning, exactly—we all knew we had to do the job—but it was tedious, sweaty, and not in the least bit creative. I'd be wearing jeans and a T-shirt, and all I could think about was how unglamorous it was, how I wanted to be back at the office in my elegant layers. But this was about business, not façade. I know that now, but I didn't know it then.

When Ralph did the men's clothes for *The Great Gatsby*, Robert Redford became his fan and his friend. Whenever he was expected to arrive, the news would fly all over the floor—"Robert Redford's coming!"—and we'd all go on alert. Even when he wasn't coming up, we loved to flaunt Ralph's star power. "Sorry Ralph can't be here," we'd tell our customers. "He's up with Redford."

One day he and I rode up on the elevator together. I was so impressed that I couldn't breathe. There he was, looking as great in person as he did in the movies. I'd always imagined him to be six-foot-two or -three, but he was about five-ten and a 40 regular. My height. My size.

A couple of weeks later, there in the showroom were two tuxedos marked Robert Redford. One was a peak-lapel, the other a notched-lapel. I wandered over, touched them, and, just for fun, tried one on.

It fit close to the body, as if it had been made for me. A *great* tuxedo. I look as much like Robert Redford as I do the man in the moon, but when I put that tuxedo on, I *was* Robert Redford! That's what clothes can do.

"He's not taking those two," somebody said. "They're yours."

Which is how the Lebanese dude ended up with two tuxedos made for the Sundance kid.

There were other celebrities drifting into our lives, too. Woody Allen would drop by, looking just like *Woody Allen* in his little Ralph Lauren tweed jackets. Candice Bergen was incandescent, and I remember seeing Bill Cosby and Diane Keaton. It wasn't exactly a cavalcade of stars, but it was still pretty exciting.

Even long-distance.

One day Ralph was sitting in my office when Dinah, his executive secretary, transferred one of his calls to my phone.

Naturally, I picked it up.

"Hello?" I said.

"*Hel*-lo! Is Ralph in?" It sounded just like . . . Cary Grant.

"Who's calling him, please?"

"Cary Grant."

TWELVE

Pal Joey

THERE WAS ENORMOUS energy in the place. We projected an uptight, crested image—with Clotilde the model in her beautiful tartan, looking as if she'd just flown in from Scotland, and Buzzy the all-American JFK facsimile in his wholesome Shetlands—but in truth, the tweedy hormones were ripe and raging. The girls (all the Buffys and Muffys and Miffys) would prance around in their chinos and jodhpurs, with their hair all wispy and big hoop earrings and Polo'd to the hilt, and the guys would be trying to get their tweeds straightened out, you know?

They also beguiled the out-of-town salesmen who came in for Market Week and stayed for weeks at a time. These guys were bigger than life, and they had a romantic edge. Maybe back home they were just "Yes, dear, I'll do the dishes for you." But when they came to New York they were visiting dignitaries, the Polo elite, almost like rock stars to the girls.

Jim, blond, good-looking, and the primary chick magnet, covered the Midwest territory. He dressed traditionally, right out of the heartland, and was big on button-downs and chinos. Billy Joe, the West Coast guy, was funny and flamboyant. He was big and handsome, a rugged Gary Cooper type, and he loved dressing the role of the L.A. Polo guy: cool, hip jeans, and a tweed jacket with no shirt under it, but a serape over it. Edwin came from Atlanta, with the accompanying accent and charm. He was probably the best salesman ever—a big writer (i.e., he could really write business, like an order for 250 dozen ties at a time). Larry, from Paducah, Kentucky, had an accent so impenetrable I needed a translator to talk to him. He'd usually write the orders wrong—"I didn't know ah was s'posed to do it *that* way. What about *yew*? Did *yew* know?"—but he was lovable.

John, in the New York office, was Ralph's idea of clothes reincarnate. He was very WASPy—handsome, blond, perfect—but with humor. There was nobody who could do what we called "Old Polo" the way John could. He'd take an old seersucker suit, because he knew Ralph loved that, and vintage it up with a tie from five years ago, a frayed button-down, and white bucks. John was originally from Pittsburgh, but he'd fortunately outgrown Pittsburgh style. To be blunt, Pittsburgh wasn't quite up to our standard. Any time we saw a guy in a brown suit and a yellow shirt, we called him a "half-Pittsburgh," and a guy in a brown suit, yellow shirt, *and black shoes* was a "full-Pittsburgh." That's about as bad as it can get.

Robert, our sales manager, majored in cotton pocket squares. No one else came close. He showed just enough of the white points on a handkerchief to let you know it was there, but it was perfect. And then there was me, Mr. Eurotrash—the guy who yearned to do Polo a little more European. I was sort of the international connection.

The Magnificent Seven. Plus our leader of the pack—dynamic, saddle-shoed Marty Staff.

Whenever Market Week rolled around, Polo became a Tower of Babel. As salesmen we all shared a sensibility and love for the product, but we spoke in different tongues. These good ole boys would be going, "Hey, how yew doin'?" And I'd start coming back with, "What are you guys *tah-kin'* about?" It was ridiculous. The farthest south I'd ever been was Greenwich Village.

Everybody came early, worked late, wanted to play. We had breakfast together, lunch together, sales meetings together. When the day was over, the girls in merchandising and design would bring the samples into the showroom, the guys would say, "Sit down and have a drink. Let's go out to dinner," and the next thing you knew everybody was with somebody.

If a girl came to the office in the same outfit she'd been wearing the night before, we figured she'd probably stayed at one of the guys' hotels. If one of the guys came in in the same outfit, he'd probably stayed at one of the girls' apartments. I didn't have a tally sheet as to who was doing what with whom, but it was the 1980s and a pre-AIDS mind-set, and when you put that many beautiful people in one spot with so much energy and creativity coursing around, sparks are going to fly.

Romance permeated the place on the clothes side, too. Ralph was constantly poring over illustrated books about films, cars, old hotels, Europe, so a lot of the creative stuff that happened within the line was referential—and reverential.

He didn't want to be just another Jewish kid from the Bronx. He wanted to be (and wanted everyone else to be) Gary Cooper or Clark Gable. So when he started his collection, it was about a lifestyle that wasn't a real lifestyle. It was a fantasy land, Disney World, the world as seen through his eyes—like *The Purple Rose of Cairo*, where the heroine steps into the movie. But it was real and right for Ralph. We'd come through the 1950s, when men wore dark little innocuous suits with dark little innocuous ties and everyone looked the same, and the 1960s, a very ugly time in style, with the knit suits and body shirts and body jewelry. Now here he was with his glamorous dream that anyone could buy into.

Anyone but the Brits.

When *Chariots of Fire* came out in 1981, we all went to see it. It was a visual spectacle, very lush, and a treasure trove for Ralph. British as it was, the sophisticated preppiness was also very American. I'm thinking about the tweed jacket, the belted-back jacket, the argyle sweater, and the Fair Isle sweater. Alas, the Fair Isle. At some point later on, we learned that Ralph wasn't doing so well in the U.K., and here's why: Customers didn't need Fair Isle sweaters like the ones their grandmothers and great-grandmothers had been knitting in Scotland for hundreds of years. They weren't about to embrace the Anglo-Saxon concepts that Ralph Lauren was reinventing. It was coals to Newcastle, Fair Isles to Fair Isle.

I never consciously thought, "Well, today I'm going to be an aristocrat," but life's fine things were becoming more and more available. I could have *five* Ralph Lauren suits now, or even ten. They weren't free, but we got great prices, because Ralph always wanted his staff to *look* like his staff. There's no question we were all vying for his attention, and everybody wanted to out-style and out-peacock the next guy. I think he took great pleasure in seeing who did it well and who didn't.

Ralph himself had no problem cutting a swath. He was unremittingly motif-driven. Whether he was the country squire or the cowboy, he was the star of his own movie. On Monday, he might show up in a very fitted, double-breasted, dark gray chalk-stripe flannel suit. Tuesday, he might wear fatigues with an olive Porsche watch and a day's scruff. Wednesday, a black-and-white herringbone sport coat, white shirt (with a soft, hand-washed collar), and silver tie.

"In that outfit," I once remarked, "you should be driving a silver sports car."

"No," he said. "When I wear a tie, I'm in the backseat."

No one has done a greater job of inventing the myth of Ralph Lauren than Ralph Lauren.

*   *   *

I was having a wonderful time, but getting itchy. I'd been with Polo about a year, I knew the sales game inside out, and I was ready for more. Ralph and his brother, Jerry, the easygoing, fun-loving head of men's design, knew it, too.

I had a feeling in my gut: I can do this; I can bring something to the table.

The invitation came at the end of 1981, when they asked me to be associate director of design. It was a confirmation of all those feelings, instincts, tweaks—all those years of looking at the Polo ties in Louis's window, trying on the first Polo jackets. I'd worked my way in from the outer fringes, wound through the sartorial maze to the source. I was joining the design team of one of the greatest designers of all time!

I was involved with every product in the menswear line. Everything that Jerry worked on—from concepts to colors, from the rough sketches done by illustrators to the prototypes submitted by the licensees who made luggage, hosiery, belts, and small leather goods—I worked on with him.

We had adjoining offices and interacted all day long, unless one of us was traveling. Nothing was too much. Whatever time we have to start, whatever time we have to finish, just bring it on! Design meetings took hours, but we were pre-editing for Ralph. We rarely disagreed and never butted heads. Although I was dying to go to Ralph directly and prove myself, it wasn't the right thing to do. This wasn't a who's-got-the-better-ideas-for-Ralph? contest. I was always looking for the alternative, the unexpected, and there were times Jerry would edit me out early. But other times he'd say, "Joey likes these colors" or "Joey likes these patterns for sport coats." He was very generous and always gave me a chance.

For a knit-shirt meeting, for example, the product manager of the knit department would pin up paintings of different stripes—two-color stripes, multicolor stripes, ombre stripes, hundreds of them on eight- by ten-inch square cards—on a blank wall (and if we knew that

Bentley green, say, was what Ralph was feeling that season, we'd make sure a lot of the stripes had that color green in the combination). The merchandisers or design assistants would pin up miniature sketches of shirts—a long-sleeve polo, a short-sleeve polo, a turtleneck, whatever. Once we had all the paintings and sketches up, Jerry and I could start to move them around, mixing and matching stripes and colors with fabrics and styles, adjusting, rethinking, improving. "How about adding more color to the two-color club stripe?" or "Let's do a solid ground with a single-color stripe three inches apart. Make the stripe an inch and a half wide."

We had silhouette meetings ("Should we have more shearling coats? Do we want suede vests?") and sock meetings. Most cable socks are jacquarded, or engineered through a machine, but we were still buying genuine hand-tied cashmere cables from Corgi. They cost about $75 retail, and we sold maybe a couple dozen pairs at most, but we wanted to have them because we knew Ralph wanted to have them.

The menswear business was exploding, and Jerry was pulled in a million directions, so sometimes he'd let me preselect the tie colors and designs—either in New York with the fabric suppliers or in Como, where I'd browse through the old leather sample books. These books, with their yellowing pages and handwritten notations, are filled with little square swatches of all the mill's products, and when the mill removes one for you (they don't just snip off a sample, like at the wallpaper store), it's only for reference and must be returned. There are thousands of such books, all over town. Each silk company has its own and often buys more to enhance its library. The old bookstores sell others. These archives are a major resource for neckwear design, and we all use them for inspiration.

We weren't doing literal duplicates, though. If I found a design that was too big, we might reduce it. If I found one in only two colors, we might add three or four more. I translated print ideas into wovens, and wovens into prints. It was almost an investigative process, delving and probing and deciphering, and extremely fulfilling. I was plumbing the past, seeing the connection, and rejiggering designs in a whole new way.

In Como, we always dealt with the same elegant gentlemen, and we liked them enormously. Though they were all competing for our time and business, they were the most decorous group I've ever seen, coated in their English tweeds and walking their ancient streets. I still work with many of them today.

When we traveled to London, we'd visit silk manufacturers, fabric companies, and mills. There was a print house called David Evans and another called Vanners that did beautiful wovens, club ties, and stripes. We'd walk down Jermyn Street to Turnbull & Asser, stroll up Savile Row with its legendary tailors, stop in at an antique-button shop or thrift shop, energizing us all and fueling Ralph's vision. The smallest things could inspire a whole collection. That's how it is.

"I want a bathrobe for Christmas," I told them one year, because every day I'd come into the office all dressed up, feeling good, and have to strip. Being a 40 regular is a great advantage for me now, because I can try on my prototypes and samples and see how they fit and feel. But at Polo, it was a great advantage for *them*.

In addition to my round-the-clock work for Jerry, I became a fit model.

"Hey, Joey, would you try on these pajamas?" Off came the black-and-white herringbone jacket and the beautiful pink shirt, the sleeveless sweater and silver tie. On went the pajamas.

It was the beginning of a whole new sideline. From then on, every time they needed a fit model, who did they call?

"*Joey*. Let's see the button-down." Or "Where's Joey? Get him to try on these chinos." It was funny, but it was also a drag getting dressed over and over again with a shirt and a tie and sweaters and vests. When he could see I was flagging, Jerry would look at me sympathetically and call off the dogs. Then, half an hour later, it was "Joey, could you try . . . ?"

One day we were doing a safari group.

"Hey, Joey," he said. "Do me a favor. Put on these leather shorts."
I took off my clothes, put on the leather shorts. They were a beautiful
whiskey color, but kind of heavy and stiff.

"And do me a favor. Put on the safari shirt." A leather safari shirt.

"So," he said. "How do you feel?"

"Like a briefcase."

When we had lunch in New York, it wasn't at "21" or The Four Seasons.
It was at a conference table or desk in the office. And it wasn't rabbit ter-
rine or lacquered quail. It was peaches and cottage cheese. I don't think
it had anything to do with dieting. This was a cultural thing, a throwback
to childhood in the Bronx. Jerry liked it because Ralph liked it, so I liked
it because Jerry liked it because Ralph liked it. It was messy, and sticky,
but you know what? It wasn't bad.

In building that empire, there was enormous pressure on all of us,
so meals like this were among our only chances to really goof around.
We had deadlines, and deadlines were important, but there were days
when Ralph didn't want to talk about polo shirts. He wanted to talk
about the right shade of green for the Bentley, or the brown-leather interior for the Mercedes. For me, it was a fantasy come true just to be
part of the conversation.

Once in a while, he'd invite the team to a dinner party at the apartment on Fifth Avenue. But for us the enticement wasn't the food. The
first thing we wanted to do was go see his closet, like little kids in a toy
store. I remember wood shoe trees with wonderful crocodile shoes,
beautiful tweed jackets. It's not that he had a million things; it's that
what he had looked so smart. Ralph doesn't need the *newest* thing. He
has his favorite suit, his favorite jacket—it could be five or six years
old; he doesn't care. If he likes it, he likes it, and that's confidence.

In or out of the office, we were in his thrall. We worked long and
hard, and competed to work longer and harder. "If *you* can do it, *I* can
do it. You need to get there *early*? I can get there earlier than *you*. You
need to stay *late*? I can stay *later*."

There were days I was so tired I could barely function—one reason being that I was now a commuter. After a year of apartment-dwelling, Lynn and I had decided to move back to Massachusetts.

"I don't care where you live," Peter Strom told me, "as long as you're here to do the job." He was great about it, and Polo paid for the move. We bought a cute little house in Weston, but I saw it only on weekends. Every Monday morning at four o'clock, I was driving back to New York to stay at the Parker Meridien hotel on West 57th Street, where Polo had generously installed me.

The strain of a three-days-a-week marriage was really getting to us. We didn't have kids, Lynn was lonely, and we knew we'd better move back to New York to save our relationship. But not to the city.

Manhattan has incredible energy, but it's like an elevated heartbeat you can't bring down. For an American designer, there's no place in the world like it—the fashion shows, the retail, the culture—but I need to get away from it, too. In other words, it's a great place to run a career, but I wouldn't want to live there. Lynn feels the same. So we built a charming little farmhouse on a beautiful piece of property in Pound Ridge and had the best of both worlds.

If my schedule was full, Ralph's was fuller, so design meetings usually didn't start until eight o'clock at night. That's crazy, because with the creative process you need to be fresh. It was inefficient and often unproductive.

We worked so late and got so giddy we didn't know what the hell we were doing. We'd walk out of there like zombies—sometimes frustrated, sometimes not sure we *had* it, sometimes going, "This is unbelievable!" and taking those concepts to the meeting next morning when we would develop them and bring them to Ralph for his approval. His approval was everything.

It was an all-nighter.

For months, we'd been working on designing the ties, the suits, the shirts, and now we were setting up displays for a sales meeting in a large conference room at the Warwick Hotel, because we'd outgrown our showrooms. Jerry couldn't be there, so I was in charge for the first time. There were a bunch of ties on one table and a bunch of shirts over there and a million swatches: all the raw materials with which I was now going to create a mosaic.

After dressing and pinning the mannequins, I started arranging the groups—country gentleman, Duke of Windsor, evening, texture on texture, tweed on tweed (nobody out-tweeded us). For his presentation to the salespeople, merchandisers, production team, and executives, Ralph would need everything at his fingertips. The mannequins were his demonstration piece, his slide show, and as he delivered his message for the season he'd want to walk to the flannel suits and double-breasted vests, to the stripes-on-stripes and black ties.

At eleven at night, panic set in. Still a long way to go, and the curtain was due to rise at 8:30 A.M. By two o'clock in the morning, I was a monster. I wouldn't let anybody touch or criticize anything. I'd helped design the collection, I'd put the looks together, and this was my moment. I wanted so badly to please Ralph, to justify the faith he had in me, to impress a man I'd worshiped since 1967.

By four o'clock, everything was perfect. The suits, the vests, the ties. It was all very Polo, very Ralph Lauren, but the styling was a bit more theatrical, more international, than anything we'd done before.

At 8:30 Ralph walked in.

"*Wow.*"

Maybe I really *was* good at this.

I kept spreading my wings, trying to expand the boundaries of what I thought Polo could represent. I wasn't reckless, but I was eager to press on. With the success of the logo'd Shetland sweater, which followed the polo shirt, I felt it was time. What could I come up with to make the program work even better?

We'd gone from seven to twenty-two solid colors in the sweater, but my retail experience told me we couldn't just stay the same, season after season. We had to jazz it up. I saw the next logical evolution as a regimental stripe, a horizontal version of the diagonal stripe so commonly used on ties. The people who'd done well with the solid, I figured, would now buy the stripe; we'd just keeping moving them along. We did color combinations like navy, burgundy, and olive; navy, burgundy, and ivory; and the signature purple and green. They took off.

Spurred by that success, I dove off the high board and started pushing a series of cable sweaters in what Murray Pearlstein and I used to call "petroleum" colors because they look like they have a dull, oil-like film over them: gray and melancholy blues; dusty, antique pinks. I thought they'd be a nice change after so many years of doing preppy navies, burgundies, peppermint-stick pinks . . . you know, Ralph colors. And I tried hard, but no go.

I didn't feel shot down, because this was Ralph's place. But more and more I was thinking along different lines. Not necessarily better, just different.

My most "different" idea was the African collection I persuaded them to do, a gorgeous group in black, deep indigo blues, dark berries, and wines. It integrated English and African styles and evoked wonderful khaki suits of the colonial period, so I thought it would fit right into Ralph's world. It didn't. Nobody out there wanted that ethnic color palette, not from Ralph Lauren, and not for spring. I hadn't considered that a big part of his business came from traditional areas like the sun belt and Southern California. I was thinking rich, dark colors, and they were still thinking Ivy jivey—a country-club palette of pink and purple and lime green that's very feminine for men.

Another misguided idea in the African line: the jute sweater. It was beautiful to look at, but no one could wear it. It was scratchy, it was itchy, and it must have weighed forty pounds. We should have had it framed.

The reaction was terrible, across the board, and the collection was a catastrophe. But because we opened as many as fifteen different groups a year—a Palm Beach group in pastels, an Oxford group in navy and white, this African group, and so on—it didn't have an enormous financial impact. "Africa" didn't represent the entire season and the entire offering; it was one small group in a group of groups. But it may have the distinction of being the biggest bomb.

It was what *I* believed in, but it wasn't right for Ralph. I didn't understand then that while it's good to stretch, you have to know when to stop. Whether he goes younger or older, men or women, Ralph knows who he is and what his label's about. He and Jerry have it balanced perfectly. The "Africa" debacle showed us where the borders were, and that we'd entered unknown territory. (Some things just take a little longer to catch on. Twenty years later, in early 2004, *Women's Wear Daily* would run a piece about the "new" colors being introduced by Pecci Yarn at the Pitti trade show in Florence, a palette reflecting "the earthy ethnic tones of North Africa." That's what happens with designers. We might have flashes of brilliance, but they often flash at the wrong time.)

The Laurens didn't cut my head off. They didn't kick me in the gut. In fact, we laughed about it. But I'd arrived at another crossroads.

I wasn't thinking about a Joseph Abboud label. Not then. But there were colors and concepts that I felt the market needed—even if Ralph didn't. I'd look at yarn swatches on manila cards—petroleum blues, mossy browns, inky grays—and see them as baby cable knits and V-necks, turtlenecks and sport coats.

Logic would have said, "Joe, you're with a great company, you're right next to the king, don't be a jerk." But logic had nothing to do with it. Our visions were diverging, and it wasn't just color coming between us. It was also shape, fit, and the positioning of a collection. Tradition was the essence of Ralph Lauren, and I liked edge. The clothes I wanted to design weren't right for him. But they were right for me.

THIRTEEN

The Game of the Name

ALONG CAME MY CHANCE, in the form of an old friend.

"Come with me," said Barry Bricken, who was very big in trousers, "and I'll give you your own label."

Barry and I had met at Louis when the store bought a lot of his product, and we'd become good friends. When he was in Boston or I was in New York, we'd hang out together, playing squash, going to restaurants, seeing movies. And we'd stayed close. So in 1984 I left Ralph, who was in the designer business, to go with Barry, who wanted to be in the designer business.

When we parted, Ralph gave me an antique gold horseshoe lapel pin, and Bobbi Renales, then a product manager and now senior vice president of design, gave me *The Fountainhead*. It was just a paperback, but it's still one of the most important gifts I've ever received. The novel was a lesson in trusting your instincts and pursuing your dreams, and it came to me at precisely the right moment. I'd been a good piece of Polo. But now I'd find out what I could do on my own.

Barry had a New York showroom and office on Fifth Avenue near 43rd Street, with a warehouse and corporate offices in Baltimore, where we'd have to go for sales meetings. He knew I loathed Baltimore, so on one trip he invited me to spend the night at his parents' house.

I'm really choosy about my surroundings and where I sleep. If I go to a hotel and don't like the room for some reason, I can't stay there. It's my own neurosis. As a kid, I couldn't even sleep at other kids' houses. I've always needed familiar things around—parents, wife, my own bed, the smells of home, the open windows, whatever. I do hotels when I have to, but I'd rather be home.

I didn't want to be rude to Barry, so I said okay and he showed me to this room. In the corner was a child's very low bed and a pale lime-green bedspread with little knots and little balls. I hate lime green. There were all these toys lined up. Everything was neat and clean, but it was the longest night of my life.

I wanted to be back in New York, taking off on my own path. Not that I didn't have doubts. I knew how to play with swatches and design a suit, but what was there that I didn't know? I had the Louis and Ralph degrees in my back pocket, but this was a start-up and the pressures were different. Now *I* was the guy who had to choose the right factories and decide how much fabric to buy. This time *I* was the grown-up.

I'd go forward the best I could, because what was the alternative? If I didn't know something, I'd learn it. Other people had. How hard could it be? So at a little desk in the merchandising room, I started to formulate my plans. Reaping my past experiences, I summoned up the tie connections, the sweater sources, the mills, and the muses.

My first collection was an homage to *The Fountainhead.* The "Roark," designed for a rugged individual, was a sexy cotton shirt like something Gary Cooper might have worn, and it became our number-one seller. Oversized, with two pockets and a soft collar, it was the beginning of the unconstructed look in dress shirts, and it was widely copied in the market. (I'm not going to give you a list of copycats, but when you do certain things, they just get into the vocabulary.) It had less resemblance to the regulation dress shirt than to a grandfather's shirt found in a trunk in the attic, because we did it with irregular antique stripes, like mattress ticking, of faded indigo and brown against tea-stained backgrounds of ivory and straw. This wasn't a shirt you'd wear to a formal shindig. This was a shirt you could fall asleep in. The "Keating" (named for Roark's rival) was, like its namesake, conventional, with one pocket and a structured collar with stays. It sold well, too.

I felt enormous freedom, and enormous pressure. Creatively, it was all up to me.

"So," I asked my friend Barry after a year or so, "what about my label?" The jackets, sweaters, ties, and shirts were selling at Saks, Louis, Mark Shale, and other great specialty stores.

"I've changed my mind."

"*Changed your mind?*"

"I've given it a lot of thought," he said, "and this is my company. So no label."

We were in his corner office, and the guy was telling me our deal was no deal.

Never go into business with your friends, I'd been told, and now I was finding out why.

"Give me my label or I'm leaving."

"Don't be ridiculous, Joe. This is the best job you'll ever have. Walk out the door and you'll never do anything in this business."

I wanted to punch him, shake him, beat him up, knock him down. I'd left a great job with Polo to come *here*? For *this*?

I'd never had a lawyer, never had a contract. I had verbal agreements, handshakes, *jobs*. If someone said, "We'll pay you X, and we'll want you to do this," that was good enough for me. Until this. Now it was too late. I was screwed.

I walked out the door and over to the Fifth Avenue Racquet Club. I couldn't slam Bricken, but I could slam a squash ball. After slamming and sweating and using up the fury, the picture is always clearer.

If I set my mind to something, I'm going to do it. And if someone tells me I *can't* do something, I'm going to try even harder. When Barry told me I had no future, I was out of there, even if I had to pack cartons for the rest of my life. Just hearing that son of a bitch say, "This is as far as you'll go," was all I needed. It was the best shove of my life.

From the frying pan right into the fire.

I'd met Milton Freedberg, who made tailored clothing, by buying product from him for Louis. I was young and impressionable, and when he took me to ball games and fancy restaurants or sent steaks and Madjoul dates at Christmas, he made me feel important. He'd become a friend and counselor. I'd lost Murray as my mentor, but now I had Milton.

I called him that devastating afternoon from Bricken's switchboard, and he rose to the occasion. "Come talk to me," said this second manufacturer who wanted to be in the designer business. "Why don't we start a Joseph Abboud label?"

Well, okay! Here comes Joe Abboud, gun for hire. You want to start a collection? I'm your man!

And once again I made a deal with no lawyers or contracts. It seems unbelievable now, but I was an artist, a guy trying to put his name on the label, and so shortsighted I wasn't thinking about business. I figured the Barry scenario had been an aberration, and that this time I was going to be cradled by someone who really cared about me.

The company was Freedberg of Boston, an old-fashioned manufacturer with headquarters and a warehouse on Shawmut Avenue, two doors away from where I had gone to kindergarten. I'd walk off the elevator through a sea of suits to the back office where, surrounded by pizza boxes and half-eaten sandwiches, I could devote myself to the next beginning of my life as a designer.

Sometimes I'd wander upstairs to the floor of fabrics, where the air was thick with the soapy, fresh smell of wool and lanolin. I loved moving among 50- and 100-yard bolts of raw flannels, tweeds, and linens that lay on the floor, so heavy they required several guys to heave them around. Little white tags hung from the end of the rolls, like toe tags at the morgue, identifying the mills that had woven them. In an otherwise homely room, with worn wood floors and fluorescent lights and a view of the Southeast Expressway, this was a playground of ravishing textures.

But most of the time I worked in the New York showroom on Sixth Avenue, with the designers I'd brought with me from Barry Bricken—including Mark Scarborough, a talented guy who was helping me organize everything. That's where I designed the first Joseph Abboud tailored-clothing collection. And where, at last, I got my first label: navy and burgundy with my name in gold.

At that time there were two very divergent strains in menswear: the traditional preppy look (aka the Ivy League suit or the sack suit), which was tight and boyish, and the flashy pseudo-European look, with its hard shoulders and soft fabrics. The preppy suit was one of the ugliest things that ever happened to men. It was small at the shoulders and fat at the waist, with the emphasis in the wrong place. And it made everybody look like Wally Cox. Or a pear.

The preppy suit is why I started my business.

To the press, the buyers, anyone who asked, I described my collection (for spring 1987) as "Modern American." It had classic roots, but the natural shoulder was wider and more comfortable than that on a Brooks Brothers or Rogers Peet suit. The fabrics had a traditional American feel, but with a twist. I'd been seduced by the sexiness of what Europe was doing and knew that American men could handle it.

I did linen-and-cotton sweaters in black and khaki, navy and ivory, khaki and ivory, which were new color combinations. Linen suits, silk sweaters, dress shirts with soft collars and no pockets. My jacket silhouette was soft, non-vented, and unlined—a marriage of dressed-up and comfortable. It wasn't some cool *Miami Vice* thing. It was a business suit to fit a guy and his life. This doesn't sound revolutionary now, but it was then. I'd found a new zone of opportunity, a place no one had been before.

"Recently I saw a new collection that would attract the most conservative of men if he could only see it, try it. Even the man who is unconscious of words like sportswear or casualwear would fall for it. It's the look and the feel that would envelop and snare him," wrote Clara Hancox, *Daily News Record*'s influential menswear columnist. "Abboud's creations come on so gently, so discreetly, yet so beautifully, that they grab you before you know you've been grabbed." She *got* it.

My first fall collection was inspired by Hollywood in the 1930s and early 1940s: the drape, the shoulders, the ties, the double-breasteds, were the *ne plus ultra*. So I did my own riffs on those black-and-white memories, doing things like linen glen plaid double-breasted suits and linen ties in the colors I'd imagined since childhood. I also did a chestnut-colored suede jacket with gussets on the side and a belted nonvented back. It was made by a furrier in France, a real artisan's shop.

Some called my clothes too editorial. "Editorial" means it's a nice concept and looks good on the page, but it's not going to work in the real world. "Editorial," in other words, means not commercial. But buyers and merchandisers liked them, and we sold to virtually every great store in America.

Reminds me of the moment in *Mississippi* with W. C. Fields and the piano player in the saloon.

"What's that tune you're playing?" Fields wants to know.

"It's brand new, Commodore. They call it 'Swanee River.'"

"No good," Fields mutters. "It'll be forgotten in two weeks. People can't remember the tune." And out he goes—"*Way down upon the Swanee River . . .*"—warbling it under his breath.

Even other designers liked them.

True story: A buyer from Marshall Field's, the large department store in Chicago, is visiting a competitor's showroom in New York.

"And here's our 'Joseph Abboud' model," says the salesman, showing him a soft-shouldered, full-chested, non-vented silhouette in a textured earth tone.

"Well, if it's a Joseph Abboud model," the buyer replies, "we might as well buy it from Joseph Abboud."

And he did.

We were a small team, and we didn't have enormous financial strength. From the front we looked glamorous, but peek around the corner and you'd see a stick holding us up. Our "office" was a third of the showroom. Our "furniture" was junk we found at the freight elevator en route to the trash, tossed out by another company that was remodeling. But we were having a wonderful time.

We didn't have salesmen yet, so I was designing and pretty much selling the collection myself. I was traveling to the factory and the mills, talking to the press, writing the orders. Elated, exhausted, I'd work late most nights, and when I got home to Westchester, Lynn would be waiting for me.

We had survived the commutes and the moves, and we were closer than we'd ever been. Our life together is founded on a mutual love and knowledge of the fashion world, and once we could share that again, we could share everything. Lynn's take on the industry is hilariously insightful. She understands the business, the players, and the politics. She speaks the language. She knows what gets me crazy. And she can write orders a hell of a lot faster than I can.

She'd come downstairs and sit at the counter with me while I wolfed down peanut butter and jelly. I remember standing there with a glass of milk in my hand and a wilted shirt on my back, saying, "Do you think Ralph and Ricky are doing this right now?" This wasn't dinner at "21" or champagne at the Ritz. This was Lynn half-asleep in her nightgown and me half-dead. It was very, very nice.

In August 1986, we joined the Designers' Collective at the Berkshire Hotel in New York to present the spring 1987 collection. This was an opportunity for buyers and merchandisers to sniff out emerging designers, place orders, make appointments to visit the showroom. It was a crowded, exciting experience.

There must have been 100 exhibitors spread out over four floors, so the buyers could get off the elevators and work the rooms. The staff was nice about moving some of the furniture around, but no matter how much uncut sport coat fabric you draped over the air conditioner and how much dress shirt fabric you used to disguise the horrible light-blue synthetic curtains, it was still a hotel room, and you still had to walk around the bed. And you still had the blazing red "Exit" sign opposite the door, which jangled my nerves even from a distance.

We had two adjoining rooms: one for the clothes and one for the out-of-town customers to hang out, take notes, and write their orders on the spot. When Mark told me the exhorbitant cost (something like $1,500 for the three days) I almost had a heart attack, but this was all in the line of duty.

We'd always been good at making rock soup, and we decorated the place with tables, sheepskins, and kilim rugs from my house. Buyers were coming and going, I was busy answering questions, describing the collection, being an ambassador, and in came Richard Bowes, a great merchant from Bergdorf Goodman—with Dawn Mello, the president of the store. Of all the gin joints in all the towns all over the world, she'd just walked into mine.

She stepped into the collection (and in her elegant beige suit, she really did fit right in) and went straight for the rugs. Those kilims—woven in ochres and burgundies, russets and terra-cottas—were the hook. As soon as she saw the connection between the rugs and the clothes, the interplay of serene colors and primitive patterns and ethnic textures, she understood the spirit of the collection.

She didn't just buy a couple of jackets or a few sweaters. Within the week she offered me my own boutique at Bergdorf Goodman.

*   *   *

There were some unique handcrafted pieces in the collection that we labeled "Wearable Art," and they were signed by the craftsmen who made them. In addition to the hand-framed sweaters developed in Scotland from the Nantucket stones were the sweaters being produced by the little old lady knitters I'd met in London during my days with Louis.

Mark and I would go to their dingy office, hand over our sketches, and Margaret and Peggy would quickly knit up samples using whatever yarns they had with them. There we were, hip New York designers, developing great product for the great stores, and watching them plunge into their shabby bag-lady satchels to sift through the jumble within. The method wasn't scientific, or even well organized. The satchels were full of we knew not what—a little crusty sandwich, a few tea bags, a lace hankie. But then, at last, out would come all these yarn color cards from venerable English spinners.

I'd say, "Peggy! Give me that!" and grab a card away from her. Every time she took out her knitting needles to show me a snowflake motif or something, her salt-and-pepper wig would shift off center.

After we'd gone through all the yarns, I'd ask, "Do you have any more in there?" and one of them would reluctantly pull out another. Never mind that it might have been a gorgeous yarn and I'd kill to use it. "It's itchy," she'd reply, "and the women complain because they get calluses from it, so why don't we just use a fluffy one instead?" I *loved* it.

Then and there, they'd pull out their knitting needles and some ball of yarn to produce a quick knit-down, which is a little sweater swatch, so we could get a rough idea of how the colors and patterns would work together. Later, the final knit-downs would be done with the color keys denoting the hundreds of combinations, because in every sweater of the same design, the cashmere—and the wool, and the silk—has to fall in the same place. A few weeks later we'd come back and spend more time working with them, saying, "The zigzag is too big," or "Take out this stitch," or "The way you've seamed the shoulder will affect the comfort and the fit of the sweater. Can we change *that* so that we can do *this*?"

Those hand-knits were like minestrone: There was a little silk and wool knob, there was an emu yarn, there was a cotton, there was a Rowan Donegal, and so on. They were true works of art, with all the irregularities and the bumps, and you could practically see the women's hands in them. But we couldn't depend on them for consistency, because the knitters lived in a vacuum. You can have the best *concept* in the world, but if the technical execution is off, you end up with a lousy fit—and an unworkable waistband. We veered between leaning on them and indulging them.

Sometimes the sizes were wrong. If a "medium" came in too small, we'd just change the size tag.

Sometimes the color combinations were wrong. "Peggy," I'd cry over the phone, "what happened?"

"Oh, dearie," she'd say. "It's dark here at four o'clock, and the women are getting on, and they don't see the colors properly." What do you think would have happened if I'd called Bergdorf Goodman and said, "Sorry. Mrs. So-and-so chose brown instead of burgundy because she couldn't see which was which in the dimming light"? But sometimes the botches were more beautiful than what we'd requested.

We had a limited production supply, and we knew that this ancient craft was fast becoming extinct because the younger generations had no desire to follow in their mothers' and grandmothers' needlesteps. Meanwhile, we were getting huge reorders for hundreds, thousands, and had to deliver.

"Peggy, where are the *sweaters*?"

"Oh, luv, there's a terrible blizzard here, and the truckers can't get to the houses." I had Saks and Louis choking me—"Where *are* they?"—and I'm explaining, "Well, they didn't shovel the path, so we can't pick them up."

It was great and tragic at the same time.

*   *   *

Right about then, I was also having meetings with Chanel about designing men's ties, scarves, belts, and pocket squares. A relationship with such an international powerhouse means real validation—especially so early in a career. It says something to the market. It tells the silk houses in Como, who tell Ralph Lauren, Armani, Valentino, Zegna, and every other big designer in the world, that Joe Abboud is on the map.

Comes the day of the final interview. I'm about to hop an early-morning flight from London to Paris, and I'm all spiffed up in an oatmeal-colored suit with a burgundy tie. The kid's really in the picture now.

I hail a cab for Heathrow, and about two-thirds of the way out on the M4, a gasket bursts. Oil splatters all over the windshield and hood of the cab. I'm still early, but I'm getting nervous, and the driver offers to flag down another cab.

He can't. It's turned into rush hour, and every cab is taken. Finally, a good Samaritan stops. My driver says, "This gent has a flight to catch, and I wonder if you might take him?" The guy says yes. So I get out of the broken-down cab and into an old pickup truck, trying not to smudge my suit.

When we get to the airport, I start running like hell because the gate is about to close.

"Ticket, please." I give up my ticket.

"Passport, please." I give my passport.

"Visa, please." I don't have a visa. No one told me I *needed* a visa.

"You need a visa. Or you can't go to Paris."

I tell them I'm en route to one of the most important meetings of my life and I ask how I can get a visa right away.

"You can't. It will take at least three days, maybe a week."

The woman at British Air tells me I can go to Immigration or Customs or whatever it is back in London . . . but that I'll never get it.

Great.

I ask about the next plane to Paris. She laughs. "Twelve o'clock. You won't make it."

"Just put me on it."

Now I'm sweating in my silk-and-linen suit. I call Paris, get Béatrice Bongibault, Chanel's *Directrice des Activités Mode*, and share my dilemma.

"You'll never get a visa," she advises. "*Impossible.*"

I run outside and get a taxi back to London and go to the visa place. There are lines around the block, like people waiting to see Madonna or the Beatles, and now it starts to rain. The suit is wilting. I'm panicking.

"I really have to get to Paris," I tell a guy on the line. "It's an emergency."

"Everybody here has to get somewhere," he says, unmoved. Same with the next five. Finally, after a lot of hustling and jostling, I get to the right counter and learn officially that the visa will take two days.

"Isn't there anything I can do?" I cry. "This is life or death!"

And why this happens I don't know, but people behind the counter get a supervisor, they listen to me, they call Béatrice in Paris, they understand how important this is, and *they give me a visa*. I look at the visa, I look at my watch, and it's now eleven o'clock. I call Paris.

"Béatrice, I'll be there."

"*Impossible,*" she says again.

I run downstairs, grab another taxi, race back to Heathrow, board the plane, and guess what. I make the two o'clock meeting. It's a great meeting, and worth all the sweat. I get the job.

While I was growing into a contender, Milton Freedberg was growing *noodgy*. Suddenly he had a gold mine on his hands, and he wanted it all.

In February 1987, he handed me a Federal Express envelope and told me to sign some papers, "just a formality" suggested by his lawyer. Inside were three copies of a legal document I was supposed to sign, and a memo and a letter I was *not supposed* to see. In his haste, Freedberg had forgotten to remove them.

The document, drafted in the form of a letter from me to Freedberg, included this: "I hereby give you my permission to apply for and obtain federal registration in the United States Patent and Trademark Office of Joseph Abboud for clothing and related goods and agree that you shall have an unlimited, free and irrevocable right to the name Joseph Abboud exclusive as to all others. I agree to federal registration and use as above stated throughout the world and further agree that I will not myself, directly or indirectly, use the name as a trademark or otherwise in the clothing field or give my permission to others to do so."

The memo detailed the lawyer's recommendations as to how to lock up the name—my name—and the cover letter said, "Please keep *this* letter and my memorandum absolutely confidential but send the three copies to Joe together with the corporate check for $10.00 explaining that trademark counsel requested the change and compliance with the technicality of paying consideration."

In other words, I was being offered $10 for my name.

The Joseph Abboud label means nothing, in my opinion, without Joseph Abboud. It's just another twelve letters. But Freedberg wanted it because he saw the potential. It wasn't that he didn't want to *use* me; it was that he was going to own my name and tie me up. By signing those three pages, I would have been signing away my birthright.

Freedberg was sitting behind his desk looking at me, and I was looking at the letter he didn't realize I had. I couldn't believe it. I'd been betrayed again, by a guy I'd trusted. I suddenly got this terrific, physical pain in the pit of my stomach, because I was afraid he'd snatch it back.

"What's wrong?" he asked, impatient now. "Why don't you just sign?"

"I can't," I said, and went out of the room to make photocopies. When I came back and handed him the originals, he turned ashen.

"I need to see a lawyer," I said. Freedberg said nothing. What was there to say? He was nervous, uncomfortable, a guy who'd been *caught*. He looked guilty, and I'd never seen him look guilty before.

I took those copies, unsigned, and walked out. But I didn't know which way to turn.

FOURTEEN

Getting the Business

AFTER FREEDBERG TRIED to usurp my name, I got smart and finally sought legal advice. Obviously, I needed a formal agreement. My first reaction was to cut my losses and run. But we had a thriving business going together. I really didn't need to leave; I just needed protection. While the cold war raged long-distance—Freedberg was in Boston, I was in New York—I remained dedicated to getting the collection ready. To me, the collection is an entity, a living thing, and I couldn't abandon it. So I kept going into the office every day, still getting my paycheck and still designing, while my lawyer worked to redefine the relationship—on paper, this time.

While the legal eagles pecked and scratched, the clothes were going great. When *Esquire* ran a piece on the world's ten top designers in its September 1987 issue, I was there along with Ralph, Armani, and Versace. "His designs are clearly inspired by the thirties," the magazine said, "with quality fabrics, baggy pleated trousers, three-button jackets, elegant sportswear, and fine detail work. Place him a bit to the left of Ralph Lauren."

The clouds were lifting. The Freedberg people were still on my case, but now other companies were knocking at the door. Hart, Schaffner & Marx, a well-respected clothing manufacturer that owned hundreds of retail stores, was interested, and so was Zegna, an old-world Italian fabric maker that was moving into apparel. It was thrilling to be approached by such prestigious houses.

Just as Ralph had rescued me from Grieco, another silver-haired angel landed on my shoulder: Guido Petruzzi, at Gruppo Finanziario Tessile (GFT), the power behind Armani, Ungaro, and Valentino. Eager to enter the international market, GFT was looking to acquire new American designers. Marco Rivetti, whose family owned GFT, and Petruzzi, who was the president of GFT USA, were convinced that we could have a big business.

I had no contract (and little contact) with Freedberg, so why not flirt with these guys?

Here's why not: When Freedberg heard about it, he turned around and sued *me,* claiming he had rights to my name, or trademark, which he did not—since I'd never signed his legal document. In a dizzying round of musical lawsuits, it then became *my* turn to claim Freedberg owed *me* money—royalties on sales of the products.

His side was asking, "Have you been negotiating with other companies?" and, "Were you planning to do another business while you were working with us?" and I was saying, "Yeah, and when do you want to talk about that letter?" Every time I did, they'd shut up and end the depositions for the day.

With tally sheets and balance sheets we went through all kinds of financial machinations to determine who owed what to whom. Ultimately, we worked out a settlement (which has to remain confidential), and we made them go away. I probably could have pursued it further, but I wanted to get on with my life. Now I had a *real* relationship with a *real* sponsor. Now I had the global presence of a giant.

Everyone knew that you didn't choose GFT; GFT chose you. And here were Rivetti and Petruzzi with an irresistible serenade: I'd do the designing; they'd put up the money and take care of business. We'd each own a percentage—60 percent for them, 40 percent for me—and I'd get a royalty based on sales. (They called it a royalty; I called it a monthly paycheck.) At last, a structured, formal deal.

It sounded perfect. As my strategic partner, they'd bring in great financial strength, great market expertise, and great manufacturing. They'd buy the fabrics, build the showrooms, and place my products in the international marketplace. They'd make some of the clothing for America and Europe at the factories in Italy and clothing only for America at the factory in New Bedford. Joseph Abboud would be the first designer label to come out of that factory.

On April 1, 1988, we signed the deal: JA Apparel was official, with Guido Petruzzi as CEO and me as executive vice president and designer. In addition to menswear, we planned to do a women's collection and a home furnishings collection, and open freestanding Joseph Abboud stores in America and Europe.

I'd started a small business with Freedberg, but I'd never before been a founding partner in a true corporate structure. I didn't know what the hell it meant, and I didn't know what I was doing. What did I know about joint ventures? I just figured we'd have these clothes made, sell them, and make a profit and split the money. All I knew was, I'm Joseph Abboud, the guy with his own company, and now I can spend all my time putting colors together, putting swatches together, doing shapes and silhouettes, and designing tie fabrics. A kid in a candy store.

And where was I starting out? Not in the garment district on Seventh Avenue, but in a sleek skyscraper on Fifth Avenue, where I am today. To go from the tacky Freedberg showroom to this was going from off-Broadway to Broadway. I was on top of the world, and I knew it.

I'd sit at a long metal folding table, all by myself in a front showroom. We hadn't yet started to decorate, and our half of the twenty-fourth floor was as long and bare as a bowling alley. But I had thousands of swatches in front of me, and I was putting together the first Joseph Abboud collection (for spring 1989) without interference from *anybody*.

We hired Bentley LaRosa Salasky to design the first corporate headquarters for Joseph Abboud. Decisions, decisions. Should we paint the walls dark beige or light beige? Should the tables be two feet high or three feet high? Where did I want the shelves? *My* choices, *my* decisions. I wanted a residential feel in the place, and the first things I bought were two beautifully framed sketches of horses that I found at an antiques shop in Pound Ridge.

I remember thinking, "Okay, I've got a space and a salary and a contract. Now, the hard stuff." Which meant structuring a team—a COO, an advertising agency, the works—with Guido as my guide. Unfettered by decrees like "It has to cost $78" or "We can do only three shearlings this year," I bought thousands of yards of fabric—and it was okay. I went to Scotland and bought silk and wool yarns, linen and chenille yarns—and it was okay.

That first season, we sold 2,100 suits and jackets, great numbers for a new company. So if we shipped a little late, if we had an occasional bump on the shoulder, even if we screwed up with an idea once in a while—an all-white collection called "Gymnasium," for example, was a stunning flop—well, in the beginning, when the buzz is still hot, the market is pretty indulgent.

The first ripple in these peaceful waters came when we launched the tie collection in Europe that year. Spain, Germany, Scandinavia, and Italy were buying, but France wasn't. Why not?

"The buyers love the ties," confided my Italian partners in neckwear. "But they don't like the name. Abboud. It's Middle Eastern."

What?

"Okay," I said, turning on my guy, whose fault it wasn't. "If I put my hand over the label, the ties are beautiful and you can sell them. But if I take my hand off, they're not as good. Right?"

He nodded, embarrassed.

"That's my name. If it won't sell ties in France," I told him, "I guess we won't sell ties in France."

And we didn't.

But why not? GFT had the clout and I was their boy—what was the deal? I didn't understand it then, but I think I do now. Maybe it wasn't just the French who felt hostile. Maybe it was GFT, too. The name was Abboud, not Abbodini. Lebanese, not Italian.

It was painful, but just a blip (or so I thought), and we proceeded with plans to launch the first women's collection in 1990 and to open the first Joseph Abboud store in Europe. GFT's strategy was to expand the label globally, and that meant establishing a presence in Italy, its home, where it was strongest. First stop: Rome, with stores to follow in Milan, Florence, Bologna, Paris, and London.

This was a quantum leap in my career. For an American, to open a store in Rome was to join the realm of the internationally acclaimed designers—the Valentinos and Armanis and Versaces. I was no longer the American stepson; now I was truly part of the family.

For such a golden opportunity, we chose a prime spot: the Palazzo dell'Armi Silvestri on the Piazza San Lorenzo in Lucina, just off the Via del Corso. Every building in the neighborhood looks like a museum, and so did ours. I remember walking through the first time and thinking, "This room will be for the custom tailoring, this room for tweed jackets, this room for ties." Since we wanted to create our own look for this significant venture, we hired the architectural team of Franco Mello and Loredana Dioniglio.

Franco and I studied the work of Pierre Chareau, a whimsical, innovative French designer and architect of the 1920s and 1930s, to create a spare, modern showplace. The soft-edged fixtures were made of an antique-blond wood, the walls were walnut, the furniture was cherry. The stone floor had a geometric design made with marble the color of amber. An open steamer trunk displayed shirts, sweaters, jackets, ties. All around were stone carvings, neoclassic statues, and—most beautiful of all—a tawny brown alabaster vase that Franco gave me to commemorate the event.

The opening was announced for February 22, 1991. The pieces were in place, the goods on the shelf. All we had to do was put some change in the cash register and open the door.

It didn't happen.

GFT postponed the opening until fall.

Then the fall opening didn't happen.

And that was that. GFT had decided not to open the store. Ever.

They never told me why—really. In their typically nonconfrontational manner, they claimed they were suffering from overexpansion, they'd acquired too many factories all over the world that they couldn't use, they had financial problems, and there were lease issues. Those were their explanations for aborting the store.

But they didn't offer the only one that made sense: resentment. No designer wants to see another designer make good. Nobody says, "I hope you make it, Joe, because you're part of the GFT family, too." You kiddin' me? They wait for you to crash and burn. It's human nature—especially in this business. We were new and getting attention, and some in the GFT fold were mightily aggrieved. If you're intuitive, you don't need to be told when the air has changed. The Rome store, the occasional *frisson*, a series of clicks and flashes, and I knew. But nobody said anything.

Then somebody did.

"Who is this . . . Joseph *Abboud*?" the great Valentino had asked Guido Petruzzi when my star was beginning to rise. "Why are you promoting *him*? You should have him design *my* collection instead." Valentino. When Guido told me this, my instincts were confirmed.

Valentino, being Valentino, had a lot of clout and pulled a lot of strings at GFT. I never designed his collection . . . and my store never opened. That's all I can tell you.

All that remains of that cataclysm is the beautiful alabaster vase. Every time I look at it I see the people and dreams and mannequins and fabrics and a moment in Rome when everything was possible. I've had angels on my shoulder, but this is a genie in a bottle.

FIFTEEN

Model Behavior

"GET ME THE TIGHTS! *Now!*"

"My mascara is *where?*"

"Owww! You're pulling my *earring!*"

It's Fashion Week in New York, fall of 1992. My first big women's wear show, first time out on the pussycatwalk. It's a big deal, a glamour thing, a who's-who thing, and a hell of a scary place to be.

There are so many women's shows vying for attention every season, and only so many time slots. Since the major-league fashion editors can't attend them all, they have to make choices. I've lucked out. In this particular slot, which happens to be the very first one of the week, they've chosen mine.

Fashion Week is not for the fashion weak. You're dealing with a tough crowd. The bony socialites, Goth-eyed party girls, and restless movie stars are there for the flashbulbs and fever. The buyers are there to see what you're all about and to make a very important decision: Is your collection going to replace somebody else's? Are you hot enough, new enough, creative enough to displace a more established designer? The Seventh Avenue spies are there for inspiration. And the fashion press is there because everybody else is.

I'm nervous. Very nervous. Is Anna Wintour coming? Did the *New York Times* get the right invitations? Where's *Women's Wear Daily*? Are people curious about the clothes, or will they think I'm just some fabricated designer being foisted on them? Are they thinking, "You may be a hotshot in menswear, Mr. Abboud, but that doesn't mean you can design for women. Menswear is menswear and women's wear is women's wear"? It's a different set of standards. A different ball game.

Am I good at this? Am I *really* good at this?

The women's wear press is tuned much sharper, strung much tighter than the menswear press. And these journalists are jaded. They've seen a million shows, and you'd better show them something that turns them on or they'll jump in with, "That was Armani two years ago" or "Valentino five years ago," or "This looks like Calvin Klein doing Helmut Lang."

They're good at that.

The press wants cutting-edge, experimental, avant-garde. They look beyond the clothes. They look at the *message*. They look at the model.

In the fashion industry, on the women's side at least, the model is more important than the clothes. In the fashion industry, the model *substantiates* the designer. So to put my first women's collection on the radar screen, I've bowed to my junior designers and bagged us a Big One: Naomi Campbell.

"She costs a fortune," my team tells me, "but she's worth it."

She isn't.

Backstage at a fashion show is a frenzied circus of breast implants and lip jobs, stuff flying and folks sweating. Have the clothes been altered?

Are the clothes pressed? Will the clothes be treated with respect? I'll never forget watching a magnificent one-of-a-kind $4,000 embroidered top get snagged on a model's earring and destroyed before my eyes.

Are the clothes even on the right girls? In this field, the models you see may not be the models you booked. Big names and big budgets are invariably able to have and to hold. If someone like Ralph or Calvin wants certain models for his show, and doesn't want them to appear in anybody else's show that day—and twice in tomorrow's *Women's Wear Daily*—he'll book them for a few hours longer than he actually needs them and lock the competition out. (This is more common in women's shows than men's, because the models with famous faces are usually integral to the designer's image. In men's, most of us couldn't care less.)

It's a sterile, humorless environment where nakedness is anything but sexy. When they get out on the runway, these stalky, marble mannequins will be poised and beautiful. But backstage they're wild. I know a lot of guys who wish they could wander back and see them getting undressed. I want to see them getting dressed. *Now.*

Out front, the press marches in and scans the turf. Air kisses are exchanged. In days past, the runway shows were populated not only by stars and star editors, but also by the society dames—Babe Paley, CZ Guest, Nancy Reagan, Betsy Bloomingdale—and their bachelor escorts, or "walkers." Society (or whatever "society" means these days) still matters, of course, because it gives the press something to write about. Celebrities matter even more—the Madonnas, Gwyneths, Demis, Beyoncés, and Britneys du jour—no matter how unsavvy or poorly dressed they may be.

Everyone takes a seat—and not just *any* seat. You want the heavy hitters in the front row, but you'd never put the top editors at *Vogue* next to *Harper's Bazaar, Women's Wear,* or the *Times,* any more than you'd put *GQ* next to *Esquire* or *DNR,* or Saks next to Bergdorf's, Bloomingdale's, or Nordstrom. If they *are* in the same row, you separate them with licensing people and lesser press and celebs; otherwise you place them across the catwalk from each other. The seating plan is as scrupulously coordinated as a surgical procedure, as artfully played as a chess game.

Backstage is twitchy. White knuckles, jittery vibes. Where's Naomi? We can't start the music, dim the lights, open the curtain. We can't do a thing until she arrives.

And it's show time.

No Naomi. We wait some more. Still no Naomi.

Panic sweeps through the dressing rooms. She was going to open the show and close the show. We can't go on without her, because she has four crucial outfits that have been sewn to her body and won't fit anyone else the same way. She's famous for her tantrums, but not, as far as I know, for jilting designers. This is a first. Lucky me.

If she had a problem, I would have fixed it. If she'd wanted more money, I would have paid her. But no one knows a thing. Including her agency, which is doing nothing to help us except offering to send over another girl. Great. We don't have time to do alterations here.

My career is flashing before my eyes. The audience has become a buzzing swarm. And still no Naomi.

I'm sweating, they're fidgeting, and the place is turning into a pressure cooker—in every sense. Woody Hochswender, fashion writer for the *New York Times*, rushes backstage. Do I want to take a shot at Naomi? "No," I tell him, mad as I am, tempted as I am, easy as it would be.

Forty minutes later, when it's clear that she isn't coming—no explanation, no apology, no call, no nothing (then or ever)—we grab a model from our group and squeeze her into the four crucial outfits that don't fit her exactly right.

Fifty minutes late, the show goes on.

But none of it matters. Not only has Naomi's defection screwed *me*, but—because Joseph Abboud is the first show of Fashion Week—I've managed to throw everyone else's schedule on its ear.

A wonderful way to begin.

*   *   *

High maintenance, maximum exposure, trillion-dollar contracts. Such is the state of female modelship. The women's movement has long pushed for equal pay. Not a problem in the fashion business: The men don't even come close.

Turn on TV or pick up a magazine and you'll find out everything you need to know about the female superstar of the hour. Heidi and Claudia, Elle and Gisele can trade on their celebrity for years beyond their modeling years, but how many male models can do the same? Poor guys. They leave the radar screen the minute their careers are over and become stockbrokers, doctors, or tree surgeons.

The women's wear industry has a greater attraction, a bigger audience, more zealots and devotees. Nobody depends on models for their literary views or their political savvy. The focus is on one thing: their looks. And they're kids! The waifs we send down the runway in $8,000 dresses are somewhere between eighteen and twenty-five. Let's remember that.

Glory is the lure, and the pressure is intense. Will they be used in a Ralph or Calvin show? Did they gain a calorie at Club Chicaroo last night? Did they talk pretty enough to the right agent or promoter or garmento? It all matters very, very much, and the narcissism is almost understandable. The industry has let them know how much more important they are than the clothes they're wearing.

In comparison, menswear is almost genteel. The highs and lows are less dramatic and the models reflect that. They do their job, they show up on time, they handle success better, and they don't pull Naomi Campbells on you.

Most male models, believe it or not, are straight. If they look effeminate, it's because too many of them are still going through puberty. A few years ago the fashion-show cognescenti grew tired of brawny all-American guys, so the industry went after a new crop of young boys who'd be grateful for the chance. What a mistake! We ended up going from hunks to waifs—about as far from the Joseph Abboud image as anyone could go. These were scrawny teenage boys, not even developed. They didn't look good in men's clothing, because they weren't men. We had to do so many alterations it was ridiculous.

There are still a lot of kids out there, gawky and goofy, tripping over their own feet like big puppy dogs. And it doesn't work for me. A guy can look great for a print ad, but put him on the runway where your clothes have to flow with the movement of the body, and you're dead.

Here's what I *want*: somebody who looks as if he belongs in the clothes. Not affected, spike-haired, sideburned, pouty-lipped, or pink-cheeked, but a masculine, good-looking guy—black, Asian, white, blond, brunet—who can carry a perfectly tailored suit. He's almost impossible to find. The obsession with youth is one of the reasons so many menswear shows look contrived. The models and the clothes don't mesh, and the models look uncomfortable. How could they not? When you put a $3,000 pinstripe on an eighteen-year-old kid, there has to be a disconnect. The ideal model is in his mid- to late thirties. The young guys aspire to *be* him, and the older guys think they still look like him.

Here's what I *get*: a guy who says he's six-foot-four, 224 pounds, and a 41 regular—and isn't. A lot of models are over-built and really geared to do bathing suits or underwear. You can *never* trust the sizes they list on their head sheets. "What size are you?" you ask. "Well, what size do you need?" they say. It's an enormous waste of time.

If we know exactly who we want, we'll just say, "Send Marcus or Troy." When we don't, the agency will send over a bunch of head shots for us to choose from. It's a small world, and most agencies know the designer brands and who's appropriate. If a guy's got nose rings and piercings and tattoos, he might be right for something downtown, but not for us.

The guy I put in a leather jacket is not the same guy I put in a three-piece suit. I want to know if he can deliver the message I'm sending. Can he walk? This is more difficult than it would seem. I've never been one to hire the "hot" model just because he's hot. He's got to work for the clothes. My greatest concern is not his looks but his ability to move in a sophisticated way.

Proper casting is an art, and not every agency is artistic. I remember some young guy showing up late for a show once, just before we went on. He had a scruffy beard, looked drugged, and refused to shave. He didn't understand that the show was about *me*, not *him*. I said to my producer, "If he doesn't want to do it our way, he's gone," and so he was gone.

I love good models. But they're only canvases.

A men's fashion show is divided into three parts. There's the opening, which is dramatic and sends some kind of message. (One season, in order to kill the cliché about my doing nothing but brown, we opened with edgy black leather jackets to the tune of "I'm a Slave to Love" from 9 1/2 *Weeks*.) The middle section, the biggest piece, contains most of the clothes—suits, jackets, sweaters, outerwear. And the finale is evening wear.

In styling the show in advance, I look at the clothes not the way you do in a store, but theatrically—how they'll play on the runway, one right after the other. The first group has to make a statement, hit the audience over the head. Then I have to change the message but keep the evolution going. If we do gray suits, for instance, I can't just show them with white shirts and striped ties; I have to make them *interesting*—maybe do a gray-on-gray thing, with gray shirts and gray woven ties.

A women's fashion show is a frightful experience, but a men's fashion show is an oxymoron. Guys are like cattle. They get mixed messages and don't know what to believe. If we put on a show with feathers and war paint and rattlesnakes, we'll get press from reporters who like the edge, but the consumer won't have a clue what we're doing. If we put on nothing but navy blazers and pinstripe suits, we're knocked for being old news. So we don't know what to believe either.

One year we showed luxurious robes made of suiting fabrics—wide chalk-striped gray flannels, velvet paisleys, plaids—worn over shirts and vests, as if the guy had come home, taken off his suit jacket, and thrown on the robe. I thought it was a nice cinematic reference, but instead of evoking Nick Charles in *The Thin Man* (as Ralph has done so well in his windows), I invoked the scorn of Constance C. R. White in the *New York Times*. "When a designer makes a bathrobe as a signature," she wrote, "one senses that there's trouble ahead." Uh-oh.

But the year we lived most dangerously was when we showed silk-tie evening vests with velvet sweatpants. It wasn't real, and it was really bad. We were trying to stay hot and make some noise; it hadn't yet dawned on us that that rarely works. I think there's something beautiful about the male shoulder and the male arm, and I loved the idea of silk vests on bare skin. So out went our guys to the tortured strains of Celine Dion's "The Power of Love." The vests were beautiful, and this was a time when more was more, but we didn't need to show all twelve of them. Even worse, the sweatpants were made of that lightweight liquid velvet, and you could see the outlines of the guys' family jewels because they weren't wearing underwear. Unbelievable.

We're minutes away from show time. Right now the men's suits are perfectly pressed, the shoulders look great, the shirts are on their hangers with not a wrinkle in them, the shoes are untied and ready to be stepped into. But in the heat of the battle—what with the alterations, the speed, the heat—they'll loose their energy. Clothes can take just so much. The dressers have done their thing, but half the time the ties aren't right, because they're working on three or four people at once, so I go around retying every tie. Then I *loosen* it so all the guy has to do is sort of slide it up.

There's something intimate about this, so you try and be cool. You don't want to breathe in the guy's face because you don't remember what you had for lunch, and you don't want him to breathe in yours. You just hope he's got good hygiene because you're up *close*. You don't want anybody to get the wrong idea. So you're fussing with the tie and rumbling, "Man, you look *good*," in a basso profundo.

The one thing I won't do is button their pants. That's one place I won't go.

Except when I have to. I'm focusing on the guys ready to roll, and out of the corner of my eye I'll see a guy who can't get his shoe on or his shirt buttoned. That's heart attack time. That's when I don't care what I touch, and how I touch it. That's when the poor guy gets yanked in seventeen directions. There are times, and there are *times*.

The lights go down, everybody's quiet, the music starts. The first twenty guys are dressed and ready to go. They're smoothing their hair, loosening up, and it's a good moment. After the lights come up, three or four of them will start their little parade and another four or five will join them.

I'm the last guy they see before they go out. I'm the fail-safe. "Relax," I tell them, because their instinct is to stand upright and throw their chests out, which is terrible for the clothes. "Be friendly and handsome and charming. And just walk casually." No matter how much altering the tailors have done, a coat can still be too short or too long. So I say, "Leave the jacket open and keep your hands in your trouser pockets" (which will keep his pants up), or, "*You*, you've got gloves on, so you can put your hands behind your back and just kind of stroll."

But even as I check every guy, I can't actually see him move until he's out on the runway. And then it's too late. When everything works the way it should, it's great. But that's only 75 percent of the time. The other 25 percent, I'm watching a guy with pants too long and his hands in the wrong place and I'm thinking, "Get this guy *off*."

When the lights come down again, we'll set up a new scene and open to a new color palette, with sportswear and tailored in olives, russets, golds, bronzes, and all those designer-designated colors—"birch" and "medium birch" and "light birch" and "dark birch." I might mix double-breasted suits with sportswear. If the black leather jackets at the beginning were urban and edgy, the suedes and leathers will be country and relaxed.

"Where's Todd? Where's Todd? He's next!" Eight models are lined up and ready to go. Todd, who's in the third spot, is nowhere to be seen, and the others can't go until *he* does. There's a lot of that.

The last part—fifteen outfits or so—is formal evening wear. It's always a sumptuous masculine statement, best made in black and white and gray. The most important thing is to have a powerful ending, because that's what the audience leaves with. And for emotional effect lights can work wonders, but music has even more impact on the audience. As Guy Trebay wrote in the *New York Times* after a recent Paris season, "Like scores for film or theater, the music at fashion shows sets a tone or conveys an atmosphere or supports a creative message or else helps the models rhythmically hit their marks. Not coincidentally, it also helps to keep the audience awake."

Before a show, we'll spend hours in the studio narrowing it down to six or eight tracks that will enhance the spirit of the collection. Sometimes it's tweedy and romantic stuff, sometimes it's mean, but that's almost secondary to the big finale—when you want something uplifting to goose the crowd. Is it big enough? Full enough? Will it jerk some emotion out of somebody? I don't usually like instrumentals (although *Carmina Burana* got a good reaction and good press one season) and prefer a song that really resonates—for the audience and for me.

The big rush is the twenty seconds before going out for my bow. There is nothing, absolutely nothing, like it.

The last few models come in from the runway. The lights go down and then come up again. Now's the moment for me to start fiddling with *my* hair. The music swells and rises to fever pitch.

Then it's my turn.

SIXTEEN

The Show on the Road

A FASHION SHOW COSTS at least $250,000 (and two or three months' work) for twenty minutes in the spotlight. Some shows can be done for less, but many are done for more—and with all the models, fitting times, sets, producers, lighting, and music, some are done for much, much more. One of Sean Combs's shows reportedly ran well over a million dollars.

Over the years, I've presented my men's and women's collections on runways and playing fields, in marbled halls and dusty villas, whatever suits the suits best. At one time we were mounting shows in Italy twice a year—at Uomo Pitti in Florence, and in Milan, the corporate home of GFT. But we played other towns, too.

Taking the show on the road is a logistical nightmare. In the New York showroom, the design team assembles our forty most "editorial" outfits and lays them out on the floor. We want to keep all the pieces together, because we'll never have time at the other end for re-creating and restyling. Once the outfits are organized, the PR assistants hang them on hangers (with the appropriate ties, belts, or scarves), put them in garment bags (with the shoes and socks on the bottom), and pack them in hanging cartons—listing every single item, down to the smallest pocket square.

As a precaution, we always carry extra clothes with us (at least another 20 percent backup), in case something gets ruined in pressing or lost in transit or simply doesn't work when we get there. We also take lots of belts, scarves, gloves, and hats which we don't yet know how we'll use, but we want to have all the raw materials we'll need.

We don't take the models, though, because that would be an enormous expense, so we can only hope that those we've lined up (or will see, interview, and hire) at the other end will fit into the clothes. To be honest, for women's shows I actually prefer out-of-town models. In New York, they're eighteen, nineteen, or twenty, and obsessed with themselves. In San Francisco or Denver, they're thirty-something and have husbands and kids and lives apart from the runway. They're trim and beautiful, but womanly. They have wisdom in their eyes and the kind of sensuality that comes from self-confidence. And the customers relate to them, too. There's something to be said for not always being able to troop the talent.

When the clothes arrive at our destination, they're invariably out of sorts—fallen off the hangers, in a heap at the bottom of the bag, wrinkled and weary. The more clearly marked the cartons are to Keep Upright, the more likely they are to be thrown on their sides, so the contents have to be pressed and steamed and revived.

Then we can think about putting the show on the stage.

After we'd established a terrific retail relationship with Japan, we were invited to do a men's and women's show by the ministry of culture's Association of Total Fashion. The government wanted to showcase an esteemed European designer and a brand-new American designer, and they chose Pierre Cardin and me. We'd each do two shows in a huge exposition hall in Osaka.

Cardin was one of my idols, but our clothes were worlds apart. His (mostly women's) were architectural and futuristic; mine (a coed collection) were much more earthy, natural, and contemporary. His were bright reds and brilliant yellows and jewel blues; mine were taupes and ivories. As we were setting up, I froze as he walked over to my racks and touched the clothes. "This," said the great Cardin, stroking my shearling, "is very beautiful." I thought I'd died and gone to heaven.

In America, you don't get to do serious dress rehearsals. You hire the models, race through the run-through, and hope for the best. In Japan, we *got* the best, every step of the way. The ministry had asked that at least half our models be Asian (the others would be Eurasian and Caucasian), and I loved the idea of seeing my clothes through the prism of a different culture. The producers asked thousands of questions—about the level of the music, the flow of the fabric—and the answer to each question produced a little explosion. There was exquisite attention to detail, to the way every single piece should be styled and worn; I'd demonstrate how to tie a tie or scarf, and it would then be sketched, in three or four steps. They put American producers to shame.

Our first rehearsal was a dry run to coordinate the action with the music—and I mean coordinate with a stopwatch. The second rehearsal incorporated the models walking around holding a piece of clothing on a hanger. The third was a full dress, using the actual sixty or eighty outfits. It was impeccable except for one mishap: an untied shoe. When we went backstage later, the young dresser was sobbing. I put my arm around her and told her it didn't matter, but she was almost too tense to be reassured.

The show was as well choreographed as a Fosse musical. The technology was state-of-the-art, and the sets—using stones and birch trees, scrims and wind machines—were strikingly sensual. The runway was so long you could have launched a 747 off it. I usually prefer a more intimate setting, but that long runway was heaven on earth. It gave us dimension and kept the models on view for a blessedly long time.

Once upon a time I'd been eighteen years old in Boston, getting beaten up in my first Pierre Cardin jacket—and now here was Cardin himself, an icon in a perfect double-breasted suit, congratulating *me* on a beautiful show.

It's stressful enough throwing out the first pitch at Fenway Park, but even that was nothing like throwing out the first ball at a polo tournament in the middle of a marsh in Perth. It was 1992 and I was in Scotland to show my collection in a charity event for the Special Olympics.

In Japan, the show had been held in an enormous space, and we had a big back room for wardrobe and makeup. In Scotland, we had a tent on a polo field, and the field was practically under water. The harder it rained, the muckier and muddier the terrain, which was already ripe with the droppings of pheasant and sheep.

But sometimes miracles happen. Just in time, the rain stopped, the clouds blew off, the sun came out. And the show went on. I'd tailored it for the setting—lots of shearlings and sweaters—and it was the right stuff in the right place. Afterward, when the bagpipes played "Amazing Grace," it really did seem that God was on our side.

Now it was time to start the polo match (Scotland versus Kenya), an honor I couldn't refuse. So what if I'd never played polo? So what if I hadn't been on a horse for twenty-five years? Was I going to say no? No.

So Mr. Designer dresses the part. I'm wearing a windowpane tweed jacket with bellows pockets, elbow patches, and a suede top collar, and all the creases are just right. The plaid tie is knotted impeccably and drapes perfectly toward the left. I have cavalry twill trousers, chukka boots, and a pocket square. No true equestrian would ever wear such an outfit, but it looks gallant to me.

The moment arrives, and some gent in a kilt says, "Bring auld Daisy over here"—this sweet gentle creature. But another gent, who's seeing some chichi poo-poo designer in his tweed jacket, says, "No, no. Put him on *Diablo*."

I'm high in the saddle, feeling like Errol Flynn, and Diablo decides he's having none of it. He paws the muddy ground, gives a snort, rears back, and takes off. I have a death grip on the reins but I can't control him, I'm yelling for help, and a couple of Scotsmen have to come rescue me and lead me back. Just like a little kid on a pony ride.

It pulled me up short. I felt exposed and ridiculous, like I'd been caught with spinach in my teeth. More than that, it was a pure illustration of the contrast between image and reality—sort of an object lesson in the ways of the fashion industry.

New York, New York. We were under a blue whale. A blue whale that weighed ten tons. It was 1992 at the Museum of Natural History, and our biggest show so far. We'd want music, but nothing loud enough to jostle the whale. We'd want applause, but not so wild it would loosen his moorings. We were in this room not because we wanted to be, but because it was the only room available. As far as venues go, you often have to take what you can get.

There was no nautical motif happening, just the tailored Joseph Abboud collection with its muted tartan evening jackets and beautiful paisley scarves. We did make some scenic changes, but they were on land. After bringing the lights down, we rolled in a set of terra-cotta rock slabs, and the models stepped onto the runway through a craggy mountain pass. That's where we launched J.O.E., a casual sportswear line that related to natural elements. There were stonewashed jeans in olives and khakis and browns, and sweaters of natural-dyed yarns. As for the name, J.O.E. is ostensibly an acronym for Just One Earth, since I love earth colors (and since we couldn't go with something like Joe's Own Equipment, although we thought about it). But mostly it's a decorated nickname because, aesthetically, I think the letters look better with periods. Sometimes these things are just that simple.

Meanwhile, the whale stayed put, and the show came off great.

Another memorable scene from New York: two brown-and-tan J.O.E. bandanas tied around the lions' necks in front of the New York

Public Library on Fifth Avenue. Within that magnificent white marble beaux arts edifice, we twined flowers and vines around the railings of the marble staircases and placed eighty mannequins wearing eighty outfits in the center of the grand foyer. It looked like a gallery, with one group in ivory and khaki, another in indigo and navy. Breathtaking, really.

I showed in Milan as a guy from out of town, a designer without a showroom, so the plan was to set up in a medieval stable with stone arches and niches and vaulted brick ceilings. Would it be dramatic enough for the international buyers? Unquestionably. Hazardous to the collection? Absolutely. Every surface, every brick, was veiled with a patina of dust. If a garment even touched the wall or floor, it came away smudged.

On a rainy afternoon in January, Milan is about as dark and dreary as a place can be. We'd been working all day—putting stuff on the shelves, setting up displays, arranging the flowers, moving the chairs— and we were still at it when the models started trickling in around three o'clock to be seen. By dusk there was such an avalanche of guys they were lined up out the door and hanging off the rafters. Every agency in town had responded to the call, and 300 contenders showed up.

We needed two.

But we didn't want to hurt their feelings, so we saw every one. The guys we liked we spent a couple of minutes with. The guys we didn't like got thirty seconds. The light was fading and we still had to keep doing what we were doing—picking shirt-and-tie combinations and putting the outfits together. So while I was tying ties and draping clothes, my fingers getting perforated from the million pins I was push- ing into the mannequins, I was looking at the guys' books and trying jackets on them.

"Hi, how do you do? Try this on. Turn around. How does it fit? Walk for me." It was endless. *Endless.* Theater of the absurd. And a waste of time, because most of them were dead wrong anyway. Here were all these Italian guys with tattoos and spiked hair, and we were looking for Douglas Fairbanks Jr.

We returned to Milan in 1991 with our show more together. We set up a series of twenty-four vignettes in the archways of another ancient building. The lighting and flowers were perfect; the music was great (Ennio Morricone's score from *The Mission*), and so was the reaction of the press, who found our hoary surroundings novel and refreshing.

We were showing leathers, suedes, knits, tweedy jackets, double-breasted models, and non-vented stuff. Buyers from the world's great stores were zeroing in on what we were doing and wanted to buy it.

But they couldn't.

The mid-level management at GFT had a preconceived notion of what would sell in Europe: basic dark business suits. For a corporation that had grown up in fashion, it was astonishingly stupid. The people at GFT were playing it safe, and they were wrong. When you launch a new collection, new means *new*, but everything the customers pointed to was out of reach.

They'd say, "I love that sweater."

"Well, you can't buy the sweater," GFT would tell them. "It's just for display. But how about that gray suit?" The retailers didn't *want* another gray suit. They wanted the unfamiliar. They wanted to buy the *excitement* in the collection.

I assumed the GFT guys knew what they were doing. They didn't. We sold a few things, but only a few, and the show was a disaster. Everything about it was wrong. If I'd thrown a designer hissy fit then and there, it would have been for the right reason.

I had one of my best road experiences with a bunch of guys who spend their life on the road: Wynton Marsalis & Company. Wynton sees his jazz the way I see my clothing. It's American, it's elegant, and it has a rich core. So during one Fashion Week when we had a great space in Chelsea, we invited him to play.

In the center of the room we set up tables with flowers and candles, like a club. Standing in bleachers on both sides were 100 mannequins in highly styled pastel clothes with double-breasted vests and shiny silk ties, all in the Joseph Abboud spirit, but pushed further.

"Do you want a specific performance time?" I asked Wynton.

"No," he said. "I'll just play through, and let people talk and have fun."

"You won't be offended that they're talking?"

"That's what jazz is all about. We play it, they talk through it, it's fine."

So while the crowd kissed air and rubbed elbows, five musicians were onstage in ivory linen dinner jackets with black trousers, six models in evening wear stood around the piano listening, and Wynton was center stage in all-ivory with his handsome face and gleaming trumpet.

He liked the look and asked me to design tuxedos for the Lincoln Center Jazz Orchestra on tour. *Okay!* I thought about the big bands of the 1930s and the "roaring twenties" style of *Cotton Club*, but I had my own take (a mix-and-match thing): elegant light-colored suits and double-breasted vests with a brazen style that was definitely not what you'd see on a Wall Street guy.

I designed the stuff for specific cities, events, and themes on the tour. Each musician got three three-piece tuxedos in ivory, colonial khaki, and black. There were so many possible combinations I had to write an agenda: "On Monday night in Chicago, wear the ivory dinner jacket and the khaki trouser. On Tuesday night, the black jacket and the white trouser. On Wednesday, the all-black suit," and so on. Talk about making beautiful music together.

In October 1994, I'm off to Australia on a tour with my men's collections. My sister Mara says, "Why don't you look up the family?" Family? What family? We know that our Lebanese great-grandparents had emigrated to Melbourne and lived graciously outside of the city, but that's all we know. "Latoof," Mara reminds me. "The name was Latoof."

First stop, Sydney. It's a great occasion, with fashion shows, personal appearances, Australian *Vogue*, all that stuff. When I take a break, I go look in the phone book. No Latoof.

We move on to Melbourne. Again, the phone book. Again, no Latoof. But when I mention this at a dinner party that night, one of the guests perks up.

"When I was a lad in Melbourne," says this proper Englishman in his late sixties, "there was a sign on the roadway that read LATOOF AND CALLIL. I think I know a member of that family. Adrian Callil. He owns a restaurant. Why don't we have lunch there tomorrow?"

The next day I meet Adrian, and he's a real piece of work. He's flamboyant, kind of mysterious, a wheeler-dealer, and his pocket square's too big (a warning sign, if ever there was one). When I tell him my grandmother's name was Theresa Latoof, none of it rings his bell, so that's that. But when I get back to my hotel, there's a message from a guy named Richard Fakhry. He's Adrian's cousin, and he might have some information about my family.

By 11:30, I'm on my way to a rendezvous with a stranger. It's pouring rain, everything's feeling kind of cloak-and-dagger, but when I meet this guy he looks *familiar*. As well he should.

It turns out his grandfather had a sister—Theresa Latoof Fakhry. And he pulls out a picture. It's the same picture that sat on my mom's bureau in Boston. The same picture, with the diagonal tear running through it, of her mother—my grandmother.

A lightning bolt shoots through my body. On this tempestuous night on the other side of the world, where I still can't believe I have a relative with an Australian accent, Richard and I fill in the blanks and solve the mystery that's baffled my family for ninety years.

"By the way," says my new second cousin, "you know what Theresa's father did for a living, don't you?"

No.

"Your great-grandfather owned the largest men's tailored-clothing company in Australia."

SEVENTEEN

Us Versus Them

THE FASHION INDUSTRY is no longer confined to a clump of office buildings on Seventh Avenue. Designers and garmentos are no longer faceless toilers behind the scenes, and models are no longer anonymous clothes hangers. Fashion has become a frenetic culture whose players dance through the spotlight and wend their way into gossip columns the way Joan Crawford, Lana Turner, Tony Curtis, and Clark Gable used to. Think about it. Does anyone recognize the movers and shakers in the world of breakfast cereals? Does anyone care about the sex lives of America's office-furniture manufacturers? It seems that everyone cares about ours.

We've become celebrities—especially to ourselves. (Why else would Tom Ford, upon leaving Gucci as creative director, sign with CAA and assume Hollywood was waiting for him?)

About 240 of us belong to the Council of Fashion Designers of

America, or CFDA. It's not a club where we sit around and smoke pipes and fall asleep by the fireplace, but a not-for-profit association that supports fashion designers. For young new members (who are accepted on the basis of their creative achievements, not their commercial success), joining allows them to mingle with established designers, get advice, learn. We also help them obtain pro bono legal services and health benefits. For all members, the CFDA provides solidarity, making the American design community a force to be reckoned with.

The sense of self-importance in this industry can be unhealthy, so when the lords and ladies come together for a meaningful cause, it's wonderful. Our fairs, presentations, and philanthropic events have raised a lot of money and awareness for AIDS and breast cancer, and two weeks after September 11, 2001, we held a press conference to publicize a T-shirt that was being sold to benefit the New York City police and fire departments—a good cause, with everyone really caring. But even then the pecking order was in play.

There we were, over 100 of us, with the big names—Ralph, Tommy, Donna, Diane, Calvin, Oscar—in the first row. I wasn't in the first row. Would I have liked to be? Of course, but I was in the third. Was it the wrong time to be upset? Yes, but there you are. I like being perceived as a regular guy, but I'm a regular guy with an ego.

First row or fifteenth, we all like our pedestals. And our press. And our accolades. Just like other celebrities. Consequently, the CFDA Fashion Awards—the most prestigious awards in the industry—are our Oscars.

The awards ceremonies are held every year on such prestigious turf as Avery Fisher Hall at Lincoln Center, the Lexington Avenue Armory, and the New York Public Library, and they attract a boldface crowd of movie stars holding hands with the designers whose clothes they're wearing, fashion editors and design-school students, window dressers and wannabes sashaying, stroking, posing, and posturing. They can be interminable (one year somebody quipped that the *Titanic* went down faster), and there are annual debates about duration. In 1999, the dinner went on for seven hours, and it was well past midnight when John Fairchild finally got to present the Lifetime Achievement Award to Yves Saint Laurent, who was frail anyway. We were delighted he was able to receive it before his lifetime ended.

By 2002, the invitation list was so swollen with those from the outside—the TV people, the society people, the movie stars—that it became a publicity stunt. We'd become so enamored of the Oscars, Emmys, and Grammys and television coverage that we'd "lost the mission of the event," as the executive director, Peter Arnold, put it, and forgotten who the awards were really for. So in 2003, he and Stan Herman, the president, cut the list down significantly and brought the event back to us in the industry, so we could honor our own.

One of our own was Oleg Cassini, up for a special tribute that year. Dressed in a beautiful black tuxedo, black shirt, and black tie, with that incredible silver hair, he represented the true international playboy . . . the true ninety-year-old international playboy. Practically springing to the podium, he regaled us all with romantic memories of Gene Tierney and Grace Kelly. That was the highlight of the evening for me. As if he didn't already have a place in my heart.

The first designer shirt I ever owned was by Oleg Cassini—a mustard-colored dress shirt with a semi-spread collar from Milton's in Quincy. When my sister Jeanette gave it to me for my fifteenth birthday, I thought it was the most gorgeous thing I'd ever seen. For weeks I kept it in its plastic wrapping and black box. I wanted to keep it pristine and look at it for a while before taking it out and touching it.

Whenever I got something new, I'd do that. Wait a month, two months, visiting it, cherishing it, keeping the Shetland from Filene's in its tissue paper so I could savor the smell of new wool. I wasn't just putting off the pleasure; I was paying homage. And I still do it—even with my own stuff. I've had a couple of suits for over a year now that I haven't yet worn. I'm waiting for the right occasion. I don't know what that occasion will be, but I'm waiting for it.

So Cassini. A few weeks later, I met him at a CFDA party and told him about the shirt. He smiled charmingly and appraised me in my flannel double-breasted suit. "You are a very elegant man," he said in his suave continental accent. "You're dressed properly for the 1920s or the 1930s, for tonight, and for the future." I know compliments shouldn't mean anything, but when they come from your heroes, they do.

When I won my first CFDA award for Best Menswear Designer of the Year in 1989, I asked Bryant Gumbel to present it to me because we were pals.

"In a public domain that too often confuses being creative with simply being different, Joseph's look is traditional without being sedate, stylish without being faddish," he said in his introduction. "By the time I met him almost four years ago, Joseph was just getting started under his own label. He was anxious to get on with his designs, and I was undeterred by his refusal to make something akin to a stylish thirty-six short portly. Soon thereafter I lost weight, he struck a marketing chord, and together we got through the Seoul Olympics. What was a business relationship has now gone way beyond that. I am delighted that friendship is timeless, always in style."

When I won again the next year, I called Ralph. I didn't want to put him on the spot, I said, and if he wasn't comfortable with it I'd understand, but I was asking him to present the award because he meant so much to me. He didn't say yes or no. He just told me that he'd been having some issues with the CFDA . . . and this and that . . . and I knew I'd thrown a dilemma at him. So I said, "Ralph, I want you to stop right now, because I'm going to withdraw my request." I think we were both relieved.

I didn't know many celebrities then, and I didn't think it was fair to ask Bryant again, so who was I going to call? Everybody had ideas, but nothing lit my fuse until Bob Franceschini, my PR guy, suggested Kim Cattrall, who'd just come and gone in *The Bonfire of the Vanities*. We'd never met, but she was interested—I have no idea why. Maybe it was because actors just like being part of the fashion community.

She came across as sort of a sophisticated girl next door, very vivacious, very funny—and there's nothing more attractive in a woman than a great sense of humor. We agreed that she'd do it and made an appointment for her to come to our sample room to be measured for a dress.

A few nights later, the phone rang.

"I'm taking a bath," she said. "With candles. And I'm going to write something for the awards. Do you mind?"

"Kim, you're so kind to do this," I said, with superb detachment. "Do whatever you want."

On the night of the awards, she came out looking lovely and sexy in a short black V-necked dress from my women's collection. She started to speak, and my collar started feeling too tight.

"I first discovered Joseph's designs on a lovely spring day, shopping at Neiman Marcus, and there it was on the rack—unmistakably his. It was at this point that I went to my closet and I pushed aside my Gaultiers, my Armanis, my Chanels, and all those other European designers to make room for one of *ours*: Joseph Abboud. . . .

"Gosh, I feel hot in his creations! They enhance what is uniquely mine, and what more could you ask for but self-expression in your choice of fashion. Joseph Abboud is a designer who understands his consumer as well as his art, and tonight you are honoring him again for the second time as Menswear Designer of the Year.

"As a friend of Joseph's, I know how much more there is to him than just his brilliant designs. There is a certain timeliness to everything he does, everyone he touches. There will always be a place in my wardrobe for Joseph Abboud . . . and in my heart."

She was oozing, playing the sex kitten, seeing how far she could push it. Years later, she'd shimmy through *Sex and the City* and share her expertise in a book called *Satisfaction: The Art of the Female Orgasm*. But back in 1990, her innuendos came out of left field. The audience was scandalized, with lots of "oohs" and "whoos." Lynn appeared cool (she's never let that kind of stuff bother her, and having given birth to Lila the month before, she was especially serene), but I was still worried about what she was really thinking. Bryant, who was sitting with us, let me know he considered it a tad over the edge. His wife, June, looked absolutely mortified. I was squirming. But what could I do? And how was I going to *follow* it?

In the image game, you hope to present grace under pressure. I know I did, even if I didn't have a clue how. To add to the awkwardness of the situation, I'd broken my left hand playing squash (not good, since I'm left-handed) and was in a cast. To get me into my tux, we'd had to cut the sleeve and throw a black-and-ivory silk foulard scarf around my neck as a sling. Feeling clumsy and embarrassed, but tremendously honored, I left my seat and went onstage.

"Thank you very much," I said to the inquiring minds before me. "This is very tough to follow, but I want to thank Kim for flying in from L.A. to present me with this award. It really means a lot to me."

But the award itself meant a hell of a lot more.

In Hollywood, you see actors frolicking together at discos and dinner parties, but there is no love lost among designers. You see it when they make eye contact and decide whether they're going to give you a kiss or pretend not to see you. I love Ralph, but I'm not Ralph's best friend. I'm extremely fond of Norma Kamali, who's talented and freewheeling and spiritual. We once did a charity fashion show together at Our Lady of Lebanon church in Brooklyn (Norma's also Lebanese), and recently sat on opposite sides of Fenway Park tracking each other by cell phone (she shares my love of baseball, even if she's a Yankee fan). But I'd never call us intimates.

Designers are great white sharks, and we roam the waters ourselves. We may bump into each other once in a while, but we don't swim in the same circles. We often pretend to like and admire each other, but sometimes we don't even bother to fake it. The fashion industry is as hardworking, incestuous, and political as any other, and it's virtually impossible, given the size of designers' egos, to sincerely wish someone else well, because behind every false tribute is "It should have been me."

EIGHTEEN

Down to Earth

I WORK IN AN ephemeral business, but I like my feet on the ground.

I mean that I like to be the guy in the perfect suit while everyone else is wearing a 1980s broad-shouldered, low-gorge Hugo Boss suit in some Eurotrash off-green fabric. I mean it literally, too: I love maneuvering boulders and building stone walls. When I buy 200 tulips, I'm out there all night until they're planted. When I see a tree branch out of place in the backyard, I'll climb up and remove it. When I get a statue or a vase or a chair, I'll move it around and study it from every angle until it's exactly right. I may sound obsessive, but I don't think I'm crazy for wanting my surroundings to feel right.

Home is where my heart is, and I'm not the only one. September 11 brought a lot of people home, people who'd been running off to Gstaad whenever they weren't working. And they started seeing what they had.

158

There's been a sea change. Home style is in the air, it's on the air, and it's for everybody. People are picking up ideas from *House Beautiful* and *Elle Décor*, from Crate & Barrel and Pottery Barn, from designer collections like my Environments—and they're probably spending more on furnishing and decorating their homes than on dressing themselves. Home is the next fashion frontier.

It's also a wonderful place to experiment and break the rules. Some people don't trust their own instincts, so they hire decorators or watch TV makeovers and dream of fairy godmothers wielding magic paintbrushes. But home is a personal place; it should reflect us, our taste, and the things we love. Like fashion, it's a means of self-expression.

I know mine is for me.

I've designed my ideal environment (with Lynn's blessing). Inside and out, the French country house we built in 1993 is an homage to nature. The walls are fieldstone, the floors are slate and pine and limestone, there are beams of South American hardwood and cabinets of ash. Upstairs and down are fireplaces, carvings, columns, and gates. I really love gates.

And earth colors. My career is based on them. I hate a primary, lipsticky, synthetic red, but I love the orange-red of Japanese maples in fall. My blues and greens are natural blues and greens—not acid, electric, or citric. If I use purple, it's mixed with tan. If I do pink, it's smoky and veiled.

I'm probably most connected to brown, a blessing and a curse. Brown, of course, is never just brown. It's a million different shades, from café au lait to mud. At the moment, it's *au courant*. It's shaken off its stigma and caught on everywhere, from UPS delivery trucks to the lacquered walls of chichi interiors. But people have associated me with it for years. Once, some guy at a Neiman Marcus trunk show told me, "I'd really love to buy your clothes, but I don't wear brown." (At that time we were selling over 100,000 suits a year, 80,000 of which were navy and gray. But what the hell.) And then there was the period when

Calvin Klein was calling me "the clown of brown"—until the industry decided that "brown is the new black," and he joined the crowd.

But the truth is, the beauty of brown is timeless. I remember being in Coco Chanel's apartment in Paris on the rue Cambon. When people think of Chanel, they think of black and white, but this was all brown and beige and suede couches and a lot of wheat and straw—the warmest colors you could imagine. She knew.

Black is always interesting, always complex, though, especially when woven. Some see it as an absence of color, but I see it as a *saturation* of color. There are smoky blacks, jet blacks, a million different blacks, and you can create a color chip and a lab dip for any one you want. But with dyeing, there's no guarantee you'll get the fabric to match the chip. When you dye different garments the same black—a gabardine pant to go with your nice linen blazer—you'll never be able to coordinate them perfectly, because different fabrics absorb the dye differently. With weaving, however, you can take seven, eight, or ten different-colored yarns and create a shadow-and-light effect that really works, like in a great painting. Move the fabric one way or the other and you can see *into* it. That's a great black.

I like textured black: a black-on-black cable-knit sweater, a black chenille sport coat, a black quilted-suede jacket. The guy who walks into a formal event wearing black tweed or cashmere when every other guy's got a rented tuxedo is the one to watch. He's stepped out just enough, but not too far.

For a very long time, we went through this black period for both men and women. Everything was cooler-than-thou. Everything was "I'm so chic. I'm so Prada. I'm so Gucci." It became a uniform—and a paradox. Everybody was so busy being original and cool, that everybody looked alike. Now individuality is in vogue. But black will come back. It always does.

Whatever color is in, whatever color is out, in menswear there is one abiding truth: Men will buy anything blue. It's safe. It's neutral. It's easy. It's authoritative. It's almost *contagious*, like a cold that never quite goes away. If a man has a blue suit and a navy blazer, he's going to be properly dressed just about anywhere.

Blue is the most popular color in the western world, and the most popular color in clothing. Every guy who envisions himself a success in business has a blue pinstripe suit— power!—and the navy blazer remains one of the most important items in a guy's wardrobe, whether he's eighteen or seventy-eight. (As long as he leaves the brass buttons at Harvard Square. They're not classic, they're pretentious and anachronistic—like fedoras at a baseball game. A blazer should have matching buttons or, for something a little different, an oxidized darker button.)

The smart dresser, the guy who really understands blue, will take a beautiful navy cashmere blazer and wear it with a pair of pure, classic blue jeans. It takes a lot of confidence, because men don't think outside the box. They don't know how to *use* their clothes. But that guy? He's very, very cool.

Historically, light blue used to be worn only by peasants because the cheaper dyes used by the lower classes faded fast. Now light-blue denim is synonymous with America, I don't care where in the world it's made and worn. It represents the hardworking ethic—the workman, the cowboy, the rugged individual—and freedom, not to mention the freedom and comfort it acquires after being washed a thousand times. There's also a *cleanliness* associated with it (despite the derivation of the original American name "dungarees") and an outdoorsy romanticism.

When designer jeans first showed up in the late 1970s—from Gloria Vanderbilt and a bunch of other people in the same zone—they were stretch, pressed, glitzy, and grotesque. Then in the 1980s, Calvin entered the picture with the Brooke Shields campaign, "Nothing comes between me and my Calvins." Of all his "creative" achievements, that campaign was one of the most brilliant. Do I think the jeans were particularly great? No. But it doesn't matter. The ads sold them. The jeans could have been *anything*.

What's the difference between one jean and another? Between a designer jean and an army-navy-store jean? Let's talk real. A designer name can warrant a higher price, because you're buying status. It takes a confident person to know he doesn't have to pay over $100 for a designer's name on his butt. But a lot of people need it, you know?

To me, that's not what jeans are about. I design them, but it's not about "designer jeans." They're a piece in my collection because I love them. So I'm not going to renovate them in strange ways—unless you consider other colors strange. I'm a big proponent of ivory denim, black denim, olive or brown or gray denim—with the same comfort and ease of blue. It's not as if I made it up: Levi Strauss made his first jeans out of natural canvas in off-white and different browns.

We've moved beyond the traditional five-pocket jean. Today there are all kinds of acid washes and enzyme washes, colors and finishes, shapes and opportunities. Denim today is a whole new world, a completely different animal from the period of Gloria and Calvin. But when all is said and done, the lasting pieces are the originals. When I want to buy a pair that aren't my own, I'll go to Gap or Levi. I just want a 501, the real thing. I don't think you're ever too old to wear them.

Every season a designer has to come up with about five hundred names for one color, because there has to be some easy association for the press and the press releases. What the regular guy might find fey and confusing is actually necessary where commerce is concerned, even if he doesn't know what we're talking about. We're not going to do any nail-polish names, like lilac and periwinkle and cherry blossom, so at least he can attempt to relate. What we all want is rough, tough, hands in the dirt, anything that proves fashion isn't feminine. So we sit around the design studio and start out seriously, playing word games and dredging up adjectives. But after a while—once we're into "Is that 'Tabasco'?" and "Would you call that 'vermicelli'?"—even *we* get hysterical. And thirsty.

A light maroon, or mauve, becomes "antico," like a vintage wine. In the browns we'll go for "bourbon," "whiskey," "tobacco," "rye." Or "earth," "clay," "peat," "bark." As the collection expands, so does the spectrum. So now we add "light bark" and "dark bark." But by the time we have "light bark," "bark," and "dark bark," even we can't remember what anything is. Or in the gray family, there's "thunder gray," "iron gray," "lightning gray." Now what the hell color is "lightning gray"? But when the buyer's in the showroom saying, "I think I'll take 'thunder' and I'll take 'lightning' and I'll take 'coal,' " it's hilarious seeing these meaningless words make their way onto an order form.

A designer never says "green" or "blue" when he can say "spruce" or "cobalt." Sometimes this works, but sometimes you lose people. When we did a Scottish collection years ago and described some item as "gorse," nobody knew what it was.

But I did.

In the early 1990s, the British government invited Michael Kors, Marc Jacobs, me, and a bunch of other designers from all over the world to visit the fabric mills of Scotland. I'd say that Scotland is the most beautiful place I know. It has a strength and a melancholy beauty that are almost mystical. And the mills are a constant source of surprise. When I look through their big leather sample books full of wonderful tweedy swatches, I'm always amazed by the bright colors, interesting patterns, and unique, not-so-safe stuff.

Every day we were going to different places, and every night we'd reconvene in the manor house where we were staying. A lot of the designers were comedians, but Michael was the funniest—and incontestably the best mimic (he does a brilliant Donna Karan). He'd do great at stand-up if he weren't doing so well at fashion.

One of the field trips involved a helicopter ride. I'm almost allergic to planes (as Mel Brooks once said, "If God wanted us to fly, he would have given us tickets"), but this time I decided to go for it. It was one of those bubble-front jobs, and I was in the front seat next to the pilot; I think Michael was behind me. We lifted off, and the pilot said, "There are two things we must always watch for: Tornados and telephone lines."

"I didn't know you got tornados here," I mumbled.

"No, no, no," he chuckled. "Not the tornados you have in the States. The Royal Air Force Tornados." He meant the fighter planes that fly about 100 feet off the ground at, say, Mach 1. "They're a very great danger indeed."

But the menace faded fast, because suddenly I was having an experience right out of *Gulliver's Travels*. As we floated over the hill roads, village after village appeared before us—church steeples, cottages, patchwork farms, sheep . . . Scotland *coming at us*. And then I saw these fields of yellow. I'm not talking about a patch of yellow, or a lonely crowd of daffodils. I'm talking about acres and acres blanketed in blossoms of a bright, yolky yellow.

Gorse.

The designer gives well-considered names to his colors and spends unfathomable time on the undertaking because: (1) He needs to romance the buyer who will then romance the customer. (2) He needs, when he appears on the *Today* show, to sound lyrical. (3) He and his PR team need to produce a "run of show" that will go on every chair at his fashion show so the insiders girdling his runway will know what to call the stuff they've come to see. A few selections culled from Fashion Weeks over the years:

FALL OUTFIT 15:
  Maple cable rib funnel neck sweater
  Honey reversible shearling vest
  Tobacco covert pile knit sweatpant

SPRING OUTFIT 12:
  Rum mélange linen/wool/silk twill peak lapel jacket
  Chili ombre plaid linen camp shirt
  Iridescent palm wool/linen trouser
  Henna suede cross sandal

SPRING OUTFIT 18:

Hay linen three-button suit
Straw cotton/linen shirt
Celery chevron silk tie
Olive suede woven sandal

The fashionistas are crossing their legs, leaning forward, checking their lists, whispering, "Is that the barley or the wheat? The chrome or the aluminum?" and *I* can't help them.

And none of it matters anyway. The customer walks into the store, looks around, and says, "I'd like that blue shirt and those brown pants."

NINETEEN

All Those Ties

I'M PUTTING THE neckwear collections together, so I'm booked at
the Barchetta Excelsior on the town square in Como, Italy. This is
where all the tie people hang out, and we're all here to see the same re-
sources. Is Ralph Lauren here? Is Jerry Lauren here? Is Giorgio
Armani here? Everybody's sniffing around, wanting to know who's
doing what with whom so they can go after them, too.

Aldo, the manager, is known for wearing nice ties. So when I come
down one morning, being the charming guy I am, I say, "Hey, Aldo,
that's a beautiful tie," because it's my tie.

"*Grazie, signor*," he says. "It is one of my favorite ties." And I'm
feeling great.

He turns it over, and what do I see? A Hugo Boss label! Well, I go
berserk. I go *crazy*. I cancel my appointments for the morning. I call Augusto Micheli and Luigi Terconi, who work with me on my designs and

colorations, and yell, "This guy's wearing my tie with a Hugo Boss label!" There follows a big uproar. And how could it not? The tie world is a very incestuous place, where not only does every tie maker know every other tie maker, but they all have access to everyone else's strike-offs (the silk swatches from which the ties are made) because they're all using the same printing houses. People shouldn't have access to them, but they're there, and they do. It's like looking through your father's top drawer. You're not supposed to, but you do.

It seems that since my tie maker and the Hugo Boss tie maker are sister companies, they've decided to keep my strike-offs in the family—thanks to a little guy I'll call Benito, who helps develop neckwear for Hugo Boss. I learn that Benito has been going through the stuff after hours and stealing my fabrics and designs for Hugo Boss. But I can't fire him or kill him, because he's not working for me. And I don't sue him because it would be complicated legally *and* personally. Not only would I have to do it in Italy (a nightmare in itself), but we have a lot of friends in common. And, in fact, I like the guy.

So I can't get no satisfaction there, but I get some later. I'm looking through a men's fashion magazine, and there's an Italian tie manufacturer (not Hugo Boss, but a name I'm not allowed to name) advertising six ties—six *Joseph Abboud ties*. That's when I finally go to my lawyer.

"You can't copyright tie designs," he tells me.

"I'm going after them anyway."

"You don't have the rights to a paisley. You don't own a stripe," the manufacturer's lawyer tells me.

"You're absolutely right," I say. "But that's not just *any* paisley. That's a paisley I designed."

"What makes it *yours?*"

"Let me show you the artwork where I position the motif and how I color it." I'm remembering the long nights sitting at a high table in the Como showrooms with hundreds of little color tabs, keying the color positions, putting the burgundy next to the navy next to the cream next to the gold, and anticipating the printing process well enough to know that I have to put a gold in a certain position and one color on top of another color without touching a third color. I can't tell you about the brain cells I must have killed, coloring those ties until eleven-thirty or twelve at night, combination after combination.

What surprises me is that they haven't even had the decency to change the color key! They've used the exact colors I have in my sketches.

We sue, they settle, and all of Como reacts. The tie makers and their spies have been put on notice.

But piracy—or the suspicion of it—comes with the territory.

Around the same time as my contretemps with the ties, Yves Saint Laurent sued Ralph Lauren for copying his black sleeveless tuxedo gown. I thought the lawsuit was mean-spirited and unnecessary (not to mention rigged: It was heard in Paris, where Saint Laurent fever ran high and copyright laws support claims that our copyright laws do not). In fact, the two dresses were not the same—they were made of different fabric; Saint Laurent's had pockets, gold buttons, and wide lapels where Ralph's did not—but that didn't matter. To no one's surprise, the lady judge (who happened to own two boutiques outside Paris) decided in favor of Saint Laurent.

It was an uneven playing field, and Ralph should never have lost. Here's why: Nobody owns the rights to fashion elements that float from year to year, decade to decade, century to century. The arsenal—basic paisleys, traditional tartans, tuxedos, regimental stripes, etc.—is available to all designers. If it weren't, the whole industry would start suing itself. The tuxedo represents a number of things—black wool or barathea, satin lapel, single-breasted, double-breasted—and they're basic common denominators. None of us is the sole proprietor of any one of them.

*   *   *

For years, tie designers using stripes and paisleys and other prints had kept to an antiseptic color formula known as cool color-warm color (a blue, a yellow, a green, a red, and so on), so when they touched, you'd see the contrast. It didn't matter where these colors fell in the pattern, or how many there were—could be four, could be six; it just required using as many cool colors as warm colors, for balance. Such rigidity made for a lot of nebulous ties: not really good, but too timid to be really bad.

I had other ideas. And with the guidance of Augusto Micheli, I made them happen. As managing director of Miozza, a company that specialized in printed-silk neckwear, Augusto was a legend (and a legendary eccentric) in the tie world. He'd worked with Ralph and Jerry Lauren, which is how I'd met him, and with Valentino and Chanel, among others. When I started designing ties, he took my hand and led me through Como's doors (through the gates, really; it's a walled city), brought me in, and introduced me to the players. Paying me one of the greatest compliments of my life, he said, "I think you have read Latin, because the only way to change something is to first understand its foundation." He meant that I understood the paisleys, the printing technique, the color process—the essence and structure of neckwear—so I was able to push it forward and give it my own interpretation.

Nothing prints like silk. The heavier the silk, the better the print. The more colors within the print, the more expensive it is to produce. Every season I was giving Augusto forty different print designs with five or six colors each, and that's a lot of print designs. But Miozza's technique, called application printing, was very traditional. There was just so much we could do with those forty designs, and I needed to expand the range. I wanted to try other processes as well, and I wanted wovens. Every silk manufacturer has its own distinctive look; to trained eyes, it's a recognizable "handwriting." My ties and I were ready for another "handwriting."

Augusto understood my desire for variety, but he was fiercely possessive and kept me on a chain. He was afraid the other tie people would approach me and take away his business. The value to him wasn't just in the size of the account, which was substantial (it might be hundreds of yards of fabrics that would become thousands of ties); it was also in the prestige of the customer. We were hot. So I had to have breakfast, lunch, and dinner with him. One of our favorite spots was Harry's Bar in Cernobio, in the foothills of Como, where we'd sit on the little piazza overlooking Lake Como, savoring figs and ham and pasta. But all the important tie people were regulars there, so we were hardly invisible.

I loved Augusto and was very cautious about going to other people. But Luigi Terconi, one of the other famous tie guys in Como, had something Augusto didn't have: the allover paisley. I coveted it. The allover paisley doesn't have a ground color. The shapes flow into each other, like a stir of molten metals. The printing process is very complicated, and if everything isn't just so, the paisleys can look garish. But when Luigi's company, Interseta, did the job, the paisleys were masterpieces.

Luigi had come courting, and I secretly wanted to date him. The union would benefit us both. I'd get to add a new "handwriting" to the repertoire. He'd get to tell his customers around the world that his ties were being sold at Bergdorf's, Saks, and Neiman Marcus. So I had to tell Augusto. It was tough, like telling my steady girlfriend I wanted to see other women. He was crestfallen, but supportive. He knew I had to play the field.

So I went with both of them, and that was good for us all. I experimented with colors, patterns, and combinations not traditionally found in neckwear. My palette used oxblood burgundies, golds and coppers and bronzes, blacks and khakis and olives . . . and half-colors such as taupes, stone-grays, and browns. I moved the patterns around, taking them from regimented and geometric to organic and asymmetrical, introducing elongated paisleys and ovals instead of circles, and realigning them so they ran not straight *down* the tie but off to the side a little. Never diagonal, but definitely off-center.

Once upon a time, ties were hand-printed with wood blocks, so the patterns were irregular and the lines imperfect—which was the beauty of them. When technology and precision printing came along, the prints got rigid and constipated. I couldn't dig up the old wood blocks, but I could revive their effect. So to make my ties look hand-printed, I altered the *filetto.* which is the dark outline of the paisley. By "breaking" the *filetto*, I made the line appear irregular instead of continuous, hand-drawn instead of mechanical. I also changed its color from black to burgundy, olive, gold, and bronze. At the end of the day you were still looking at a paisley tie. But it was a whole new species.

The dense, luxurious silks for my woven ties came from Bianchi, the most expensive mill in Como. The patterns were so tightly woven that the most delicate motifs—every little paisley, circle, and square—looked crisp and clear. And the colors were lustrous, including bronzes, olives, siennas, cinnamons, olives, and an oxblood the color of Chambertin.

Bianchi made vestments for the Vatican. I figured if it was good enough for the pope, it was good enough for me.

"There are a thousand reasons to love the ties of Joseph Abboud," wrote François Chaille in *The Book of Ties.* "One of the principal being that his creations disprove the assertion that there is no middle ground in the United States between screaming bad taste and puritanical conformism. While his American counterparts invented the bold-look tie, Joseph Abboud . . . takes great pleasure in subtle Mediterranean nuances, and in refined patterns with soft contours and burnished colors suggestive of Italy."

I wasn't making pronouncements or staking a claim. I was just doing something I liked. But because the colors were unexpected, the combinations and patterns unique, my first collection of ten designs had a real impact. If you had an eye on the new lines in the next few seasons, you noticed that Hugo Boss wasn't the only company in the world looking for design concepts like mine. (No wonder Augusto is fond of pointing out that most designers he knows are just two steps above prostitutes.)

Plagiarism is hardly a sincere form of flattery, but sometimes it can be accidental. When I discovered that Luciano Barbera had some of my ties in *his* line, I called him up. After spending all those nights, hour after hour, creating that stuff, correcting the designs, doing the color keys, I just felt that it was *my* work he was stealing and I wanted him to know that I knew.

"Maybe you're not aware of this," I told him, "but I designed those ties. Those are my colors." I know my tie designs like my children.

Luciano is one of the classiest men I've ever met. He's not the most well-known designer in the world, but he's very well respected on the inside. He's in his late sixties and very elegant, one of those Italians who are seduced by all things English. His company, Luciano Barbera, is like a smaller version of Zegna. His father was Carlo Barbera, and the family business was making gorgeous fabrics until Luciano blossomed as a designer.

He was embarrassed when I showed him the ties, and said he *hadn't* known, and I believed him. But someone knew. It was a beautiful design, and it didn't just land on his desk.

No lawsuits that time. Luciano apologized and said it wouldn't happen again. And it hasn't.

The thing is, I *like* Luciano. I've liked him for a long time, ever since our first meeting in the mid-1970s when I was buying fabrics for Louis Boston. In those days, before all the mills started accommodating their customers by bringing their fabrics to Como, which is bright and gorgeous, Murray and I were traveling to the mills themselves up in the Biella region, which is beautiful, misty, and sad.

It's five o'clock in the afternoon, in February, dreary as all hell, and we're here to see Luciano Barbera's fabric collection. We pull up in a dead fog, and it's a castle. Like a scene right out of *Young Frankenstein.*

We ring the bell, and this little bent-over guy (Igor?) opens the door. He's about ninety years old and wearing a work apron. He ushers us in, very, very slowly. He leads us up a winding staircase to a sort of tower. And he introduces us to Luciano, who brings out the swatches.

The light is so dim it's like having a blanket over your head, and the swatches are so little—and so tweedy and muddy *anyway*—that we can hardly see them. With a straight face, Luciano's holding them up with those poetic Italian hands of his, saying, "Isn't this the most beautiful coloration?" and we don't know what we're looking at. For two hours, Murray and I are buying fabrics we can't see, in the murk and the rain and the fog. But Luciano believes it, and we believe that he believes it, so we believe it, too.

A suit is a suit. Blue, gray, it's not a personality-defining thing. But a tie, with its texture and pattern, is. It's the icing on the cake (except when it becomes the cake itself, and the guy doesn't understand that the tie is meant to go with the outfit, not the outfit with the tie). The beauty of a tie is its length, its shape, and its movement, so avoid the horizontal motif. A design running across it defeats the beauty, and with all those little stripes going the wrong way you've got a test pattern.

Every tie sends a message. It reveals a guy's mood and self-image. The guy in the striped rep tie or club tie is telling you he's an intellectual, a college grad. The guy with the small woven motif is a conformist. The guy wearing a print—paisleys, florals, circles, squares, diamonds, or many of them in combination—is a little frivolous, a little playful. The guy with the naked lady on his chest is very frivolous, very fast. The guy in the solid tie—well, there are two solid-tie guys: One is saying, "I'm so cool I don't need pattern," the other can't figure it out and doesn't know what else to do.

Knit ties are a very small niche. I've designed them, I've worn them, and there are fifteen or twenty of them hanging in my closet at home—some striped, most solid—that I just look at. I'm occasionally tempted to do them again, and one of these days I will. The whole purpose of fashion is to free yourself from having to conform all the time. Break it up a little. Get a life.

Whatever the design or material, the tie has to be properly pressed.

You want to see the roundness of the edge, see it drape. If it's over-pressed, it lies flat. You also want it to hang properly, which means aligning the front and tail end so the lengths are even. (It's these details that separate the men from the boys.) Just like hems, ties change with the times: They're long or short, they're wide or narrow. If you watch old movies, you can get absolutely dizzy studying this migration.

A lot of love and care goes into tying a tie, and most guys are lousy at it. The most important part is making the perfect dimple. As you pull the tie through, you use your finger to guide it. Then you make the two sides of the dimple bow out so it falls right in the middle. The dimple hitting on the side is unacceptable. Multiple dimples are unacceptable. Then you gently pull—not yank—to work the knot.

If a guy can tie a good knot, he can throw out his chest with pride. One of the best practitioners I know is Don Imus. For all the emphasis on cowboy shirts and authentic jeans, for all his laughing at designer fashion, on special occasions he'll wear a tuxedo jacket or cashmere dinner jacket and tie a great tie.

Knots have personalities, too. I like a four-in-hand, which is once around and through, and the knot is neat and narrow—but not so tight that it will kill the tie. It has a perfect dimple, and it's sophisticated, the knot of Harvard and Yale, Rex Harrison and Cary Grant. The Windsor (a half-Windsor takes an extra loop, a full-Windsor takes two extras), which looks a little gangsterish, a little slick, was named after the Duke of Windsor, who was anything but. In fact, the old boy didn't even wear it. Suzy Menkes, author of *The Windsor Style*, explains that "The Duke's famous 'Windsor knot' was achieved by having his London shirtmakers Hawes and Curtis put a thick interlining in his ties to make the knot fatter." You can't get a good dimple with a Windsor, because it creates this big triangle—a knot that looks like a block of wood at your neck.

Bow ties belong nowhere but with tuxedos. Guys who wear them by day are trying too hard. Unless their glasses are dangling on a cord and they're parsing Ezra Pound, they look pretentious. And if you have any kind of ethnic background, like me, you look like an organ grinder.

But the worst thing I can think of is pre-tied bow ties. Ninety-five percent of American men—maybe more—don't know how to tie a bow tie. I don't know why. It's as simple as tying your shoe, except that the shoelace is around your neck. You make a loop, wrap one end around the other, pull it through, and you've created a bow. Anyone can do it, but the real art is the fluff. You have to play with the bow a little bit, tighten the knot, and tug gently so the wings are dimpled and symmetrical.

But guys are afraid to try it, so most bow ties sold, even for expensive tuxedos, are pre-tied. We sell them, out of necessity, but I hate them. If your tie is pre-tied, you can never be cool. You can be PeeWee Herman, but you can never be Frank Sinatra in the wee small hours of the morning. What do you do, take off your pre-tied bow tie and drop it on the bar? It looks like a dead butterfly.

TWENTY

Designs on Women

CONFESSION: I LIKE DESIGNING for women *more* than designing for men.

Here's why. One, women are smarter about style. Two, they have more options. They can wear their hair up or down. They can wear more makeup or less. They can look great in jeans and a T-shirt or in a satin gown. They can do whatever they want—except be sheep. Three, I love women.

Women's wear drives the fashion industry. Menswear isn't even a close second. Think about the CFDA Awards: The biggest attention-getter is the Women's Wear Designer of the Year (as opposed to the Oscars, where the last performer's award goes to Best Actor). There are a lot more women's designers than men's designers, so the women's business is much more competitive. It's not exactly that menswear designers are laid back, but we are less uptight and worried about our public image. The pecking order and position-grabbing are definitely less intense.

Menswear is less interesting, largely because men are less interested in it. The design changes are too subtle and too gradual to make great copy, unless we're talking about men in skirts or high heels, and most male consumers are staunchly unconcerned with what the fashion editors write—which is why if out-of-town editors can make only one trip to New York, it's going to be for the women's shows, not the men's. Male consumers like a suit or they don't, and they don't need to be told why. Female consumers, on the other hand, *do* want to read all about it. That's what sells magazines, and magazines sell clothes.

When I joined GFT, I was finally in a position to move beyond menswear, and we launched the first women's collection in 1990. The collection was expensive (more expensive than my menswear), in the same price range as Calvin, Armani, and Escada. We weren't just scraping along in the back room of the menswear business anymore. We were really *doing it*. Our main customers were Neiman Marcus, Saks, Nordstrom, and upper-end specialty stores all over the country.

I'd always been aware of women's clothes, of course, and followed what the designers were doing. And I knew that my fabrics offered a different palette that would apply beautifully. Back in my days with Freedberg, I'd done some sweaters and jackets, but that was just menswear for women. This was a clean slate. I knew I still had a lot to learn, and I learned on the job.

In menswear, we develop prototypes in the factory. In women's, we created samples in the sample room on Fifth Avenue. In menswear, the options are limited and the silhouettes simple. In women's, you're doing sexy *and* you're doing corporate; you're thinking about age and mood and build. Men want practicality and timelessness. Women want sensuality and innovation. In men's, a print fabric is a tie or maybe a shirt. In women's, it's a dress, a blouse, a skirt, a scarf; it's 8 million things. I was cross-dressing, pulling elements from one to give the other. The possibilities were endless!

I did adaptations, borrowed references. The designers and merchandisers in the women's division loved one of my men's jackets, so we translated it almost literally. We used the same antiqued leather and color combinations, but made it a little longer and took out some of the bulk. I did women's tuxedos with pants, with skirts, in ivory, in black. Borrowing from a men's tie, done in black and brown stripes on an ivory base, I designed a women's bias skirt, pants, halter tops, tank tops, pajamas—exploding the stripe and using a textured tussah silk instead of pure tie silk. It was so beautiful that I then moved it back into men's and designed some scarves.

I think most women dress with fantasy (and maybe a specific man) in mind; that's how they bring excitement to a relationship. Sometimes it's a sultry evening gown; sometimes it's a cloud of new underwear. (With a guy, it's a whole different thing. He goes home and puts on his BVDs. He wants to go to bed with the girl, but he's not about to go out and buy some exotic Tarzan leopard print. He may throw a little powder on there, but that's about it for the romance. If men dress with fantasy in mind, it's for a featured role at the Met.)

One day, I'd be untangling men's shoelaces for *DNR*; the next day I was explaining to *Women's Wear Daily* how texture and fabric inform a woman's lifestyle. I was moving back and forth, and the energy of doing both was fantastic. When you design both men's and women's, you're dealing with two thought processes, two messages, different channels of distribution, different buyers, and different management; each collection should stand on its own. (It doesn't always. Example: the men's military-style jackets with big gold buttons—right out of Michael Jackson's closet—that Tom Ford did a couple of years ago at Gucci. Who were they really for? What normal guy was going to wear them? It was an extension of women's-wear thinking, and it didn't work.)

In men's, the colors are muted and subtle. But in women's, they could be edgy and bright, burnt and hot. We did a heather-tweed jacket with suede piping and a poet's neck, resplendent hand-embroidered evening jackets, trousers, halter tops, and dresses using wood and copper beads. The clothes were beaded in India and sewn in Italy. In our sample room, twenty to twenty-five people did the pinning and draping on mannequins and gorgeous fit models. More than designed or manufactured, the garments were actually *crafted*, and we never produced more than twenty-five or thirty of any one piece. There were no hard architectural lines. The shapes were simple, soft, and organic, because there's nothing more seductive than a woman moving gracefully and the fabric moving with her.

In the design studio, I learned how women see their bodies. Unlike guys, they know their assets and liabilities and how to flatter them— when to go short to show off the legs or long to cover them, how to accentuate the waist, expose a little cleavage, reveal a shoulder, camouflage a belly. Even those who aren't *au courant* and don't know about fashion seem to understand this instinctively.

In the sample room, I learned about fit models and *their* bodies. They're crucial to the draping process, but you have to watch where you put your hands. A fit model named Karen was one of my favorites. She was not a shy girl, and between fittings she was usually swanning around naked, except for her wonderful little G string. I tried very hard to be professional, but she was so ravishing, the scene was so intimate, that I couldn't look her in the eye. I'd try to be clinical about it—this was not soft music and a lap dance; these were our *jobs*—but it was hard to concentrate sometimes. So when I had to adjust something on her, I'd stare at her shoulder or her hem and make sure that when I touched her, I touched her *waist*. Occasionally there was an accidental bump-in, but it wasn't a mistake I felt bad about.

My roots are in retail, and I know that the battle is won or lost not in the design studio, not in the showroom, but at the counter. So it's crucial to meet the customers.

One time-honored tradition is the trunk show, where the designer brings his or her new collection to the store (in trunks, once upon a time) to meet and measure a congregation of loyal customers invited by the store's personal shoppers: "Joseph Abboud is doing a trunk show, and Joseph will be here personally to meet you and talk about the clothes." A men's trunk show is an excuse to have a gathering and a glass of wine, and that's about it. Men come, look at a swatch, and have to think about it. They don't ask questions or spend three or four hours trying things on and learning stuff. Women do. They pay more attention to detail—to the fit, the shape, the fabric, the lining, the way a button hole is sewn. They pick up on new concepts and experiment with odd color combinations. They aren't afraid of novelty. If they want more pants or skirts in next season's collection, they'll say so. In just one trunk show at I. Magnin or Neiman's, I was doing $500,000. Trunk shows for men mean nothing, but for women they mean business.

If you're a male designer, women want to talk to you. I don't think most of them expect to meet a heterosexual designer, and a lot of them would ask, "Are you sure he's not gay? Is he married?" The customers would ask the salespeople, and the salespeople would ask my people. For some reason, that was part of getting to know who the designer was. Women seem to feel more comfortable discussing their bodies and their flaws with a gay designer, whom they consider nonthreatening, but I was there if they wanted me.

One day we were at Neiman's in Dallas and our sales manager said, "There's a young lady waiting to see you. She wants to show you her book." The chick probably wants to be a model, I figured, and I'm this nice guy who likes to help people, so why not? She was a knockout—long blond hair, probably in her late twenties. She handed me her book, I opened it up, and it was full of naked pictures.

They weren't exactly pornographic, but they weren't what you'd expect in a model's book either. Everybody was standing around looking over my shoulder, and I was saying, "Well, your hair really looks good here," trying to be Mr. Professional. It was funny in a way, but embarrassing. And endless. She asked where I was staying, but I'm not some rock star who sees a girl in the crowd and has her sent up to the room.

Sometimes a woman will hand you a note; sometimes she'll mail it. "I never do this, but I met you and I'd love to see you again. Here's my number, and . . ." It's flattering, but if you compromise, you compromise yourself.

By the mid-1990s, we had a $10 million to $12 million wholesale women's business (which would be a $25 million business at retail). But as we were beginning to soar, financial problems were grounding GFT. The head office in Milan started downsizing and closing factories, the lifeblood of our production line. For a young company like ours, this was disaster.

Women's didn't break down all at once. It was more like a tree dropping its leaves. First there were no more factories, then no more sample room, then no more marketing and advertising. The restrictions became tighter and tighter, the collection became smaller and smaller, and we were no longer on a level playing field with Calvin Klein or Armani. I wanted to continue with it, but GFT didn't. I wanted to continue with our retail venture, particularly the store in Boston, but GFT didn't. They just wanted to produce my menswear.

For a few golden years, we'd been totally aligned in everything we did, but by 1995 we were virtually estranged. By 1996, it was over. Whether I agreed or not, GFT was stepping out of my women's wear.

But I wasn't. I made a licensing agreement with Pellari, a wonderful little company in northern Italy. I'd design the collection and Pellari would manufacture and sell it, paying me a royalty for the right to use my name. We weren't dead yet.

In 1996-1997, we relaunched the collection. Rose Marie Bravo, then head of Saks Fifth Avenue, was delighted. She knew we'd moved away from GFT and she was cool with that. When I made the new presentation to her, she brought her people in, committed to over $4 million worth of volume, and asked us for an exclusive. I said yes.

It was one of the biggest mistakes I ever made.

Neiman Marcus had also been a terrific customer, and they expected to carry the new collection, too. But we now had to tell Neiman's they couldn't. I wasn't at that meeting, wasn't there to convey the facts properly and hold discussions, and I should have been. I could pass the blame here, but I don't want to do it. Someone who was working for me on the management team said, "I can handle it beautifully," and I trusted him. Mistake. He didn't handle it beautifully, and my absence came off as cocky. I take full responsibility for it. Neiman Marcus was Neiman Marcus, not chopped liver. But Saks had made us an offer we couldn't refuse. Although it sounded like a good move, in the long run it was anything but.

Soon—too soon—after making the commitment, Rose Marie left Saks and went to Burberry, leaving us in the lurch. While the multi-million-dollar purchase was still firm, support within the ranks was not. Stores depend on the designer's marketing and advertising to help promote the collection, and our advertising budget was much too small to please Saks. We did what we could, "contributing" hundreds of thousands of dollars through discounts on the clothes, but it didn't matter. As soon as there were problems with delivery, with selling, with fit—the kinds of problems that inevitably happen and can be overcome if the store wants to overcome them—Saks backed off their commitment. They didn't want the exclusive anymore, didn't intend to put the collection in many of their stores. We couldn't persuade them. What were we going to do?

The arrangement lasted for about two years. We tried to woo Neiman's again, kept inviting them to see the collection, but we'd burned that bridge. I was willing to eat all the humble pie they dished up, but we'd alienated them *real good*. They weren't interested, and I understood completely.

We still had twenty-five or thirty specialty stores across the country buying the collection, but specialty stores can buy only so much, and without the critical mass of one major champion you can't sustain a sizable business.

Finally, Pellari couldn't keep it up and neither could we. It trickled out and broke my heart. It still does.

Women's is the greatest failure I've ever had.

TWENTY ONE

The Reality (and Realty) of Retail

THE STORE WINDOW—backdropped, propped, and provocative—is theater. "It's a fantasy world, and when people stop, you have to reward them," says Tom Beebe, who did just that as the wittiest of display directors at Paul Stuart for fourteen years (and now creative director of *DNR*). "You want to pull them in beyond the glass."

Uh-uh, says Geraldine Stutz, the ingenious merchant who reinvented Henri Bendel in the 1960s. "Windows are not meant to sell merchandise or even to show it," she quirkily observed to *Women's Wear Daily*. "They are two eyes to communicate the spirit and point of the store."

I'm with Tom. Whether or not they're *meant* to show and sell, they do. Back in the Louis days, with Murray on my back, growling, "Don't tell me about your mistakes. Make them into winners," I learned fast. If we had a suit or tie or color that wasn't moving, I'd put it in the window and out it would fly. (I got so good at display, in fact, that one night in the 1970s somebody backed a truck up to the front window, smashed it, and stole the whole works—except for *one tie*. Really ticked me off. It was a *great* tie.)

When a new collection comes into the store or a designer comes for a personal appearance, the clothes are probably going to make the windows. Whether they appear in one window or seven depends on the agenda of the store's fashion director and display team. It also depends on how much of the collection they've bought (they don't buy two sweaters and feature them), and on the moment and the season and the message they want to deliver to the public; they may, for example, want to show just formal wear for the two weeks before New Year's. In other words, it's survival of the fittest. All you can do is pray they really *get* your stuff and show it well. You don't want them to just stick a bunch of mannequins out there with some swanky props and open the curtain.

When I worked at Surman's as a kid, everything was in the window—and I mean *everything*, the way it was at Woolworth's or the local hardware store. But if you show everything you have, nobody can see any of it. The display has to breathe. Barneys' windows are so cluttered I don't know what I'm looking at anymore.

"You've got to focus," says Paul Stuart's Cliff Grodd, putting it into perspective. "If you simplify things, they have more meaning. The consumer doesn't have a lot of time."

On the other hand, the Dolce & Gabbana model of showing just one white shirt is ridiculous. It's not even cool to be *that* cool. The one shirt. Please.

What's inside the store matters, too, of course. Let's take a field trip to Saks Fifth Avenue in New York. To Men's Sportswear on the seventh floor. To the Joseph Abboud shop.

It's not really a shop. It's an area, a space. Stores don't want to build walls for you anymore. They don't want to give you an *environment*. You may be able to put in some freestanding fixtures, like the beautiful walnut-and-bronze display tables that were designed by Jim D'Auria, who's our guy, but you can't touch their floors or their walls. So most shops are generic spaces except for the designer's name dangling overhead. That's "name recognition." Ergo, it's a shop. It may not have four walls, but it's a shop.

Getting a good space isn't a matter of happenstance or luck. It's a question of whether the chairman thinks a Joseph Abboud shop is valuable to his store, how our brand relates to the guy next door, and—let's be honest here—how much we're willing to pay.

In the better stores, you'll notice, Ralph Lauren usually has the biggest space. Look at his shop, his positioning, the amount of inventory. The tables are merchandised well; they're artfully coordinated, so that several different items (the shirts next to the sweaters next to the corduroy pants) all work together. The props, the paneling, the fixtures, the photos—it's all part of the "negotiation." Such spreads cost him dearly, but the biggest space means the biggest presence, so he gets paid back in spades.

Every store is unique, and it's basically a day-to-day skirmish. If you have a prime space like ours at Saks, it means you're viable. By viable, I mean able to prove ourselves by *selling through* to the consumer—pleasing him and having him continue to ask for our brand. It takes a lot of time to get that kind of positioning, and even after you get it, you can lose it if you don't perform. Bad sales might be the store's fault—and so what? No matter whose fault it is, if you don't perform and the numbers don't add up, you start to lose real estate. So you're always fighting the battle with the store's head merchandisers for territory and position.

Are they going to put me all the way in the back? Will they give me the right side or the left? (I'm left-handed myself, but I always go to the right first, like most people, so the right is preferable.) What about that tremendous space over there by the windows? Or, even better, how about up front near the elevators?

These things can change overnight, and you never know where

you'll land. Whether it's near the elevator or halfway to Hoboken, the goal is to snag the customer. I want him to see my name. Then see my product. Then see that he has a lot of my product to choose from. Even if he's just come in for a shirt, he'll see how everything works together because we've coordinated the colors and patterns well. Stores and designers love it when a guy comes in and says, "That sweater looks good with that pant. I'll take the jacket. Oh, and the scarf looks good, too." If you do it right, you get a multiple sale from it, and multiple sales are how you get the volume.

But what he actually gets to see isn't our decision. It depends on what the store has chosen to buy from us, which puts us in the precarious position of trying to defend our turf with weapons somebody else is choosing. If they say, "Well, it might be right for Nordstrom but it's not right for us," we could disagree all day long, but ultimately, it's not our call. That can be a huge disappointment, and we've had those. We're in some stores very, very strongly, and wish we were better in others. Next season, who knows?

Once you've won the real estate, you get down to brass tacks—literally. No Saks or Bloomingdale's is going to say, "Oh, sure, Joe, come on in. Pick the space you like. We'll build you a palace, and if it works, great, and if it doesn't, that's fine too."

No. They say, "You want a shop in our world-class store in New York City? Fine. You can build the shop yourself for X thousands of dollars, or you can help us build the shop." This means we pay to bring in our own interior designer.

So we'll call our designer, Jim D'Auria. "Saks wants to do a shop. Let's go take a look at it, and tell us what you think of the location"—not that we always have a choice, of course. We pay Jim to do the shop design, on paper. Then we try to convince the chain of command at Saks. We want the environment to say Joseph Abboud; they want the environment to say Saks. Sometimes it can take six or seven presentations over a three-month period before they'll give the go-ahead.

When we go to Bloomingdale's, it's a totally different story. They *want* my personality, and that's great for me because I have an emotional attachment to *them*.

Bloomingdale's was the first store I ever saw in New York. I was 17 when I came to the city for the first time, taking the bus down from Boston to visit my sister Mara, then an artist in Greenwich Village. She offered me the Empire State Building and the Statue of Liberty, tours of this and tastes of that, but instead, I dragged her to look at the Ralph Lauren clothes at Bloomingdale's. That was *all* I wanted to do.

There were so many Ralph Lauren clothes in so many styles it was like King Solomon's mines—different patterns and different cuts, tweeds upon tweeds I didn't see at Louis. I had loved clothes in only one city; I'd never been out of Boston. This was my first experience in understanding that one store could have something different from another store.

And something else: I knew these clothes were Ralph Lauren, even without seeing a label. The experience was foreign and new, but I knew they were his. I didn't have the money to buy anything, but to see all those sport jackets on circular racks was like a blood transfusion. I connected with Ralph's designs, and with the store, and I stayed connected.

At Bloomingdale's, we have a budget—how much *we're* going to contribute, how much the *store* is going to contribute—but it's easy. The managers there don't meddle except in technical matters, to make sure we don't use too much heat or interfere with their electrical systems. They've embraced us 100 percent, given us whatever we've wanted. We don't have to deal with design approval, and we've been able to do a new shop there almost every two years.

While we're deciding how the space will look, Jim is trying to fit it into the budget. Sometimes we have to have an "artful compromise," in which it isn't just a creative decision anymore, but a creative decision based on budget. The challenge is to use beautiful but inexpensive materials in new and interesting ways.

How do we draw customers into the shop? First, we look at the aisle configuration: which way the people are coming in. Are they coming from the Third Avenue side or the Lexington Avenue side? Then, how do we lay it out? What do we use for bait? We always try to announce the shop with some graphic feature you can see from a distance. At one of our shops, you could look straight through Armani's slick environment, decorated in black, gray, and stone, to mine—which was so nicely framed it was like seeing the Eiffel Tower at the end of the Champs-Elysées. Jim knew just what he was doing.

So we create the structure, and then it's up to the display people to prop it right and catch the customer's eye. The rest is up to the gods of commerce.

With your own shop come myriad responsibilities. First of all, you have to ensure product flow. This means keeping your stock fresh and replenished at all times, and sticking strictly to delivery schedules. Every thirty, sixty, or ninety days the big stores want new product, especially in a designer shop.

You have to pay the salesperson, aka "the specialist." He sells, obviously, and makes the inventory look good. Since he works only for Joseph Abboud in the Joseph Abboud shop, he's on Joseph Abboud's payroll. There are all kinds of arrangements here, and the financial equation can vary from store to store, season to season. What's sure is that designers and manufacturers contribute significantly (if not entirely) to the salaries of their specialists.

Then you have to pay the "retail coordinators." They also work for us, not the store, overseeing the Joseph Abboud product in every shop and department in their region. They decide what goes on the mannequins and tables, and they keep the salespeople up to snuff.

Not only are you required to bankroll the cast of characters; you're also responsible for the housekeeping. This is supposedly a collective effort by our sales force and the store, but it's generally lackluster on the store's part. Customers can be careless, and not just at the sales rack. On the best days in the best stores, I see things that are stained, torn, and askew—and they're selling for $800, $900, $1,000, $2,000. If a suit jacket sits on a hanger the wrong way for twenty-four hours, that affects the pressing and leaves marks. This is not the customer's concern, nor should it be. It's the responsibility of the store, the salespeople, and our staff.

In Japan and Europe, the housekeeping is impeccable; it's all about respect for the merchandise. Armani insists that his merchandise hang exactly two inches apart, and it does. But we in America, we as an *industry*, do a horrible job. Maybe American retailers think they're above folding shirts and neatening shelves, although Gap, Banana Republic, and Levi's have become famous for it; their jeans are lined up so perfectly they look like an art form. Sure, a store's going to get disheveled during the day. If it doesn't, you're in trouble; you're not doing any business. The job is to go back in and pull it together.

When I was at Louis, every night before we went home we had to "rack the clothes," which meant straightening every shoulder of every suit on every rack so that the next morning when the store opened, everything was perfect. It made sense, you know? People will spend more time and more money in a neat environment where they can find their size and try on a sweater that doesn't look as if it's been rolled up in a $300 ball.

No matter how viable you are, no matter how successful, there isn't a department store or specialty chain on the planet that's going to be able to show your entire collection. Even Nordstrom, my biggest customer—which has over ninety stores and has sold thousands upon thousands of my suits and jackets—can take only a portion of my collections. Nordstrom's buyers and managers know their products (and in many cases even help manufacturers develop them). The service is exquisite, and to me service is everything. The tailoring is superb. The sales staff is uniquely knowledgeable. I'd advise anyone to shop there, whether he's buying Joseph Abboud or not. But that said, any designer with dreams up his sleeve wants his own retail stores, where he can invite customers into *his* world—just as we do with our new flagship store at the Time Warner Center at Columbus Circle in New York. (The ideal is to have it both ways, like Coach, Cole Haan, and Polo do: product in our own retail stores and the big stores as well.)

For a few minutes back in the early 1990s, we had Joseph Abboud stores in Seattle and Greenwich, but they were franchise stores, not company-owned. The franchise idea works for McDonald's, but it doesn't work in the fashion business. Other people were running them (one was the corporate giant Hartmarx; the other was a small business with two stores in Westchester), and it was really their endeavor, not ours. They bought product from us, and we had a formal relationship, but it was their space, they had the leases, and they had the responsibility—until they ran into financial problems, which became *our* financial problems. When they couldn't pay the rent they had to close the stores, and then they couldn't pay for the inventory we'd shipped. We lost money, we lost market position, and, worst, we lost face.

The way to make it work is to control everything—the real estate, the image, the product, the selection, the service, the marketing, the visuals, the windows. But that's a very expensive proposition.

In 1990, we opened our flagship store at 37 Newbury Street in Boston, one of the world's great shopping streets. The very stylish glass-and-stucco building had been designed by Gwathmey/Siegel as a Knoll showroom in 1979. It was on the first block between Arlington and Berkeley, near the Ritz and the Public Garden, near Armani and Louis, about a mile from where I'd been born, and light-years away in culture.

Choosing this location probably wasn't the smartest economic decision—the space was ridiculously overpriced, Newbury Street is notoriously problematic for parking, and the store would probably have done a lot more business if it had been in Manhattan—but it was an emotional one. More than just a magnificent venue, it said: Here's a South End kid who took a very long way home.

The interior was designed by Bentley LaRosa Salasky, who had done my first corporate headquarters in New York, and we created a luxe residential ambience with beautiful paintings and antique furniture. (When I was a kid on the other side of the tracks, antique was not good. We didn't have enough *new* to start worrying about paying for other people's *old*.)

The first level (men's sportswear and furnishings) was light and airy, with kilim rugs, a leather wrap desk, and a round table displaying hundreds of ties like a kaleidoscope. Men's tailored clothing on the second level had cherrywood walls and armoires, with fitting-room doors of quilted leather, brass studs, and bronze finials. Women's, on the third, was done in blond wood and soft terra-cotta tones. A balcony drenched in bougainvillea, where customers could sit at little tables sipping coffee or tea, overlooked the street.

Perfect, right?

Right until it closed in 1995. The usual reasons were given—lease expiring, rent increase, etc.—but GFT was having financial problems and the CEO, who was maybe the fifth or sixth guy since I'd been there, had a new strategy to save the day. He didn't want any stores, he didn't want a joint venture, he wanted to be just a licensing company.

I think another strategist might have found another way. I don't think it *had* to close. But I take responsibility for the whole mess. It probably was a financial mistake from the beginning, and I persisted because I was so determined to make it work.

These days the store is occupied by Donna Karan, and I won't even take a stab at telling you what that does to me. But every time I walk by I can still see the faint imprint of my name on the stucco façade, and it's like seeing a ghost. Even though someone has tried to sandblast the letters, I can still make them out.

TWENTY-TWO

Honor Thy Customer

A GOOD MENSWEAR SALESMAN connects to the male psyche. He understands that straight or gay, shopper or retailphobe, most men know how they want to be perceived. There are straight guys who want to be flashy, gay guys who want to be conservative; it's not their sexual preference but their personal aesthetic that defines them. The salesman asks, he listens, he helps. He can discuss single-breasted and double-breasted. He knows to tell a customer that it's more important to have five *great* suits than ten mediocre ones—that he may spend more but he's buying something that fits better, looks better, and lasts longer. (European men understand this. Americans don't.) The salesman has a sense of pride and cares if you come back.

Unfortunately, there are more bad salespeople than good. There's the kind who thinks he's hipper than thou and judges you by your cover—foolishly betting his commission that you're not a wealthy, quirky person who just happens to like wearing sneakers and tattered jeans. Another type is ignorant of his terrain. This type is more prevalent in the big department stores, where most salespeople are here today for an hourly wage and over there tomorrow. If they move from ladies' handbags to men's ties to ladies' hosiery in the space of a month, how can they know what they're selling? Why would they feel any sense of commitment to the job, the store, the product, or the customer?

At Louis, I used to hold sales meetings every Saturday morning. I'd tell the salespeople about trends in fit and color, about quality and technology, about image and style. I'd illustrate my little talks by creating a designer look with different labels we sold—maybe using a Fair Isle sweater, a tweed jacket, and a tie. The point was to sell the salespeople so *they* could sell the customer. Such training should be done across the board, but it isn't. The salesman doesn't sell as much product; the customer doesn't get the right message. Everybody loses.

The good salesman has an innate sense of touch and feel, not just with fabric but also with people. He knows when to move in and when to move back. If he's tuned in, he'll know when a guy wants to have a conversation about socks or wants to be left alone. If he can read his customer (as opposed to imposing his own will), if he'll just step back and let it all come in, he'll know what he has to know right away. Most people *want* an expert to tell them why they need something. Most people *want* to be sold. But they want it done with integrity. They want to be sold by someone they trust.

You want to talk about fashion crises for men?

Two-button or three-button. Double-breasted or single-breasted. Spread collar versus point collar. French cuff versus button cuff.

The range within which men panic is very small. They're so frightened by fashion that they limit even the options they *have*. They don't realize that it isn't an either-or situation—that it's okay to have double-breasted *and* single-breasted, that they're both right at certain times, and that they can coexist.

Every so often the cover of *DNR* will ask, "Is the three-button suit dead?" My answer: It's cyclical. The two-button is always right; the three-button is always right. How many kinds of suits does a guy have? If a designer takes two-button *or* three-button out of his vocabulary, he's taken away one of the options. That's why it's important to change fabrics. It's just about all we can do.

We show off our craft in the details, like button placement, which is very important. For instance, you never want it to hit a guy on the sternum, because even if he's in great shape, the sternum is where the body projects out. So if you button the jacket *there*, it's going to hang away from the body.

Sleeve buttons are a time-honored tradition, but they can be more than ornamental. They can actually work. When I'm wearing a suit casually, I love to unbutton the sleeves and turn the cuffs back. It's kind of nonchalant, and it's a cool detail. Some days I wear them all unbuttoned, with a linen shirt and a pair of jeans, and it looks almost as if I didn't really care what I threw on. When it's warm outside and the jacket is cotton, I keep only one closed. When I wear a serious shirt and tie, I button them all.

When they're sewn on, they should be cross-stitched, not parallel-stitched, for durability and a better look. I also like to see my sleeve buttons "kissing." This means that they *almost* touch each other, but not quite. Very nice. How many buttons are right? Four. One looks cheesy. Two looks cheap. Three is a poor man's four.

To have working buttons, you need working buttonholes, so I always have mine cut through, although most guys don't see the point. I'm especially keen on the "fish-eye" buttonhole, which is long and narrow with a wide, round opening at one end.

Such matters may seem inconsequential, but they're all a part of style. Style's a very subtle thing.

So subtle, in fact, that many men can't seem to see it. What to do? Take your wife . . . *please*. Men ought to have a mind of their own, but they don't. They hate to shop, and who can blame them? It's very confusing out there, and the same gene that makes men drive around the block fifteen times because they won't ask for directions makes them hesitant to ask for help from their best resource, a salesman. So until you gather the nerve, take a woman. Most women are great tour guides to the life of style. They're in tune with fashion, they know designer names and labels, they know what works (unless they're the kind who want their man to be something he's not—to dress younger, cooler, hipper than he is—so he ends up looking like a jerk). For the young consumer, it's Mom who knows that he needs a gray suit and a navy blazer. You think Father knows best? No way. He's not so sure himself.

Guys want safe. They're dumb. They're locked into the way they think, and they have very little range, so they rely on the women they want to appeal to. Even though they think they're dressing for other guys, they're automatically dressing for women as well. They don't realize it, but they're subconsciously saying, "I'm seeking your approval. I want to look good for you, so tell me *how*." (Women like guys who dress like guys. They don't like fashion plates, and they hate fashion victims.) It takes away some of the individuality, but that's okay. The payoff is the guy doesn't have to make the final decision because the woman— the one with the taste, the walking *Good Housekeeping* stamp of approval—will.

As a salesman myself, I learned early on to make the woman a part of the sale. She'd be expecting to get blown out of the picture, but instead I'd make her my ally. Then *we'd* have the conversation, and the guy would do whatever we told him to.

The chairman of a Boston bank brought his wife in one day, and he was putty in our hands. This guy who'd scare the hell out of me in a business environment was now in *my* zone—although we didn't make him feel that way. We made him *happy*, because *we* were connecting. I said something like, "Well, Mrs. So-and-so, what do you think? He looks so good in navy. Do you think maybe we should just get a nice navy double-breasted suit so he's always got it? We don't *have* to do it, but it's probably a great thing." *Bang!* The sale was there. Then she'd say, "Well, what else? Do you have one in gray?" and I'd say, "Yeah, but you know, maybe we should do the olive in a vested suit." The dialogue created a multiple sale.

My ties are made in Italy. So are Armani's. One season a few years ago, we both used the same fabric (an honest mistake; not every coincidence is "tie-jacking"), and both ties were manufactured in the same factory—at Massimo, in Italy. Armani's linings and knots were thin. Mine had more body, better bar-tacking, and details like a self-loop in the back to pull the tail end through. His ties retailed for $105, and mine were $75. Why? We all know why. His name was bigger, his awareness was greater, and his presence as a designer had existed for twenty years before I got there. I understand that. Americans are besotted by marquee names.

But a big name doesn't ensure top quality. When a company is under financial pressure, for example, it's going to charge higher and higher prices—even when the quality doesn't warrant them, even when the materials are less expensive. Donna Karan is not the only designer who's lost customers because her prices seemed out of whack with the quality of her clothes. It was a bad rap for a good designer. People loved her styles and designs and concepts and were willing to pay for them. But they were disappointed in how the stuff wore and performed.

No matter whose name is on it, you have to pay attention to the garment itself. How do you know if a shirt or pair of pants is well made and worth the price? Feel the fabric and trust your instincts. Is it soft and comfortable or hard and scratchy? Look at how the buttons are sewn on and the zipper is put in. Are there hanging threads? Is the inside of the garment cleanly made, neatly finished? Do the linings fit nicely? Look for loose stitching (the more stitches per inch, the more durable the seam). Notice the way the item is pressed. Does the collar lie flat? It should. Try it on and see how it feels. This is not brain surgery.

There are all kinds of labels, meaning all kinds of things. *Caveat emptor.*

There's the label of a defunct designer. Perry Ellis was terrific, but the brand that survives him reflects none of his DNA. It's just a bunch of products with his name on them and no relation to who he was as a designer. (The flip side of that is Chanel. The brand has remained important because those who carry it on know who Coco Chanel was and truly understand her culture.)

Then there's the designeresque label favored by moderately priced stores. An Italian-sounding name gets thrown onto some product and the public falls for it. The product might be decent quality and good for the price, but the label is baloney. "Vermani" looks and sounds authentic, so the unknowing consumer figures it's as good as Versace or Armani. But there's a certain deception intended. The "big name" is the magnet, but it's not the real deal.

On the other side of the name game is private label, which instead of a designer name carries only the name of the store. Early in my career, I designed private label sweaters and jackets for Paul Stuart in New York. It was an honor to be affiliated with such a prestigious retailer, and the stuff was beautiful. But private label can be a crap shoot. When you buy a Paul Stuart sweater, you can rely on the integrity of the store and the quality of its products. Depending on where you buy it, the product may be well made or shoddy, a great value or overpriced. There are no absolutes. Private label isn't good or bad. It can be either. You can only go with your instincts and how much you trust the store.

Yet another variation on the label is the fictional name. This is not meant to deceive anybody, but it is made up—for a legitimate reason. When Murray Pearlstein and I were buying thousands upon thousands of expensive Hickey Freeman suits for Louis, we were prohibited from using the label. Why? Because Mosher's, a tiny little store in Newton Centre which had probably been doing business with Hickey Freeman for 100 years, had an exclusive. So we carried the Walter-Morton collection and Mosher's kept Hickey Freeman. Walter-Morton—named after the sons of the founders, Jeremiah Hickey and Jacob Freeman—was a merchandising shell game. The suits were identical, but Hickey Freeman concocted the device back in 1928 to avoid competition with itself within a territory. In the long run, it didn't really matter. The Louis customer knew Louis, knew he was therefore getting a great suit, and probably knew it came from Hickey Freeman.

And finally there's the daddy label.

One day, Ari and I are dropping off some of my suits, jackets, and shirts at the cleaners. I hand over the stuff, the guy gives me the ticket.

"Daddy, why do you need a ticket?" she asks.

"So I'll know they're my clothes, honey."

She frowns. She's puzzled. She's five.

"But you *know* they're your clothes," she says, pointing to the label. "Your name's *on* them."

TWENTY-THREE

Lowdown on the Markdown

TO EVERYTHING there is a season, except in retail. It's July 31, 150 degrees outside, and we're looking at wools and plaids in the stores. It's absolutely ridiculous that in this heat you can't go in and buy a cotton suit. Oh, you can probably *buy* one, but it's probably marked down and filthy and there's no longer a full size run. And it's depressing, because the sale cuts the season short.

We've created a plight for ourselves by training the consumer to buy out of season, and on sale. No wonder the fashion industry is in chaos.

In years gone by, most stores had two sales a year: one at the end of the fall season (right after New Year's) and one at the end of the spring-summer season (right after the Fourth of July), just before the new goods came in. That's no longer the way it works, and it's a blessing and a curse. The designers and manufacturers are in a continuous race to deliver their goods ahead of everybody else's so they'll have a longer period in which to sell them at full price before the markdowns come—but the stores can't *take* the goods early unless they move out the goods they've got! So they're forced to reduce everything prematurely.

The fashion-forward customer is an early customer, and it used to be that if he wanted something new and fresh, in the right size and color, he saw the fall clothes in July or August and was willing to pay full price. Not anymore. And why should he pay full price when he knows the store will mark stuff down in thirty or sixty or ninety days? This frenetic program of sale after sale may generate volume, but it's destroying legitimate retail by discouraging customers from ever paying full price for a product. The stores are selling below margin and *losing* money because they're sacrificing profit. How can this be good for business?

When I think about the years of planning, the care that goes into production, the packaging and thought process all the way through, and then see the clothing hurtling through the system, it's tough not to lose heart. All that time spent in creating a beautiful collection, and in two short weeks it's toast.

Some customers don't bother with sales at the full-price retail stores, no matter how frequent, because they like to hit the discount and outlet stores. It all comes down to getting a deal—or thinking you are.

The original bargain stores, such as Filene's Basement and Loehmann's, were where you really could get deals, and people actually used to wait for things to show up there. Then Marshalls, TJ Maxx, and a few others joined the mix. They all have a continual reduction program, so they keep slashing and slashing until the stuff is gone. These are where department stores and designer companies traditionally unload their end-of-season inventory. Most designers (including me) think they're too good to be in the discount channel. But we all end up there anyway.

Here's how it typically works.

A Joseph Abboud suit goes into Saks in all the sizes and newest fabrics at the beginning of a season. In a month or two, the suits start to get marked down and the sizes start to get depleted. The 46 long that's still sitting on the rack will probably find its way to Filene's Basement, where it could be 40 or 60 percent off. If it stays in Filene's Basement for another month, with the automatic markdown, it could then be 70 percent off. The customer who wears the 46 long isn't going to go in and find an enormous selection, but if he's at the right place at the right time (and there are a lot of devoted Filene's customers who know just when product goes in), he's got a good shot. The suit's not any less valuable for being there, but it's not what we call your first-end product anymore. It's been handled a lot, and at each step along the distribution route it's been handled a little less politely. But to the 46-long who may not have the money to pay full price for it at Saks, it's right there looking him in the eye.

This was the process for years. But then the big stores and designer companies started to get smart. "Why should we give the business to Filene's or TJ Maxx when we can do it ourselves?" they said, and they started developing their own freestanding off-price shops. Saks has Off 5th, Nordstrom has the Rack, and for the last fifteen or twenty years the designers have been filling the outlet centers.

So outlets are a flourishing by-product, but they've had an impact on the business as a whole by affecting the pricing structure and persuading customers that full price is obsolete. Outlets are an unhealthy thing for the fashion industry. But there's no foreseeable resolution.

We have three Joseph Abboud outlet stores at the moment—at the Premium Outlet in Wrentham, Massachusetts; Woodbury Common in Central Valley, New York; and the Sawgrass Mills Mall in Sunrise, Florida. They aren't flashy and romantic and innovative, but they do the job.

A few weeks ago I was in Manchester, Vermont, checking out the other guys' outlets. As a consumer who loves new things and new ideas, I found the scene totally uninspiring. I didn't want to buy anything. Not because it wasn't shown well or priced well. It just didn't turn me on.

Nothing screamed, "Touch me, fondle me, buy me!" The big-name stores were there, and filled beautifully, but it was all basic product. If anybody needed a nice cotton cable sweater he could buy it there, but he wasn't going to find that one dynamite jacket. That's what the outlets do: replace the individual and unique with commodities.

Designers with a million outlet stores—Ralph Lauren, Tommy Hilfiger, whoever— require a lot more than leftovers to keep their shelves filled. So they manufacture product strictly *for* the outlet stores. Before he had his own outlets, Ralph was producing slews of hunter-green blazers that went directly to Sy Sims (without appearing first at Saks or anyplace else) simply because the factory had to be fed. They were made well, but they weren't made with *love*. It was mass production, and the nature of the business. When you see thousands and thousands of them hanging in the factory, they don't seem so precious anymore. I like envisioning a little tailor with his sleeves rolled up and a band-collar shirt and a little vest, sitting down with his needle and thread to sew in the shoulder pad. And here were all these green blazers.

Another thing to watch for. You know the price tag that reads, "Originally $495, now $295"? It's the high-low game. Here's the gimmick: The manufacturer and retailer agree on what they call a "price out the door." This means that the store puts a suit on the floor for $495—but only long enough to mark it down and send it out the door. Nobody really expects (or needs) the suit to sell at $495, because the store and manufacturer make their full profit on the $295. It's just a trick of the trade to keep the customer in a markdown state of mind.

The sample sale is another popular destination, but "sample" is a misnomer. To most people it suggests custom-made samples made for the showrooms. In truth, the outlet store and the sample sale serve exactly the same purpose: They sell off excess goods.

Early on, when we had sample sales of *samples*, the stuff was all 40 regulars and 40 longs, which were mediums and larges, so if you were an extra-extra-large or a small, the sale wasn't for you. But if you were the right size, you were going into a South African mine and finding a diamond no one else would have. You might pick up an expensive shirt, a suede or leather jacket, a shearling, or a $2,000 cashmere sweater—a sweater that we might have made three of and never sold—for $150. All the products went for a fraction of their real value. That's the true meaning of "sample sale."

Today it doesn't make economic sense to do a sample sale based strictly on samples, because true samples come in only one size. So we do what everybody else does, which is to put out a conglomeration of stuff: a few true samples but mostly excess stock from the warehouse and factory so Mr. 46 regular and Mr. 36 short can find things too. Is there the occasional great piece? Yes. If you happen to be a 40 long, might you find a few things you wouldn't find at a store? Sure. But that's only 5 or 10 percent of the product sold. The other 90 to 95 percent is leftovers. Still tasty, still greatly reduced, but not exactly irresistible.

People love sample sales because there's something fun about them, and a certain energy, and usually a few celebs to keep the antennae waving. When we hold ours twice a year in New York, I'm reluctant to stop in because I hate the circus environment and hate watching the clothes get tossed around. On the other hand, it's interesting to see which are the winners and which are the losers. According to what he tries on or steers away from, the customer is telling you the same thing at the sample sale that he tells you at Saks. If you see dozens of light blue shirts at the sample sale, and no white or khaki ones, you know that of the three colors in that shirt, the baby blue was a bust. If the baby blue is piled up at Saks, too, same thing. Doesn't matter if it's displayed in a romantic environment or at a sample sale. When the product's good, it will sell. And when it isn't, it won't.

TWENTY-FOUR

Lucky Charms

ON MONDAY NIGHT, September 10, 2001, I was booked on an American Airlines 767 to California, where I was scheduled to make personal appearances at four Nordstrom stores and a Macy's fashion show. It was pouring rain—so bad the Red Sox were rained out at Yankee Stadium—and we sat on the runway for almost five hours. I'm no fan of flying anyway, and this was definitely not a good omen.

I used to love to fly. In the early 1970s, when I was a buyer for Louis, I would take the Eastern shuttle back and forth to New York all the time. One night, after a dinner date in New York, I decided to catch the last flight, the ten o'clock, back to Boston.

It was a clear night. We took off on time, the stars were bright, and everything was smooth. I was sitting next to a flight attendant in uniform (one of the Eastern personnel on board who was deadheading to home base), and life was good. Suddenly, after ten minutes in the air, the floor dropped, my stomach rose up to my throat, and I thought I was going to vomit. Then silence. Eerie, terrifying silence. No engines, no hums or roars, no nothing. After thirty horrifying seconds, the red lights above the storage compartments started flashing. Deafening alarms, like air-raid sirens, started blaring: *uhh uhh uhh*. The attendants collecting the fares left their cart, grabbed seats, and strapped themselves in. I looked at the one next to me, and the fear in her eyes made me even more afraid—especially when she gripped her armrests and started mumbling a prayer. When you see the crew in panic mode, what the hell are *you* supposed to do? "Okay, fine. We're going to die." But not until the money cart went rolling past me toward the cockpit—like the furniture sliding across the dining room on the *Titanic*—did I really believe it.

After what seemed like an eternity, the plane pulled out of its dive—which we knew because the money cart started running back the other way—and the pilot calmly announced, "Ladies and gentlemen, we had some engine trouble. We'll be returning to LaGuardia."

It was the longest ten minutes of my life. I've been on plenty of planes that have had to turn around, but this one was definitely in an emergency situation. As we approached LaGuardia, we could see fire engines and foam on the runway. I got back on the horse and flew to Boston next morning, but the spirit of airborne adventure was gone.

So here we were nearly thirty years later, in a state of raging cabin fever at JFK. Not until eleven o'clock did the plane take off. But the engines didn't cut out, and I got to San Diego.

The next morning all hell broke loose.

The first call came from home. "Daddy," Ari begged me, "whatever you do, please don't fly." Not that I even could have, since all planes were grounded. But I had to get home to my family. How? Trains, buses, and rental cars were booked solid. This was a case of supply and demand, and the only way to get there was by car. It took two days to line up the only available one: a limo, complete with two drivers, for a staggering $8,000 (and they probably could have held me up for more).

The trip took us fifty-four hours straight across—and quite a picture we made, stopping for gas and burgers at the 7-Eleven in our ominous black stretch limo, the last thing you'd expect to see emerging from the sagebrush. This was no freewheeling Kerouac saga, no folksy Steinbeck jaunt. This was Odysseus Abboud in a sweat to get home.

In those two days, the world had changed. People were cordial and caring—catastrophe does that—but the tough town had become vulnerable. Fashion Week was canceled, and Bryant Park, with its empty tents, became a ghost town. The stores were empty, too. Who'd go shopping when downtown was a smoldering war zone? My office is diagonically across Fifth Avenue from St. Patrick's cathedral, and I'd stand at the window watching daily funeral processions. Flags were flying, bagpipes were playing, crowds were weeping, and for weeks and weeks we stayed in a psychological state of emergency. Every time a siren screamed past, we'd stop and stare, worried that this was The Next One.

A few days after I returned, I got a call from the FBI. A couple of agents wanted to come up to the office. What the hell? Had a red flag gone up when they saw my Middle Eastern name on the passenger list?

"I didn't think of that," said the FBI guy on the phone. "I know you from *Imus in the Morning*."

"That doesn't make me a terrorist." The funny designer.

"We need to talk to you. We want to show you some things."

The cleaning crew had found box cutters on my plane, planted between the seats. The FBI brought a book of 200 photographs—among them, the suspected hijackers—because they wanted me to take a look and see if I recognized any of them from the flight.

But no matter what they said or didn't say, I think they also wanted to take a look at *me*. I fit the profile.

I was used to being "noticed," or observed. I'd been humiliated in the world's biggest airports for *years*. We forget that terrorism existed before September 11, but there were a lot of hijackings back in the 1980s, and whenever I came back through Milan I'd get pulled aside.

One look at the passport and they'd slap a green sticker on my luggage. I knew what that meant. Everybody else had red, white, blue, or whatever.

"What is your name?"

"Abboud. I was here a month ago," I'd tell them, but they didn't care. You'd figure they'd have me in the computer so they could say, "Here's Abboud again. He's okay. He's here every month." But no. We danced the same dance every time.

"Country of origin?"

"America."

"No, no. What is the origin of your name?"

I knew the game, and I was going to drag it out. "It's Middle Eastern."

"Which country, specifically?"

"It's Lebanese."

"Would you step over here, please?" The whole thing. They'd take me out of line and behind a curtain, ask me more questions— "How many times have you been to Italy? What were you doing in Italy?"— and go through every inch of my luggage. It was so insulting, so degrading. Where it took anyone else ten minutes to go through Customs, it took me an hour. If it happened only once, I might have forgiven them. But it happened twelve or thirteen times over a couple of years. And these guys were armed with Uzis.

But when the feds came to question me, I supported them—and not just because they were wearing great textured sport coats and my kind of print ties. I knew they were doing their job. When I told Ed Nardoza, the associate editorial director at Fairchild (the publisher of *DNR* and *Women's Wear Daily*) about my experience, he wanted the story for *DNR's* cover. I was sensitive about it for a lot of reasons—my family, my heritage, my career—and my sisters wanted me to keep quiet because they worried I'd become some kind of target, but *DNR* handled it nicely. As I told David Lipke, who wrote the piece, "I was a little surprised, but not offended. Some of my friends are more indignant, but I understand it. . . . It's just an unfortunate fact of life; you're just keyed into these things now."

Right after that, I was scheduled to go on CNN to talk about Yves Saint Laurent's retirement after forty years. But Aaron Brown said, "We don't want to talk about Yves Saint Laurent, do we? Let's talk about your background, and about the FBI." So we did. I talked about it on Mike Barnicle's radio show in Boston, and I talked about it on the Imus show. So did I use the press or did the press use me? A little bit of both. But my agenda was not about self-glorification. It was about humiliation and suspicion. For the public, the event was a hot button for the moment. But it continues to be hot for any Lebanese guy who rides a plane.

What I didn't say in any interview was that I had a traveling companion: my Beanie Baby. He's a little black-and-white dog named Spot, and I love him because he connects me to my daughters (from whose room I'd snatched him one night). They make fun of me and threaten to tell their friends, so I bribe them—promise to take them shopping at Limited Too if they don't tell anybody. Works every time.

When I flew to California that night, Spot was in my bag. If there hadn't been a thunderstorm, and we hadn't been stuck on the tarmac for four hours, and somebody in first class had actually *used* the box cutters, I could have been on a plane bound for oblivion. Was it fate or timing that saved my life?

It was Spot.

Another talisman. I was very pleased in 1998 when General Motors asked four designers—Dana Buchman, Max Azria, Vivienne Tam, and me—to design one-of-a-kind vehicles to raffle off for Concept:Cure, an initiative by GM to benefit breast cancer research (which really hits home for me, since the disease killed my mother and my sister Nancy).

My assignment was a GMC Sierra, and I decided I was going to get an Indiana Jones thing happening. I made the exterior bronze and olive, with bronze hubcaps. Inside, I did shearling headrests and textured leather seats. The back of the seats was covered in our signature plaid—a Russell plaid of beige, ochre, bronze, and russett—with saddlebags for storage. On the ceiling, I put an old-fashioned world map in ivory and sepia; on the back bed, where you haul stuff, I attached a canvas cover with leather straps. The dashboard was khaki, the steering wheel was padded in leather, and the instrumentation was trimmed in brass, like on a beautiful old yacht.

But the object of my obsession was a smooth "worry stone" (which helps reduce stress when you rub it) for the middle of the console. An irregular, organic shape at the center of this sleek, machine-tooled vehicle—the contrast knocked me out. Connecting with nature has always been lucky for me. Keeps me grounded. I got so fixated on it that I drove back to Great Point, where I'd gotten the stones for my sweaters. It was a stubborn, risky move on a rainy, foggy night, because you can't see where you're going, there are lots of drop-offs along the beach, and if you don't get stuck in wet sand, you'll get swept out to sea. I went alone because no one would go with me. Lynn thought it was nuts.

I think it was my designer genes.

Kahlil Gibran, the poet and artist, was my grandfather's first cousin. Like everybody else in high school and college I read *The Prophet*, but otherwise all I knew about Gibran was that he was a famous relative who'd lived and died before I was born. Later I learned that we had a few things in common.

He came from a town of ivory buildings and rust-red roofs, and he did his drawings in sepias and grays. My colors, all of them.

He wrote only in brown-covered notebooks. So do I.

He loved natural wood, dark earth, waving trees. So do I.

And he "cherished a collection of smallish stones, 'brought from the shores of every sea upon the planet,'" wrote his biographer, Barbara Young, in *This Man from Lebanon*. "He would finger them with more true pleasure than a hoarder of gold with his shining pieces."

Me, too.

*   *   *

Of course you *can* push your luck too far. "General Motors and Joseph Abboud are proud to present the GMC Sierra," said the announcer over the loudspeaker at Fenway Park. The truck was being exhibited on the concourse, and for the first time in my life I was on the field (this was before the opening-pitch adventure), with my wife and daughters and mother-in-law. Here came the Marine Band, and then my hero, Nomar Garciaparra, running out of the dugout to introduce himself and tell me he was a fan of *mine*! We were promoting the vehicle like crazy, even in TV commercials, for a raffle.

So what did I do next? Too much.

The following February in New York, I brought out the Sierra for another bow. During the finale of my fashion show, a General Motors guy drove it out—through smoke and music and models—on the runway.

I got slammed.

"A final cautionary note, inspired by the Abboud show, to designers during a Fashion Week sponsored by General Motors," wrote Constance White the next day in the *New York Times*. "A burst of smoke, music playing overhead and the dramatic appearance of a car on a runway do not bring to mind fashion so much as 'The Price Is Right.'"

It was the right cause, but I was on the wrong track.

TWENTY-FIVE

Whose Image Is It, Anyway?

IT WAS A NAVY-AND-IVORY lamb's-wool turtleneck with big felt letters—an ivory J and A—sewn on the front, and it changed me forever. I was four years old, and my mother had knit it for me to wear in a school picture. But I wouldn't take it off. Clark Kent put on his cape with an S and became Superman. My sweater did the same for me. Through all the years and all the collections, there has never been a more perfect sweater in my life.

I didn't know it yet, but I had a personal style.

Style ought to be personal. It defines you to *yourself*, not to somebody else. It includes all the things you choose, from the small ceramic bowl on your coffee table to the baseball cap on your head. Or the watch on your wrist. Watches are fun, like pens. At the gym, or with jeans and stuff, I usually wear a stainless-steel Tag Heuer. It makes me look like a rugged guy who can handle anything. In the office, my

Baume & Mercier with the brown face or my 1935 rose-gold Rolex with a cognac-colored crocodile band. It's one of the first bubble-backs, and Lynn gave it to me for my thirtieth birthday. What I hate on men is a delicate, thin-faced watch. They think, "Whoo, how elegant and chic." I think, "Whoo, how feminine." It's almost like wearing a pinky ring. And on a guy with big wrists and big hands, it's horrible.

When style pleases you, you've found your own. (I look at my two daughters swanning around in pink bell-bottoms and lime green-and-yellow tie dyes—and whatever I felt about those colors before, they're so right for *them*.) It's easy to fall into the hands of a hot designer and follow a trendy path, but the word "fashion" screams of sameness. Be who you are and develop your own flair.

That said, there are some universals. At some point every guy wants to be James Dean, so every guy should have a great leather jacket. If it's styled right, then it's not the hot jacket of today or tomorrow. It's the great jacket of his *life*. Of all the clothes I've designed, my favorite piece is a drawstring thigh-length jacket made of distressed whiskey-color leather. It's very rugged—I put it on and I'm Joe the Marlboro Man—and though it's fifteen years old and almost falling apart, people still ask where they can get it.

A lot of men buy clothes for an alternative image of themselves, and I'm all for that. There's nothing taboo or shameful about being in touch with fantasy; it just takes confidence. But fantasy should go just so far. When a designer decides to reprise clothes of the 1970s, the idea sounds as if it might be fun to do a fashion show around—disco stuff and all that—but the clothes won't work because they aren't right for now. How do you make 1970s-looking clothes for the twenty-first century?

Or the 1950s thing. You hear a designer saying, "Well, I feel very *fifties* this season, in little gingham-checked short-sleeved shirts and plain-front gray pants," and it's embarrassing. Those things don't translate. Fashion should make reference to the good things of the past, but it shouldn't try to raise the dead. No one wants to wear *Leave It to*

Beaver. We were kids then, and we grew out of that. It was a historically unattractive time—every man looked like a CPA—so why would we bring it back? Aren't we supposed to be an industry of creativity?

Or grunge. The worst. Nobody should pay designer prices to look like that. You can go to the Salvation Army.

Women's wear thrives on being provocative and experimental, but fashions of the moment—whenever the moment was, or is—make no sense for men. You don't tell a Wall Streeter to go shop at Gucci or Prada, because Gucci and Prada are not about the businessman. They're about the rock star and the fashion victim. So even if the names are *hot*, they're not hot for all comers. Most clothes are going to be worn on the elevator, not the runway, and the people wearing them don't—and shouldn't—give a damn about the maestro's inspiration.

I passed a Gucci window recently and saw a pair of bell-bottoms, a very wide paisley tie, and a shirt with a long collar. Now, I don't care if that outfit cost $3,000; you would have thrown it away after a season. It's like seeing a horror film where someone jumps out of the closet: It's fine the first time, but the jolt weakens with every rerun. Am I suggesting that Gucci and other luxury brands actually build obsolescence into their clothes? Yes. I'm not talking about poor workmanship here. I'm talking about ephemeral whimsy.

If you'd happened to buy a Joseph Abboud suit that day instead, you'd still be wearing it, because my stuff is designed to go the distance. The changes are so subtle that a suit or jacket of today is not so different from a suit or jacket of five or six years ago. The trained eye will notice that the button placement is a little higher or the shoulders are a bit narrower—but by two inches, not six. Does that make me a better designer? Maybe it does, maybe it doesn't. Maybe it makes me the tortoise and not the hare. But I know what the job is, and it's not to make you look like yesterday's news three months later, not to make you feel like an idiot for spending so much money, not to make you look like you came out of a time machine. It's to make you look good.

* * *

Individual style has as much to do with attitude and carriage as it has to do with shirt and tie. For me and my fellow baby boomers, John F. Kennedy was the first president whose style we really admired. (And how could we not, after Dwight D. Eisenhower, a great president but a lousy dresser?) Kennedy carried that Cambridge thing with natural-shoulder soft suits and button-down shirts. He was preppy before there *was* preppy, and it fit him like a glove.

But it wasn't the clothes themselves that gave him style. It was the way he wore them, the way he touched his tie, the way he put his hand in his pocket. Bobby Kennedy Jr. has a wonderful picture of his uncle Jack and uncle Joe when they were in their late twenties—one in a double-breasted suit, the other in a single-breasted, both elegantly rumpled. It's not what you'd see in an ad or catalog shot, but you can imagine the way the clothes must have *moved*. It's one of the most stylish pictures I've ever seen.

From the sublime to the felonious: John Gotti was a handsome guy with an out-there style and a real knack for wearing clothes. He might wear a very tailored double-breasted coat with black Chesterfield collar and peak lapel or a Brioni suit with shiny fabric, sharp cut, and square shoulders. Whatever you call it—the wise guy look, mob chic—it wasn't the black shirt and white tie from gangster films of the 1940s. It was beautiful custom Italian, not in the soft Armani image but in the high Roman style: arrogant, imperious, and very interesting. This kind of style sense is innate. It's nothing you're told (not that anybody was going to tell John Gotti about style or anything else). He always looked polished, even in a crisis—sort of the tragic hero, if you can consider Gotti a hero—and was the epitome of the boss, the guy that everybody in his line of work probably wanted to be.

We all have our role models.

The Prince of Wales. Fashion and style are part of his every waking hour, and the know-how is in his genes. His Savile Row suits are always beautifully tailored, he wears the right ties, and he understands when to mix a kilt and a dinner jacket. (Note: Don't do this if you're not from the British Isles, and preferably the prince of one of them. The sun never sets on guys who look dumb in kilts.) He appreciates tweeds, cheviots, tattersall shirts, and country shooting jackets. It would be swell to be involved in Charles's wardrobe, but he doesn't need me. Nobody tells the Prince of Wales what to wear.

John Kerry. Handsome and stately, he carried off the campaign with innate style (and without any Naomi Wolf-Al Gore-style silliness). He's Ivy League in the truest sense—on the good, not the hokey, side of preppy—whether he's at Fenway Park with his sleeves rolled up or at the Capitol in a two-button navy pinstripe. He knows how to tie a tie, how to smooth down the suit. It's the whole package.

Kevin Costner. All-American handsome, polite, sexy—the guy every girl wants to bring home to her parents—and the all-American sportswear guy. He looks great in leathers and suedes (see *Dances with Wolves, Wyatt Earp, Open Range*). He looks great in jeans and white polo shirts. He even looks good in golf clothes, which ain't easy.

Tom Wolfe. Do I love the occasional white suit? Yeah. I love it, I have it, I design it. But I see it as less dressy than Tom does. To me, it's the right suit for a party at Newport. To him, it's right for every day—with the spats and the hats—and I admire the flamboyance.

Bruce Springsteen is a different kind of hero, the workin' guy with the Frye boots and jeans the way they should be worn: tight. He's gutsy, hard-rock, sexy, gritty, and in such good shape he can wear his shirt open with vests that show his waist. If I were a rock star, I'd dress just like him. I don't have the bracelets and headband, but I do have a dark striped shirt like his, and I definitely have the vests.

Bill Clinton. He'd survived the nightmarish scandal over Monica, he was president again, and he was back in business. The cameras were rolling, the nation was watching, and out he came in a dark navy suit, a snow-white shirt, and a solid red tie—to stand smack in front of the American flag. Translation: *I am America*. It was a brilliantly staged moment, and an indelible image.

Ernest Hemingway. The ultimate masculine vision. The cowel-neck sweater wasn't a "fashion" cowel-neck, but a fisherman's sweater. The safari shirt wasn't something he bought in the designer department at Saks. The rumpled linen suit wasn't rumpled because he was cool and Armaniesque; it was rumpled because when you're in Havana, that's what linen does. I'd design him a linen suit—a big hopsack weave—in tobacco, light beige, ivory, or khaki. It would be strong and powerful. The knees would bag out, and he wouldn't give a rat's ass.

Hemingway had a handsome, weather-worn face, and his beard—full and straight and cropped close—complemented a strong jawline. It sort of went with the guy catching marlins and running with the bulls. But facial hair is tricky.

I wore a beard in Paris, but that was then. Now I like the clean-shaven look. But there are guys who think facial hair is swell. If you want to look like Hemingway or Dennis Miller or Santa Claus, why not? If you have a weak chin, give it a try. You'll need a good mustache, too, for balance and because it's part of the framework. But you need to have been blessed with a good beard line. If it has holes and patches in it, you'll end up with a wispy thing that looks dirty and unkempt—unless you're Brad Pitt, who can get away with anything.

In my opinion, it's a full beard or no beard. Once you start playing with that delicate little fuzz tracing the jaw, you start to look like the villain in an Errol Flynn movie. If it's scraggly, you look like you've just gotten out of a prison camp. So it has to be shaped and well trimmed, or you get it cutting into your collar and dangling over your tie.

As for the hair on your head, it has a natural form and shape—whether it's a lot of hair or a little—so don't fake it. If you're going gray, go gray. If you're going bald, go bald. Look at Ed Harris, James Taylor, Sean Connery. Bald can be very sexy. The long hair thing is just trying too hard. If some guy is an artist and he paints by the beach, that's cool. But if you sell mutual funds, get a haircut. It's just a question of environment.

There's a cultural thing going on now where dyed hair is okay in some cases, like when pop stars and young baseball players become bottle blonds. That's fine when you're young and cool and punky, but once you get over thirty and enter the real world, you've got to go with what you've got. Don't comb it over and don't color it. When a guy dyes his hair brown, it turns a creepy red color, and the guy's face and age no longer connect to his hair. A guy in his forties or fifties with jet-black hair just looks ridiculous. And these Just for Men commercials where the gray disappears and the girl swoons? Guys are such suckers.

A woman may soften her hair color to look younger, and she also has cosmetics in her repertoire. Well-applied makeup is a beautiful thing, an art form. But when a guy colors his hair, he's still stuck with the same craggy face. His hair's brown now but he's still got wrinkles, still got a double chin. You think he's going to get the babes? He's not gettin' the babes! What's he going to do, tint his chest hair? He'd have to get into a vat! It says a lot about the guy, and it's the opposite of what he's trying to say.

Giorgio Armani, Oleg Cassini, Ralph Lauren—the grayer, whiter, and more silver their hair gets, the better they look. Then there's Karl Lagerfeld, whose snow-white ponytail is his trademark. But, you know, ponytails on guys. I hate ponytails on guys.

I'm still salt-and-pepper. Sometimes I cut my own hair because curly hair is easy. You just sort of snip and trim a little bit. I used to go to a guy in Connecticut, but it was really a woman's place, and I was paying $48 for the same haircut I'd get for $12 at a barbershop—if there still were any barbershops.

Back in the 1950s, your father took you every two weeks to get a haircut. There'd be a bunch of guys there, and maybe a couple of *Esquire* magazines, and if you got lucky there'd be a *Playboy*, but that was usually for the older guys in back. You'd sit in the chair, and in fifteen minutes you had a haircut and you were done and the next guy stood up. But there are no more barbers. Who goes to barber school anymore?

It's very weird, a guy going into a beauty salon. One woman's getting her nails done, another one's getting her hair washed, another one's under the dryer, all that stuff a guy doesn't even *know* about. When you call Information, you don't even know what to *ask* for. "I'd like Chez Hugo. It's a beauty salon."

Frédéric Fekkai cuts great hair, makes great men's products, and has a beautiful shop on 57th Street with a lot of archways, terra-cotta reliefs, and classical figures. My kind of taste, so I relate to him. But I feel funny getting my hair cut there, too—not just because it costs $180 to cut the same amount of hair that would cost $12 at the barbershop, but because the clientele is mostly female. I saw a guy in there whose kids go to school with my kids and I almost felt like we'd discovered each other in a strip joint, on the sly. We were both in our little smocks, pretending it didn't matter.

Guys are much more aware of grooming today—from our wives, from the media—and yet somewhere in our genetic memory we know it just doesn't feel right. We'd still rather say, "Yeah, I just went to the barbershop and paid twelve bucks for a haircut," even if we know intellectually that we'd get a better haircut at the salon. Maybe in 10,000 years things will be different, but the caveman in us still feels goofy in a smock surrounded by women with tinfoil in their hair.

No one yet has figured out to do a "Hey, how ya doin'?" kind of beauty parlor place for us—and I think there's a world to be explored out there. I'm not talking about a "Let's have a beer and some peanuts" joint with sawdust on the floor, the game on TV, and oversized tubes of he-man face scrub. Nor am I talking about some Roman bath staffed by sudsy chicks as haircutters, receptionists, and masseuses. What I mean is an environment where a guy could talk sports and not feel awkward, where he could get a massage or facial or body wax ("Hey, why don't you take off your *sweater?*" we used to shout wittily to the hairy football players in the locker room). A place where we'd get intelligent information about shaving and vitamin supplements. A place for guys who've finally come out of the quagmire and stopped dragging their knuckles. Why not?

Nobody's done a good job of marketing skin care and body products either, so we have to shop for men's products in a drugstore or department store. If they're there at all, they're stuck back in a corner someplace, and we have to creep around mumbling about moisturizers and secretly sniffing shampoos—the middle-aged man's version of buying a condom.

TWENTY-SIX

Campaign Promises

SINCE WE NEED to be in touch with our customers, I guess we have to do surveys once in a while to hear what they think about our ads. But for my money, focus groups are basically the blind leading the blind. One lead guy decides it's his moment to say something relatively intelligent, and the rest parrot him. These people don't do what we do every day. They're regular folks who get a few bucks to come in and talk about men's suits. And what do we learn? "That model's too young," or "Why is he on the beach if you sell tailored clothing?"

Focus groups are not gospel, and anybody who tries to base advertising on them is nuts. You've got to look at the "information" they provide on what you're doing wrong and then make your own decisions, because if you need outsiders to tell you what to be, then you can call yourself anything you want to, because you're not Joseph Abboud or Ralph Lauren or anything else. You're a product.

One of our best campaigns just *happened*. The stars were aligned, and everything came together like magic. There wasn't some group figuring out how to do it. It's 1990. We're now big players, and we have to figure out how to make our own territory and create an image. What we need is a photographer to get us to a new place, the way Bruce Weber did for Ralph Lauren. I see some l'Oréal ads—the most magnificent shots of the most gorgeous hair—and I know that whoever shot these is the guy for me.

It turns out to be Fabrizio Ferri, this bear of a man with a big beard and loose clothes—handsome, almost Roman-looking, with hair that's always perfectly disheveled. He's not in great shape, not at all, but there's something very sexy about this guy. He's one passionate artist. He's shooting hair, not fashion, but we decide to hire him. Our models are a guy named Eric and Joanna Pakula, the movie actress.

The campaign is about color and texture and sensuality, and Fabrizio wants to shoot in the desert. So we schlep five or six people and mountains of clothes out to Joshua Tree National Park in California. Our creative advertising guy is Tyler Smith from Boston, the art director I loved working with in my Louis days. Lynn's along, too, just to hang out. We've been married for fifteen years at this point, and we have a carefree life, traveling all over the world together. While our friends are having kids and staying home, we're taking off for Como, Paris, and now this godforsaken place. Lately, as we've been closing in on forty, we're starting to look at each other and ask, "What about kids?"

We get to LAX at eleven o'clock at night, everybody's exhausted, and now we have to drive to the middle of the Mojave Desert. The 29 Palms Inn sounds like some posh resort, right? Wrong. The accommodations are called "adobe bungalows," but whatever they're called, they're one-room cinder-block boxes, the worst things you ever saw.

We're out in the middle of nowhere, it's two-thirty in the morning, and now we're hearing coyotes howling out in the desert. Joanna Pakula is not a happy girl. She's terrified, and refuses to stay in her room alone. I'm thinking, We're spending a zillion dollars, we're going to shoot in a few hours, and she won't stay in the room. Lynn is thinking the same thing.

The three of us are crowded together in this austere, uncharming space, when my wife pipes up. "I don't mind," she tells Joanna. "Joseph can stay with you."

I turn around and stare at her. Joanna's a beautiful girl, and I have the feeling she might even say yes. Not because of my great sex appeal, but because she's so desperate not to be alone.

"I don't think that's going to work," I tell them both.

So we drive thirty or forty miles back to a Best Western. We put her in a choice room (can't be on the outside, got to be on the inside). It's three-thirty, and now we drive back to the cabin in the desert that's good enough for us. It has to be. It's not exactly the Ritz Carlton, but life is imperfect, and what else are we going to do? Sure, I get depressed in tacky surroundings, but this is no time to be a diva.

So we make the best of it. And here's what else we make: a baby. That's where Lynn conceives Lila, our first daughter. (If Joanna *had* been my roommate, I later reflect, would *she* be having my baby right now?) It was a night to remember in more than a few ways.

The other magic to come out of the situation was Fabrizio's baby. When the sun came up, we went into Joshua Tree, where there were salt flats and magnificent stones. The hair and makeup people had made Joanna, who was pink and blond, tawny—and Eric, who was dark, bronzy. The campaign ran in *Mirabella* and *Vogue*, and it really set the tone for us because it showed product in an uncommonly sensual way. The effect was almost surreal, with beautifully dressed models in leather jackets posing in the middle of Death Valley.

So three years later we used Fabrizio to shoot the first ads for our Joseph Abboud fragrance. This time the model was Marcus Schenkenberg, the hunk du jour. Great build, great body, and Fabrizio shot him naked, because skin was so appropriate to the product. The newsworthy thing here was that Marcus was holding the bottle, making this the first time a fragrance bottle had been incorporated into an ad, rather than superimposed on it.

I held onto Fabrizio and his magic for two or three seasons, but I couldn't keep him. He was becoming a celebrity, fast. Calvin grabbed him (which enraged me because I'd brought him into the fashion side) and usurped his primest time. When we *could* get him, the model we were using would become his girlfriend, and that detracted from the purity of the thing. Eventually, it just got too complicated.

So, unfortunately, did the fragrance.

I wanted to do one because it's part of a guy's image. Clothes, shoes, car, home, grooming, scent—they're all part of the package. You can't have a nice suit, nice shoes, nice grooming, and bad body odor. You can't have a nice fragrance, nice grooming, nice suit, and bad shoes. You just can't. It's all part of interacting and being a man. We can't wear skirts and pretty flowers in our hair. But we can wear a fragrance.

We developed ours with Givaudan Roure in Paris. It was a fascinating process that took forever. We probably went through forty different versions of the scent—weak, strong, spicy, sweet—and by a certain point I think I was able to identify every note in every sample in every unromantic little sterilized aerosol-spray test tube. I loved watching the perfumers and technicians in their white lab coats, loved reading the labels with their meticulous distinctions. In the orange section, for instance, there wasn't anything so obvious as "orange fragrance." We were seeing and sniffing "essence of California orange," "essence of Valencia orange," "essence of Spanish orange," "essence of tangerine." The final result was a brew of lemon, orange, basil, bergamot, black pepper, cardamom, angelica berry, jasmine, violet, coriander, ginger root, thyme, camomile, cedarwood, vetiver, musk, amber, ceylon, and sandalwood. Sounds like the wine list at Jean Georges.

To design the bottle—and other vessels for the aftershave, body cream, bath gel, and deodorant—we hired Pierre Dinand, who is famous for bottling such fragrances as Armani, Opium, Obsession, Eternity, Valentino, Paco Rabanne, and about five hundred more. Mine went into a bottle of deep amber, with a one-piece silver cap. The shape suggested the torso of a man, wide at the shoulders and tapering to the waist, but it was subtle (and nothing like the undulating Man and Woman bottles perpetrated by Jovan in the 1970s).

And then to market, to market.

GFT and I had always counted on building a big business in Europe, so we hooked up with a wonderful little manufacturing company called EuroItalia and planned to launch the fragrance over there. EuroItalia had been very successful with the fragrances for Dolce & Gabbana and Moschino. But their business was primarily in Europe, and ours, it turned out, was not. The Joseph Abboud brand just didn't catch fire there. The strategy was well intentioned, but it wasn't well planned. The pricing was an issue, the marketing was an issue, the name recognition was an issue—all those things, and the pieces didn't connect.

So the fragrance would be sold only in America. But that wasn't easy either. For scents to make sense here, they need big marketing bucks, broad distribution, and critical mass—and EuroItalia was no Estée Lauder. We were in the Sakses and Neimans, but we weren't in the May Companies and Federateds. We had an incredible fragrance and almost no distribution.

I'd always relied on my taste and ability to sense what people wanted, but I didn't understand the dynamics of a European company trying to launch a fragrance in America against the powerhouses that dominate the shelf space. We tried to switch to an American company, but we weren't a household name and didn't have the sort of distribution that could propel big business. Our exclusivity was a drawback. The fragrance never reached the critical mass where it meant anything to the European market. And it didn't mean anything to the American market either

As Pierre Dinand once told *GQ*, "The success of a new fragrance is really the jackpot." I didn't hit the jackpot, but I still wear the fragrance. There are a few bottles available here and there, but the deal is done and the supply is drying up fast.

One naked guy does not a successful launch make. As exposed as Marcus was, we still didn't have enough exposure. Maybe it takes a crowd.

The people at Abercrombie & Fitch thought so, until they got themselves into a controversial spin a couple of years ago. Their product was good, and they knew their audience. Their clothes were preppy and plaid, not sexy—this was no Victoria's Secret—but the advertising went off-key. And the quarterly catalog, which had virtually become a soft-porn magazine with its collegiate models exhibiting more and more skin in every issue, was finally pulled before Christmas of 2003. It was probably driving their business numbers through the roof, but it was also driving parents and Christian conservatives up the wall.

The other problem, which *60 Minutes* addressed in a segment around the same time, was the blond-and-blue-eyed concentration of the cast. I'm not being politically correct here, but I devoutly believe in the diversity of America, and that kind of exclusionary stuff in this day and age is just unreal. If we look at the makeup of today's consumers, we see that beautiful Aryans are a small *minority*. So we in the industry have to understand where the world is when we toss around these advertising campaigns. (Not that Benetton, which was cleverly inclusionary with its "mixed colors" campaign, is necessarily the way to go either. You don't have to be so obvious one way *or* the other.)

In this limelit world everybody wants publicity, but sometimes publicity can backfire. Sure, people will talk about you. But are these the things you want them to say?

The A&F thing was a walk in the park next to Calvin's romp on the wild side. After the Brooke Shields campaign, which seems almost innocent in retrospect, came a raunchier brigade hustling jeans and underwear: Marky Mark grabbing his crotch, assorted young waifs slouching come-hitherly in wood-paneled dens, and the preternaturally hung Travis Fimmel on prominently hung billboards. The ads had less to do with product than porn, and that's what Calvin seemed to be after—lapping up his role as the baddest boy of all. Disingenuously he went on Larry King to defend it, although he was eventually forced to pull the ads.

But Calvin had set the standard. When Yves Saint Laurent retired, he said he was tired of the business because marketing had replaced creativity. And that was before he'd even seen the latest issue of *Vogue Hommes*.

Am I a prude? I don't think so. But I flip the magazine open and look at these menacing shots of guys creeping out of the forest or holding naked babies in their black-gloved palms, and what am I missing? What guy who takes the train every morning is going to wear these clothes? Who are the ads for?

Here's a twiggish Dior model with a carved face who looks like a white Michael Jackson. I'm not sure if it's a boy or girl, but that's okay. The outfit is an unbuttoned white shirt, open leather jacket with lapels, and tight leather pants. Dior's a wonderful brand, a wonderful name, but what am I looking at?

I turn the page to a potential sexual escapade by the Yves Saint Laurent-less house of Yves Saint Laurent. A woman in green satin is standing next to a sofa, bent at a right angle over a guy lying down in a polka-dot velvet jacket with a polka-dot ascot. I don't know what's going to happen, but I sort of wish I were there.

I'm not quite sure where I am in the Prada ad, but I'm really having a hard time. A young man is reclining in a bathtub fully dressed, and there isn't a guy I know—regardless of race, creed, color, or sexual preference—who'd buy anything here. The button-down shirt is a traditional silhouette, but it's printed in a geometric pattern of polyester blue, mud brown, and white. The tie is black, turquoise, and lime green. Perched on his head is a little English tweed hat. I don't understand this. If I'm in the business for another thirty years, I will never understand this. Maybe it would work for Picasso. But even Picasso's wildest *fantasies* were more wearable than this stuff.

The Dolce & Gabbana ad is every guy's nightmare. It looks like a scene out of a film noir in which four men are about to kill you. After they rape you. The setting—a palatial room with paneled walls, bare wood floors, and an antique gilt bed—is in jarring contrast with some very strange clothes. One guy is strapped into a pair of pants suitable for parachute jumping or a round of S&M. Hard to tell if the buckles are attached or an accessory you'd have to buy extra.

With Louis Vuitton, the terror continues. This guy's in a suit too trim and too tight, in an open-legged stance, with a hairdo that would scare Elvis and a wonderful pocketbook-attaché that would embarrass Liberace.

But the piece that could permanently drive me away from the menswear business is the Gucci ad featuring a vampirish, genderless model in sunglasses and *Dr. Zhivago* hat, with canine teeth exposed, gripping a naked baby as if it's about to be eaten.

Okay. Here I am, Mr. Businessman from Des Moines. I've just arrived in Paris, I'm at the Ritz, and I'd like to see what fashion's all about. So I pick up men's *Vogue.* Come on, folks! Nothing in these ads looks like a man. Nothing in these ads would attract any man I know aged twenty to seventy. There is no relationship between the pages I've just described and a guy wearing clothes.

To illustrate an even greater disconnect, I recently picked up an issue of *National Geographic.* On the cover: a picture of two zebras in their natural dressing, playing together. On an inside page: a Helmut Lang ad of two white guys in unnatural dressing, scowling together. The zebras were romping. The guys looked like they'd just woken up. The zebras were wearing stripes. The guys were wearing buckles, metal, and straps. They looked as if they'd gotten off at the wrong stop. If I'm an anthropology professor at Harvard, is this my wardrobe?

Maybe it was a clever way to promote Helmut Lang's name. Being on foreign turf is always provocative, and that's one form of advertising, but if he was trying to sell clothes, he'd just lost the entire Harvard campus. This is what happens to fashion when we forget who we're talking to. If I were running an ad in *National Geographic,* I'd be showing some great tweed jacket or rugged outerwear piece, consistent with the spirit and readership of the magazine.

But maybe that's just me.

TWENTY-SEVEN

The Last Row

I WASN'T THE Best-Looking kid at Roslindale High School in 1968. I wasn't the Most Athletic. I wasn't the Most Likely to Succeed. But I *was* the Best-Dressed. And that was important to me. I owned a zone—that was my piece of the world. Dressing well opened doors for me. It didn't always mean I'd get the job, or get the job done, but it let me get my foot in.

I love clothes. And I love the creative process even more. After the clashes with Bricken, Freedberg, and Southwick . . . after all the ups and downs with GFT, I knew that I was spending too much time on the business side and not nearly enough on the creative. I didn't want to deal with another lease or license agreement. I just wanted to design, which was what I did best.

So in June 2000, at the age of fifty, I sold my trademarks to my Italian partners and associates (who had been GFT and were now called

RCS). I believed this sort of relationship would give us all the greatest platform to build an empire. By shedding the administrative and organizational aspects, I'd now be free to focus on pursuing new ideas. I could roll up my sleeves and do innovative things in the fashion world (a world that *requires* innovative things in order to survive) to the exclusion of everything else.

The creative life isn't about ego gratification, but about curiosity—the what-ifs and why-nots. That's what drives me forward and forces me to face the challenges and overcome the obstacles. That's what allows me to dream the dreams.

But sometimes the dreams turn into nightmares. The decision to divorce myself from the business side unexpectedly blew up in my face. It was a matter of corporate thinking versus artistic expression. The creative freedom I thought I was getting turned out to be anything but. After diplomacy failed, the only recourse, unfortunately, was litigation.

It was painful to spend time reading legal briefs instead of *GQ* and to meet with my New York lawyers instead of my Italian silk suppliers. But that's what I had to do. I'd made adjustments before and usually managed to find myself in a better place, and I expected, somehow, to do it again. The things that don't kill you really can make you stronger—and with the heartbreak and frustration of the ongoing battle, there were times I felt like an absolute Schwarzenegger.

In April 2004, J. W. Childs Associates, a venture-capital firm from Boston—Boston!—purchased JA Apparel, the company I'd founded in 1988, from RCS. Not only were the new owners good guys, but the new president and CEO was none other than Marty Staff, my old pal from Polo, who'd morphed from button-downs and rep ties to funky T-shirts and bandanas while building an enormous business at Hugo Boss. The fact that somebody I'd worked with twenty years ago should walk back into my life, with the same twinkle in his eye and a lot more savvy, was absolutely cosmic.

So the good news is: Nightmares do end. You wake up, it's a sunny day, and even with the vestiges of panic still dancing around the edge of your consciousness, you know you're okay. In fact, the situation with RCS had been worse than a nightmare and more like a coma or near-death experience. But the veil was lifted. I felt like Sleeping Beauty in a gray flannel suit, kissed by a saddle-shoed prince.

Out came my beloved archive of old swatch books—the DNA of my career, the history of my seasons, the roadmap to what's next—and I watched Marty and the new merchandisers getting turned on by the herringbone glen plaids, covert twills and gabardines, antique diamond patterns, sharkskin windowpanes, silken camel hairs, bleeding madrases, and vintage stripes I'd designed for my suits and dress shirts in the late 1980s and early 1990s. In came the respect and recognition for what I'd done when I started the business and was itching to do again. Back came the energy that had been gone so long from the office, and the laughs.

"I've basically invested all my money in this company. I'm broke now. That's how much I believe in this opportunity," Marty told *DNR* when the story broke. "I love Joseph and consider him a great friend," he added. "He's a brilliant designer and it would be stupid to do Joseph Abboud without Joseph on board."

Nobody wants to be stupid, so Marty and I teamed up. This time—like Ralph with Peter Strom, Calvin with Barry Schwartz, Saint Laurent with Pierre Bergé, Armani with Sergio Galeotti—I got me a partner with vision, charisma, and balls.

This time, it's our time.

An August evening, and Fred Wilpon takes me to a game at KeySpan Park in Coney Island. Fred's Mets have a minor-league team there, the Brooklyn Cyclones—named after the world-famous roller coaster. He's Sandy Koufax's best friend and an important guy in my life, too. He's wise, a mentor. He's a guy of impeccable style, the model of success in his beautifully cut Italian suits. He's the Brooklyn kid who made very, very good. He's also the older brother I never had.

I've sat in a Palm Beach Jacuzzi with Fred and talked about baseball. I've sat at the Four Seasons, in limos, and at a major-league ball-park in Tokyo with Fred and talked about baseball. Now, on my very first trip to Coney Island, I'm sitting with Fred at the top of KeySpan, the intimate little field his family built on the site of the old Steeple-chase Park.

It's a dark and stormy night, as so many nights of revelation are. Patchy sun, crashing thunder, torrential rain, then new rays piercing the clouds. Almost biblical.

The Cyclones are playing the Pittsburgh Cutters, not that it matters. In spite of the crazy weather, this is the ultimate baseball experience: a hot-dog-scented game in a small-town setting right out of the 1950s. KeySpan is so tiny you can almost reach out and touch the players. From its 7,500 seats you can see the boardwalk, the Atlantic Ocean, the iconic Cyclone (decorated with a thousand lights and looking like a Picasso mosaic), and whatever else is left of Coney's razzmatazz.

The pregame ceremony pays tribute to NAT's Kids (aka the Neigh-borhood All-Star Team), an educational-recreational program named after Fred's father that does good things for urban New York kids. This is Fred's way of honoring his dad—just as my throwing out the first pitch at Fenway was my way of honoring mine. Naturally, I men-tion the parallel. Then I mention that for this book, my sister Mara has just sent a picture of our parents taken on their New York honeymoon in 1932: Joe and Lila Abboud, young and hopeful, snapped in front of a woven wooden structure at Coney Island.

Fred points to the Cyclone.

In that instant, I see my parents. I see them strolling along Surf Avenue still reeling, hands sticky with cotton candy, approaching the grand entrance to Steeplechase Park and the Pavilion of Fun that once was *here*, almost precisely where I'm sitting. I see them hopping aboard the steeplechase ride, which once was *there*, where the outfield is now. I see them racing mechanical horses on infinite steel tracks, and galloping off into another sunset.

In this very place, seventy-two years ago.

When you knit a sweater, you finish it with something called the linking stitch. This goes into the very last row and locks the piece together. In the owner's box, Fred and I are in the very last row, and *everything's* coming together: Brooklyn and Boston (even the B's on the baseball caps are similar), family and fortune, then and now.

When we leave the ballpark, Fred and I are no longer talking baseball. But we are discussing a game plan.

"Sometimes it's okay to have your head in the *veltnroym*," he says. The word means *outer space* in Yiddish. *Out of this world.* "Now you can dream even bigger dreams, do bigger things. Choose where you want to go next."

The air smells of brine and wet sand. The streets are washed clean. And in the distance, the Cyclone threads its wonderful risky course, up and down and out of this world.

ACKNOWLEDGMENTS

WRITING A BOOK, like designing a collection, is an evolutionary process. You start with an idea, then add shape and color, pattern and passion. But you don't do it alone. The creative team who helped weave *Threads*: David Black, my agent, who got it on the runway; David Hirshey, my editor, who styled it perfectly; and Ellen Stern, my partner, who knows me better than I do.

INDEX

Abboud, Ari (daughter), 41, 43, 199
Abboud, Jeanette (sister), 48, 154
Abboud, Joe (father), 42, 46–47, 51–52, 71–72, 233
Abboud, Joseph
on advertising campaigns, 221–29 (see also marketing)
Council of Fashion Designers of America awards, 152–57
early life and family, 46–53, 71–72, 150–51 (see also individual names of Abboud family)
European buying trips for Louis Boston, 81–89, 172–73
European experience at Sorbonne in Paris, France, 65–70
on fashion design, 11–23 (see also fashion design)
as fashion designer with Barry Bricken, 113–116
as fashion designer with Ralph Lauren, 105–12
as fashion designer with Southwick, 90–91
flying experiences, 205–8
GMC Sierra design, 209–11
high school and college years, 54–64, 230
homosexual stereotype and, 33, 40, 180

on home style and earth colors, 158–65 (see also colors)
international fashion shows, 143–51 (see also fashion shows)
Joseph Abboud label (see Joseph Abboud label)
Lebanese ethnicity, 52–53, 129–30, 205–10
legal issues, 115–16, 124–28, 166–68
on markdown sales and outlet stores, 200–204
on media visibility, 32–40 (see also celebrities; press)
on models, 133–42 (see also models)
personal appearances, 41–45, 146–47
on retail stores, 184–92 (see also retail stores)
sale and restart of JA Apparel company, 230–34
as salesman at Louis Boston, 59–62, 71–80
as salesman with Ralph Lauren, 91–104 (see also Lauren, Ralph)
on selling to men, 193–99 (see also men; menswear)
on specialty stores, 24–31 (see also specialty stores)
sports and (see sports)
on style, 212–20 (see also style)
on suits, 1–10 (see also suits)

suit size, 22, 99, 107
ties, 166–75 (*see also* ties)
women's wear, 176–83 (*see also*
  women; women's wear)
Abboud, Lila (daughter), 31, 41, 43, 72,
  223
Abboud, Lila Sallah (mother), 48,
  50–51, 66, 74, 209, 212, 233
Abboud, Lynn Weinstein (wife), 87–88,
  93, 109, 119, 156–57, 213, 222–23
Abboud, Mara (sister), 48, 233
Abboud, Nancy (sister), 48, 74, 209
Abercrombie & Fitch, 31, 226
advertising, 182, 221–29. See also marketing
African collection, 111
airports, ethnicity and, 205–10
Allen, Woody, 100
Anderson-Little, 55–56
appearances, personal, 41–45, 146–47
Appolonia, 80
Armani, Giorgio, 3, 15, 36, 190, 197,
  232
Arnold, Peter, 154
assistant designers, 15, 18
Australia, family in, 150–51
awards, CFDA, 152–57, 176

band-collar Nehru jackets, 17–18
Barbera, Luciano, 172–73
bargain stores, 201–3
Barneys, 28
baseball. *See* Boston Red Sox; Brooklyn
  Cyclones
Bashford, Wilkes, 30
Baume & Mercier watches, 213
beauty salons, men and, 218–20
Beebe, Tom, 184
Ben Sussan, 86–87
Bentley LaRosa Salasky, 129, 191
Bergdorf Goodman, 28–29, 120
Bergé, Pierre, 15, 232
Bergen, Candice, 100
Best Menswear Designer awards,
  155–57
Bianchi mills, 171
Black, David, 2–3

black color, 160
Blakely, Susan, 80
blazers, navy, 23, 161
Bloomingdale's, 27–28, 188–89
blue color, 39, 160–62
Boston, 47–53, 62–64, 191–92
Boston Red Sox
  Abboud as fan of, 9, 33, 42–43, 157
  Abboud's father and, 47, 72
  Abboud's pitching of first ball, 41–42
  GMC Sierra at Fenway Park, 211
boutiques, 5, 120
Bowes, Richard, 120
bow ties, 174–75
boxers (underwear), 44
Bravo, Rose Marie, 181–82
breast cancer, 66, 74, 209
Bricken, Barry, 113–16
briefs (underwear), 44
broadcasters, 33–34, 36–40
Brokaw, Tom, 39–40
Brooklyn Cyclones, 232–34
Brooks Brothers, 30–31
Brown, Aaron, 209
brown color, 75, 159–60
buttons, 5, 161, 194–95
buyers, 25–26. 73–89, 172–73. *See also*
  marketing
Buzzy, 101

Calvin Klein. *See* Klein, Calvin
Campbell, Naomi, 133–37
Canadian Northwest collection, 23
cancer, 66, 71–72, 74, 209–11
Cardin, Pierre, 145–46
Carr, Zack, 15
Cartier watch, 10
Cassini, Oleg, 154–55
casual style, 8–10
Cattrall, Kim, 155–57
celebrities, 32–40, 99–100, 135, 155–57,
  215–17
Chanel, Coco, 5, 123–24, 160, 198
Chareau, Pierre, 130–31
Chariots of Fire (movie), 104
Clemens, Clint, 80
Clinton, Bill, 216

clothes, 49–50, 55. *See also* collections; fashion design; menswear; women's wear
Clotilde, 101
CNN interview, 209
coats, 68, 71, 91–92. *See also* jackets
collections
  for Barry Bricken, 113–15
  creating, 19, 21–23
  exclusive, 182–83, 198–99
  labels and, 30
  for Louis Boston, 60–61, 84
  Joseph Abboud label (*see* Joseph Abboud label)
colors
  Abboud's, 3–4, 60, 74–75, 111, 159–60
  blue, 39, 160–62
  collections and, 21–23
  designer palettes, 17, 22
  hand-knit sweaters, 122
  lime green, 114
  naming, 141, 162–65
  Polo logo shirt, 97
  red and yellow, 98
  stones and, 12–13
  ties, 169–72
  women's wear vs. menswear, 178–79
Combs, Sean, 143
competition. *See* rivalry
Concept:Cure benefit, 209–11
continental look, 55
Corgi, 75
corporate casual style, 8–10
Costas, Bob, 38
Costner, Kevin, 216
Council of Fashion Designers of America (CFDA), 152–57, 176

Daily News Record (DNR), 32, 78, 118, 184, 208–9, 232
daughters, 12. *See also* Abboud, Ari (daughter); Abboud, Lila (daughter)
D'Auria, Jim, 186–89
David Evans, 107
denim fabric, 162

Dent, Bucky, 9
design. *See* fashion design
designer labels, 30, 161–62, 197–99
Designers' Collective, 119–20
Dinand, Pierre, 224–26
Dioniglio, Loredana, 130
Dior, 227
discount stores, 201–3
Dolce & Gabbana, 14, 185, 228
Donna Karan, 20–21, 192, 197
dress shirts. *See* shirts
dyed hair, 217–18
dyeing fabric, 160
dyeing shoes, 55

earth colors, 159
Eisenhower, Dwight D., 215
environments, store, 27, 185–89
Environments collection, 159
Eric Ross, 86–87
Esquire magazine, 126–27
ethnicity, 52–53, 129–30, 207–10
EuroItalia, 225
European style, 78–79, 94
exclusive collections, 182–83, 198–99
Extreme Makeover (show), 40

fabric
  designing with, 12–14, 21–23, 162
  dyeing, 160 (*see also* colors)
  silk, 106–7, 140, 169
  swatches, 18, 21–22, 166–68
facial hair, 217
Fair Isle sweaters, 104
Fakhry, Richard, 151
family, 46–53, 71–72, 150–51. *See also* individual names of Abboud family
fashion design
  as Abboud's profession, 1, 230–31
  awards, 152–57
  with Barry Bricken, 113–16
  ideas and concepts, 11–14, 19–21, 94–96
  Joseph Abboud label (*see* Joseph Abboud label)
  with Ralph Lauren, 105–12
  in Paris, France, 69–70

popularity of, 40
schools, 16–17
shows (*see* fashion shows)
at Southwick, 90–91
styling as, 75–80, 139
teams and culture, 14–23
women's wear vs. menswear, 176–79
    (*see also* menswear; women's wear)
fashion shows
    GMC Sierra at, 211
    international, 143–51
    menswear, 139–42
    Museum of Natural History, 72, 147
    run of show color names, 164–65
    trunk shows, 179–81
    women's wear, 133–36, 139
Fashion Weeks, 133–36, 149–50,
    164–65, 211
father. *See* Abboud, Joe (father)
FBI interview, 207–8
Fekkai, Frédéric, 219
females. *See* women
Fenway Park. *See* Boston Red Sox
Ferla mills, 6
Ferri, Fabrizio, 222–24
fictional name labels, 198–99
Filene's, 56, 201–2
filetto, paisley, 171
Fimmel, Travis, 227
"fish-eye" buttonholes, 195
fit models, 107, 179
flannel fabric, 3–4, 12
flats, 18, 22
flying experiences, 205–9
focus groups, 221
food, Middle Eastern, 52
Ford, Tom, 152, 178
formal evening wear, 142
40 regular size, 22, 99, 107
Fountainhead, The (book), 113–15
four-in-hand knot, 174
fragrance, Joseph Abboud, 223–26
Franceschini, Bob, 155
franchise stores, 190–91
Freedberg, Milton, 116, 124–25,
    127–28
Freedberg of Boston, 116–28

Full Frontal Fashion (show), 40
Fusati, Max, 81–82
fusing, 77

gabardine fabric, 12
Galeotti, Sergio, 15, 232
Galway Bay Sweater Company, 77–78
Garciaparra, Nomar, 42, 211
gay stereotype, 33, 40, 180
GFT (Gruppo Finanziario Tessile), 15,
    127–32, 149, 177, 181, 192, 225,
    230–32
Gibran, Kahlil, vii, 210
Gloria Vanderbilt, 161
GMC Sierra design, 209–11
golf, 44–45
gorse color, 163–64
Gotti, John, 215
Grant, Cary, 100
gray flannel suits, 3–4, 12
Great Gatsby, The (movie), 99–100
Grieco, Richard and Edna, 90
Grodd, Clifford, 30, 185
grunge style, 214
Gruppo Finanziario Tessile. *See* GFT
    (Gruppo Finanziario Tessile)
Gucci, 152, 178, 214, 228
Gumbel, Bryant, 36–39, 155, 157
Gymnasium collection, 129

hair, men's, 217–20
Hall, Jerry, 80
Hamilton, George, 35
Hancox, Clara, 32, 118
Hart, Schaffner & Marx, 127
Hartmarx, 191
Head, Peggy, 83, 121–22
Helmut Lang, 228–29
Hemingway, Ernest, 216–17
Herman, Stan, 154
Hickey Freeman, 75–76, 198–99
high-low price gimmick, 203
Hochswender, Woody, 136
home style, 158–59
homosexuality, 33, 40, 137, 180
housekeeping, retail store, 189–90
Hugo Boss, 5, 166–67

Index

humiliation, Lebanese ethnicity and, 52–53, 129–30, 207–10
Hunter's mill, 13–14

image. *See* style
Imus, Don, 32–34, 174
Imus in the Morning (show), 32–34, 207, 209
inspiration boards, 22
Interseta, 170
Italy, 5–7, 107, 143, 148–49, 166

JA Apparel company, 128, 230–34. *See also* Joseph Abboud label
jackets
 band-collar (Nehru), 17–18
 Ralph Lauren's, 92–93
 leather, 68, 213
 madras, 55
 military-style, 178
 navy blazers, 23, 161
 silhouettes for, 117–18
 sport coats, 91–92
Jacobs, Marc, 163
Japan, 144–46, 190
jeans, designer, 161–62
Jewish tailors, 77
J.O.E. sportswear, 147–48
Jordan, Arthur, 59, 81, 85–86, 89
Joseph Abboud label. *See also* Abboud, Joseph
 boutiques, 5, 120
 fragrance, 223–26
 Freedberg of Boston and, 116–25
 GFT and, 15, 127–32, 149, 177, 181, 192, 225, 230–32
 JA Apparel company and, 128, 230–34
 retail stores, 128–30, 190–92, 202 (*see also* retail stores)
 ties (*see* ties)
jute sweater, 111–12
J. W. Childs Associates, 231

Kamali, Norma, 157
"Keating" shirt, 115
Kennedy, John F., 215

Kerry, John, 216
Klein, Calvin, 15, 19, 160, 224, 226–27, 232
knit-downs, 121
knit ties, 173
knots, tie, 174
Kors, Michael, 163

labels, 30, 90, 197–99
Lacoste crocodile logo shirts, 97
Lagerfeld, Karl, 218
Lanham, 75
Latoof, Theresa (grandmother), 151
Lauren, Jerry, 105–7
Lauren, Ralph
 assistant designers and operational partners, 15, 232
 channels of distribution of, 28
 comparison of Abboud and, 126–27
 fashion design with, 105–14
 Calvin Klein vs., 19
 first meeting with, 73
 mystique, 20, 97, 104
 outlet stores, 203
 personal relationship with, 155, 157
 Polo logo shirt, 96–97
 retail store space, 186
 salesman job with, 91–104
 lawsuit against, 168
leather jackets, 68, 213
Lebanese ethnicity, 52–53, 129–30, 207–10
legal issues, 115–16, 124–28, 166–68
lime green color, 114
Lincoln Center Jazz Orchestra, 150
linen suits, 12
linking stitch, 234
Lipke, David, 208
Loehmann's, 201
Louis Boston
 early shopping at, 57–59
 European buying trips for, 81–89
 exclusive collections and, 27–28
 housekeeping, 190
 Ralph Lauren clothes at, 91–93, 95–96
 salesman jobs at, 59–62, 73–80, 194
 as specialty store, 29

Louis Vuitton, 228
Luciano Barbera, 172

McDonough, Sean, 42
Magic Nesting Doll, The (book), 12
Makeover Story, The (show), 40
Marcovicci, Andrea, 80
Mark, Marky, 226–27
markdown sales, 200–204
marketing. *See also* salespersons
  advertising, 182, 221–29
  fashion shows (*see* fashion shows)
  markdown sales, 200–204
  marketability, 14
  media visibility, 32–40
  personal appearances, 41–45, 146–47
  retail stores and, 184–92
  selling to men, 193–99
  specialty stores and, 24–31
Market Weeks, 21, 24–26, 101–3
Marks & Spencer, 30–31
Marsalis, Wynton, 149–50
media visibility, 32–40. *See also* celebrities; press
Mello, Dawn, 120
Mello, Franco, 130
men. *See also* menswear
  as designers, 15–16
  as models, 137–42
menswear. *See also* collections; jackets; shoes; socks; suits; sweaters; ties
  Best Menswear Designer awards, 155–57
  blue color and, 160–61
  fashion shows, 139–42
  personal style and, 212–20
  selling, to men, 193–99
  sportswear, 45, 147–48
  women and, 43–44, 196
  women's wear vs., 134, 176–79
Micheli, Augusto, 166, 169–70
Miozza, 169
Mitchells and Richards, 29–30
Mitten, The (book), 11–12
Mizrahi, Isaac, 16–17
models
  Abboud as, 78–79, 107–8

Naomi Campbell, 133–36
  fit, 107, 179
  Ralph Lauren and, 101
  menswear and male, 137–42
  out-of-town, 144, 145, 148–49
  photo shoots with, 79–80, 222–24
Modern American collection, 117–19
mood boards, 22
Mosher's, 198–99
mother. *See* Abboud, Lila Sallah (mother)
mounted police uniforms, 63–64
Moveable Feast, A (book), 69
movies, 49–50
Museum of Natural History, 72, 147
music, fashion show, 142, 149–50

nakedness, 80, 135, 223–24, 226
names
  Abboud's, 124–25, 129–30, 186
  collection, 23
  colors, 141, 162–65
  designer label, 30, 197–99
Nance, Jim, 37
Nardoza, Ed, 208
National Geographic, 228–29
nature, 12–14, 210
navy blazers, 23, 161
neckwear. *See* ties
Nehru jackets and shirts, 17–18
Neiman Marcus, 6–7, 28, 180–83
New York Times, 136, 140, 142
New York Yankees, 9, 42–43
Nordstrom, 27, 202

Olympics, 37–38, 155
operational partners, 15, 97–98, 232
O'Reilly, Bill, 38–39
Ósiocháin, Padraig, 77–78
outlet stores, 201–3

paisley designs, 167–72
Pakula, Joanna, 222–23
palettes. *See* colors
pants, 8, 140–41, 161–62
Paris, France, 65–70
partners, operational, 15, 97–98, 232

passport pockets, 8
Paul Stuart, 30, 184, 185, 198
Pearlstein, Murray, 29, 58, 61, 74–75,
    81–89, 95–96, 172–73. *See also*
    Louis Boston
Pecci Yarn, 112
Pellari, 181–83
Perry Ellis label, 198
personal appearances, 41–45, 146–47
petroleum colors, 111
Petruzzi, Guido, 15, 127–28, 131
photo shoots, 79–80, 222–24
piracy, tie design, 166–68
Pitney, Gene, 35–36
pockets, suit, 4, 7–8, 12
pocket squares, 96
police uniforms, 63–64
Polo label, 15, 19, 73, 91, 96–97. *See
    also* Lauren, Ralph
polo tournament appearance, 146–47
ponytails, 218
Prada, 214, 227–28
Premium Outlet store, 202
presentation boards, 22
press. *See also* media visibility
    collection names and, 23
    color names and, 162–65
    designers and desire for, 16–17
    women's wear vs. menswear, 134, 178
pressing suits and ties, 4, 173–74
Pressman, Fred, 28
prices, 197, 203
Prince Charles, 215–16
private labels, 30, 90, 198
Prophet, The (book), vii, 210
prototypes, 22–23

Queer Eye for the Straight Guy (show),
    40

Ralph Lauren. *See* Lauren, Ralph
RCS. *See* GFT (Gruppo Finanziario
    Tessile)
Rector, Kelly, 19–20
red color, 98
Redford, Robert, 99–100
Red Sox. *See* Boston Red Sox

Renales, Bobbi, 113
retail coordinators, 189
retail stores
    design schools and, 16
    exclusive collections and, 182–83,
        198–99
    Joseph Abboud, 128–30, 190–92, 202
    outlet stores, 200–204
    space in, 185–90
    specialty stores, 24–31, 128–30, 177
    windows, 184–85
Riley, Pat, 36
rivalry
    between designers, 19, 157
    between design houses, 19–20,
        131–32, 134–36
Rivetti, Marco, 127–28
"Roark" shirt, 114–15
Rolex watches, 10, 213
run of show colors, 164–65

Saint Laurent, Yves, 15, 154, 168, 209,
    227, 232
Saks, 26–28, 32, 181–83, 185–87, 202
salespersons. *See also* marketing
    Abboud as, at Louis Boston, 59–62,
        71–80
    Abboud as, with Ralph Lauren,
        91–104
    menswear, 193–99
    retail store, 189
samples, 22–23, 24–25, 106, 203–4
Sarandon, Susan, 80
Sartre, Jean-Paul, 66
Sawgrass Mills Mall store, 202
Scarborough, Mark, 117, 121
Schachter, Eddie, 95
Schenkenberg, Marcus, 223–24
schools, design, 16–17
Schultz, Hans, 77
Schwartz, Barry, 15, 232
Schwartz, Bernie, 86–87
Scotland, 146, 163–64
Seal, Margaret, 83, 121–22
seam slippage, 6–7
Seinfeld (show), 34
selling. *See* marketing; salespersons

Seoul Olympics, 37, 155
September 11, 2001, terrorist attack, 205–9
Shetland sweaters, 56, 83–84
Shields, Brooke, 226
shirts
  band-collar, 18
  editing process and, 25
  Polo logo, 96–97
  power brokers and, 10
  unconstructed, 114–15
shoes, 2, 10, 55
shoulders, suit, 5–6, 12
shows. *See* fashion shows
silhouettes, 22, 106, 117–18
silk fabric, 106–7, 140, 169
sisters. *See* Abboud, Jeanette (sister);
  Abboud, Mara (sister); Abboud,
  Nancy (sister)
sizes
  Abboud's suit, 22, 99, 107
  models and, 138
  samples, 203–4
  suits, 76–77
sleeve buttons, 195
Smith, Tyler, 79, 222
socks, 75, 95, 106
Sorbonne, 65–70
Southwick, 90–91
space, retail store, 185–92
specialty stores, 24–31, 128–30, 177
sport coats, 91–92
sports
  Abboud as announcer, 33–34
  Abboud's participation in, 44–45
  baseball (*see* Boston Red Sox; Brooklyn Cyclones)
  broadcasters, 36–39, 155
  polo tournament, 146–47
  wedding and Celtics game, 88
sportswear, J.O.E., 147–48
Springsteen, Bruce, 216
squares, pocket, 96
Staff, Marty, 102, 231–32
stars. *See* celebrities
stitching
  Abboud's mother's, 50

buttons, 195
  linking stitch, 234
  pockets, 4
stones, colors and, 12–13, 210
stores. *See* retail stores
storybooks, children's, 11–12
strike-offs, tie, 166–68
Strom, Peter, 15, 97–98, 109, 232
Stutz, Geraldine, 184
style
  Abboud's, 54, 112, 158–65, 212–14
  corporate casual, 8–10
  European, 66–67, 78–79, 94
  hair and, 217–20
  image and, 1–2, 147, 224
  male examples of, 215–17
  suit button, 194–95
  ties and, 173–74
  styling, 75–80, 139. *See also* fashion
    design
success, clothes and, 55
sued coat, 68, 71
suits. *See also* menswear
  button styles and, 194–95
  first job selling, 55–57
  image and, 1–4
  manufacturing, 4–7, 77
  pockets, 7–8
  styles, 3–4, 8–10, 12, 37, 117, 214
  styling out and sizing, 75–78
Surman's, 55, 185
Survillo, George, 62–63
Sussan, Luciano Ben, 86–87
swatches, 18, 21–22, 166–68. *See also*
  fabric
sweaters
  Aran, 78, 83
  designing, 83–84, 110–12, 121–22
  Fair Isle, 104
  Filene's, 56
  knitted by Abboud's mother, 212
  linking stitch, 234
  stones and color for, 13–14

Tag Heuer watches, 212–13
tailoring, 10, 77
Taplin, Myron, 79

teams, fashion design, 11–23. *See also*
    fashion design
television, 34–40
Terconi, Luigi, 166, 170
Thorpe, John, 83
ties
  buying, 56, 57
  designing, 169–74
  first collection, 129–30
  price vs. quality, 197
  sample books and, 106
  strike-offs and piracy, 166–68, 172
  tying, 174–75
  tuxedos and, 36, 174
Time Warner Center store, 190
Tommy Hilfiger outlet stores, 203
Torres, Mike, 9
Trebay, Guy, 142
trunk shows, 179–81
Turnbull & Asser, 10, 107
tuxedos
  bow ties and, 36, 174
  French, 67
  Joseph Abboud label, 35–36, 150
  Robert Redford and, 99–100
  tying ties, 174–75

unconstructed dress shirts, 114–15
underwear, 44
uniforms, mounted police, 63–64
University of Massachusetts, 59, 62
Unzipped (documentary), 16

Valentino, 131–32
Vanners, 107
Versace, 145
visa problem, 123–24
Vogue Hommes, 227

Wagner, Robert, 80
walking, models and, 138–39
wallets, 8
Walter-Morton, 198–99
watches, 212–13
"Wearable Art" pieces, 121
weaving, color and, 160
Weinstein, Lynn. *See* Abboud, Lynn
    Weinstein (wife)
White, Constance C. R., 140
Wilkes Bashford, 30
Wilpon, Fred, 41, 232–34
windows, store, 73–74, 184–85
Windsor knot, 174
Windsor of Germany, 77
Wintour, Anna, 16, 134
Wolfe, Tom, 216
women
  Abboud and, 12, 56, 65–66, 67,
      84–85, 95, 176, 180–81
  fashion design and, 15, 43, 196–97
  models (*see* models)
  Ralph Lauren salesmen and, 101–3
women's wear
  Abboud's, 130–31, 176–83
  fashion shows, 133–36, 139
  menswear vs., 15, 176–79
Women's Wear Daily, 16, 184
Woodbury Common store, 202

Yankees, 9, 42–43
yellow color, 98, 164
Yves Saint Laurent, 15, 154, 168, 209,
    227, 232

Zegna, 127